3

May 2009

WHERE LIGHT TAKES ITS COLOR FROM THE SEA

For the LePage
family ~
Do not forget us in
California. We will
certainly not forget you!
Bon journée!
Embrace,
Rona and
Jacob
Spiegel

WHERE LIGHT TAKES ITS COLOR FROM THE SEA

A California Notebook

by James D. Houston

Foreword by Alan Cheuse

Heyday Books, Berkeley, California
BayTree Books

This book was made possible in part by
BAYTREE a generous grant from the BayTree Fund.

Library of Congress Cataloging-in-Publication Data

Houston, James D.
  Where light takes its color from the sea : a California
notebook / by James D. Houston ; foreword by Alan Cheuse.
    p. cm.
  A collection of essays and short fiction.
  ISBN-13: 978-1-59714-083-6 (alk. paper)
  1. California—Literary collections. 2. California—History
—Literary collections. I. Title.
  PS3558.O87W47 2008
  818'.5408--dc22   2007032616

Cover Art: *Monterey Bay from Santa Cruz Pogonip* by Tom Killion, 2002.
  www.tomkillion.com
Cover Design: Lorraine Rath
Interior Design and Composition: Leigh McLellan Design
Printing and Binding: Thomson-Shore, Dexter, MI

Orders, inquiries, and correspondence
should be addressed to:
  Heyday Books
  P. O. Box 9145, Berkeley, CA 94709
  (510) 549-3564, Fax (510) 549-1889
  www.heydaybooks.com

Printed in the United States of America
on 50% post consumer waste recycled
paper

Heyday Books is committed to preserving ancient forests and natural resources. We elected to print *Where Light Takes Its Color From The Sea* on 50% post consumer recycled paper, processed chlorine free. As a result, for this printing, we have saved:

  9 Trees (40' tall and 6-8" diameter)
  3,902 Gallons of Wastewater
  1,569 Kilowatt Hours of Electricity
  430 Pounds of Solid Waste
  845 Pounds of Greenhouse Gases

Heyday Books made this paper choice because our printer, Thomson-Shore, Inc., is a member of Green Press Initiative, a nonprofit program dedicated to supporting authors, publishers, and suppliers in their efforts to reduce their use of fiber obtained from endangered forests.

For more information, visit www.greenpressinitiative.org

10 9 8 7 6 5 4 3 2 1

I made the world.

And every place has a name.

This is so when you travel to other places

You can tell people where you are from

And where you have been

And where you are going.

—from *The Maidu Creation Story*

Contents

PART THREE

THE WRITING LIFE

PART FOUR

SOME FICTION

Foreword
by Alan Cheuse

1.

Let's begin in Manhattan, a beginning which, as you'll see in a moment, suggests the argument I'm trying to make. I mean, specifically, the Manhattan of brilliant cartoonist Saul Steinberg, whose poster you may have seen on the walls of folks with a New York state of mind and some sense of humor—a densely populated bustling place of commerce and energy crammed into the few square miles of a small island, with everything west of the Hudson River stretched out to infinity in great empty spaces, and only a few cities barely marked on the horizon of the great American desert. No better emblem of New York provincialism than this! If the entire East Coast flew a flag, it might show off this same emblem. After all of the great battles of the Indian wars which cleared a continent for Eurocentric domination, we Easterners don't venture very far west except for ski vacations and trips to Disneyland.

We don't travel west very often in the novels and essays we read either. A few stories by Jack London have made the grade-school literary canon. You can find some Steinbeck in high school reading lists and in the Library of America series, our semiofficial literary pantheon. But since the days of Wallace Stegner it's been a battle for books with a western orientation to make it on the reading shelves of the educated East. I don't believe this has to do with the quality of post-Stegner prose. Having decided that we've cornered the market on our national literary tradition without having to move much beyond the Chicago suburbs, we've kept that Saul Steinberg flag waving. Eastern literary provincialism, which if it hadn't been jolted out of its reading chair by the great Latin American writers some decades ago might also never have looked south past the sands of the Gulf of Mexico, has a way of pigeonholing certain books and writers and traditions, and ignoring many others.

Make no mistake about it, the East is all mobbed-up, as we say in my home turf of New Jersey, and don't think you have much chance to make your mark in the canon if you come from any place west of the Mississippi. Take, for example, the case of Joan Didion, a daughter of Sacramento. She herself has been canonized—ever since she moved to New York City—as a New York writer, while her masterpiece of a novel, *Play It As It Lays* (published in 1970), set in Las Vegas and pointing west, is scarcely ever cited. And consider, as the story has it, that the *New York Times Book Review* did not publish a review of Wallace Stegner's wonderful 1971 novel *Angle of Repose* until the news came that it had won that year's Pulitzer Prize for fiction. You may say things have changed a lot since then.

Maybe.

If there is one California-grown, longtime California writer who seems to be changing things even a little it is James D. Houston, who in the last (nearly) thirty years has published several of his novels with one of the most prestigious houses in New York.

2.

In California and other parts of the West educated readers consider Houston a natural resource. For decades his reputation has been as solid as a redwood. Novelist Oakley Hall, co-founder of the Squaw Valley Community of Writers, aptly describes him as being "in the Stegner line" of California writers, which means in the Steinbeck line as well. Although Houston, in his essay in this volume titled "Ancestors," writes about family roots going back to North Carolina, Tennessee, and the Texas panhandle, his literary kin stand quite close to his San Francisco and, later, Santa Cruz home.

When you read his wonderful novels, including *Continental Drift, Snow Mountain Passage,* and *Bird of Another Heaven,* all of them beautifully crafted love notes to California past and present; when you read the powerful story of the Japanese American internment camp in *Farewell to Manzanar* that Houston wrote with his wife, Jeanne Wakatsuki Houston; when you read his occasional essays about literature and life; and his short stories, some of them collected here, you recognize that in his depiction of the land and characters who live upon it, in his attention to the historical roots of the land and its present inhabitants, in his anger at injustice and his praise of the possibility of harmony among people and between them and the places where they reside, his literary father is John Steinbeck, his favorite uncles are Wallace Stegner and Oakley Hall, his sibling is Joan Didion (that adopted daughter now of Manhattan), he's cousin to (Northwest transplant) Raymond Carver, and a literary father himself to such younger writers as UC Santa Cruz–educated Daniel Duane and Sacramento novelist Andrew Wingfield.

Houston's notion of kinship, literary or otherwise, is, in
fact, vertical in time as well as horizontal in place. As Andrew
Wingfield has pointed out, the Santa Cruz writer, in his "Ring
of Fire" trilogy (comprised of the novels *Continental Drift, Love
Life,* and *The Last Paradise*) demonstrates precisely "how continuity can come of people's tendency to make places mean
[something]. He is certainly not the only author who under-
stands the way the land can resonate in the human imagination. In fact, he has observed in his critical work that in the
fiction of many California authors 'it is...almost impossible to
separate the places on the map from the places in the mind.'"

As Houston himself points out in "Words and Music," the
autobiographical essay included in this volume, his own California literary awakening came when he read Steinbeck at the
age of seventeen. Of course he had read his Bible, and some
of the great Eastern giants of American fiction. But while
immersed in Steinbeck he first began to make the connection
between what he saw on the page and what he saw when he
lifted his eyes from the page. "At no point," he writes, "did I
think or say aloud, 'I *know* this place. I *know* these people.' Yet
that was how his stories affected me—at that level of implicit
recognition."

This is an expression of literary kinship as pure as you
can get. Even the creek at Tassajara, Houston's beloved Zen
Buddhist retreat in the Santa Lucia Mountains (which flows
through the last pages of *Continental Drift* and spills over into
an essay in this collection), doesn't run that clear. In the very
title of this present volume we can find that same purity of
relations among the elements: *Where Light Takes Its Color from
the Sea.* And between those who have the eyes to see this rela-
tion, and to make a human, and humane, response to it, and
the power to find the right language with which to express it,
we see the links between James Houston, his tenancy of a particular place on our continent, and his own kinship with the
best American writers, West or East, who have come before.

"Earth's the right place for love: I don't know where it's likely to go better," Robert Frost wrote in "Birches" ages and ages ago. Frost, that San Francisco–born transplant to New England, headed East when he set out to discover who he was. James D. Houston, and we thank him for it, stayed put, sensing the quakes and tremors of life just by remaining in place, turning one way and seeing the beaches and ocean, bays and inlets of the coast, turning the other way and finding forests and mountains all within his vision, and making up a particular variety of novel and essay and story out of what he feels and sees that is particular to the place he inhabits, and true to the psychology that he knows is universal to us all. The critic and symbologist in me might even argue that he has taken Steinbeck's geographies and psychologies to a higher dramatic stage, demonstrating how they are not only tied to history, as the master from Salinas pointed out, but rise to the level of symbolic reenactment of inner states of being, figures in dialogue with, not enslaved to, the land.

Maybe Houston could have done much of this in the mountains and forests and beaches of Brooklyn, but I doubt it. Luckily for us, California's the right place for him. And in the pages that follow you will find a lot of that place of geographical wonder and human wonderment. Readers in New York and Atlanta and Boston and Washington and Miami (and Paris and Bombay and London and Moscow) should pay attention. He's writing about where—and how—we all live.

PART ONE

HABITAT

It is spring once more in the Coast Range
Warm, perfumed, under the Eastern moon.
—Kenneth Rexroth, "Yin and Yang" (1965)

The View from Santa Cruz

From here I can see the candy store shaped like a Dutch windmill. Atop its red, peaked roof sits an eight-sided dome painted white, with windows too small, too toy-like and too curiously placed for anyone to look through. I used to imagine someone lurked in that stubby tower watching me. But this is impossible. It's a make-believe windmill, with make-believe windows. Last year in a storm its vanes blew down. Few people think of it as a windmill anymore. It's just a candy store, with a Dutch girl on its side, and she is fading fast. All day she faces the sun. I doubt that many who pass by realize she is supposed to be Dutch.

The store is called Buckhart's, which might be a Dutch name, except that the long sign over its door features not a girl but an enormous heart, and gazing from within the heart is a well-antlered buck who looks pirated from some York-shire hunting lodge. The heart was red once. After the vanes blew down they painted it white. The buck is white. The girl is white. The eight-sided dome is white. Where the morning sun catches it, the dome gleams and leaves an angular flash on my retina when I look away.

It's a landmark, that candy store. If I want to tell someone how to find my house, I mention Buckhart's. Everyone knows where it is. "I live across the street from Buckhart's," I say. A strange identity.

A famous road passes between Buckhart's and me, an old road that curves along the coast and carries thousands of cars a day, tourist cars, visitors' cars, beach-bound and water-seeking cars. This is a seacoast town, spread along one edge of Monterey Bay. It's winter now, the end of February, a leap-year day, in fact, the twenty-ninth, the rarest day. It's winter, and the stream of cars along this famous road is thicker now than it ever was in the summers when I first discovered the town, fourteen years ago.

And what about this year's summer? Who dares predict what that will bring? It isn't a wide road, two lanes laid perhaps thirty years ago. In this state, that is a long time for anything to last. It is already 1964, and this is Santa Cruz, resort town for that great megalopolis rapidly surrounding San Francisco Bay.

A range of mountains separates us from the megalopolis, and so far we only feel the explosive overflow on weekends. It is just a matter of time, of course. Everything in California is just a matter of time. But so far this town has been spared. That's one reason I came here, to taste it again. This is why I watch Buckhart's from my window. Who knows how old it is? Forty, maybe fifty years? This house I watch from is even older. Sixty, the owner tells me. Older than Buckhart's and higher by a cupola. If I sit up here in this cupola and watch the dome of Buckhart's hard enough, I don't see the traffic. For long moments it isn't there. I burn my eyes on his gleaming dome, and the stream dies.

Buckhart, it is said, lived here once himself, roamed these redwood rooms, kept the little garden, and each morning crossed that small acre of apple trees to his store. He didn't live here long. No one has lived here long, not in the twenty years this house has been rented, not since the original candy man died and took his secret formula with him, and the deed to the land changed hands.

In the old days it was an estate, with the aura about it of a southern novel. The old Frazier-Lewis place, everybody called it. The lawn spread two hundred yards down to the sea. The grounds covered what has become several square blocks of bungalows. The lake that is now a state game preserve came with the land, a private vista from the wide front porch. In those days the candy man would go next door to his candy factory, lock himself in a small upstairs room, and mix his formula for the chocolate confection that made him famous. But the candy man died sometime before the Second World War. His sisters died without issue. The family died, and this immense house was gradually surrounded. The grandeur that depended so much on distance and perspective was lost. It became a rental property. They closed his little factory. Now its weathered wooden frame bulges next door with a hundred years of dusty, warping furniture.

The candy he made there made him a fortune, and I suspect that is why Buckhart lived here a while. He was searching for the formula that died with Frazier-Lewis. Imagine Buckhart scouring this creaking house for any scrap of yellowed paper. Sometimes late at night the wind rises from the sea in a sudden thrust that shivers the ceiling. Nails draw, floorboards settle. It is almost certain then that Buckhart is up in the attic again, creeping and tapping the walls for hollow spots that might hold the long-lost recipe for the chocolate marvel that only Frazier-Lewis could concoct.

Buckhart's hunch was reasonable, if he ever thought to search, because this is a house of gothic secrets, of hidden nooks and dark stairways, sudden rooms and unpried window seats, a house to explore on a rainy afternoon. When it was built, two years after San Francisco's earthquake and fire, it was elegant, a Victorian climax. Everyone must have built such houses that season. This town is dotted with them. From here I can see their spires, turrets and domes, gables, newel posts, and dormer windows. I can't help thinking, though, that this is, first of all, a boy's dream house. Tom Sawyer deserved it. Penrod Schofield should have planned adventures here. It is a house for Jack Armstrong to surround, for the Katzenjammer Kids to invade, for Huckleberry Finn to find floating down the Mississippi.

I have always coveted old houses, with a boy's fascination for the ancient and curious, similar to the way I once collected coins, and later old cars. Not vintage cars. Just old ones. I have sought old houses as one seeks an old man whose tales verify what sometimes seems never to have existed. Call it a yearning for continuity. In California I have watched mountains change their contour, seen orchards swallowed by bulldozers, known whole towns to sprout in a summer, watched familiar roads inflate like inner tubes to thrice their size, and felt square miles of asphalt raise a valley's temperature until seasons lose their shape. Such transformations are, of course, the experience of the Western world, in one form or another, for the past couple of hundred years. And it is nothing new to seek permanencies in a shifting environment. But in California things change faster than in most other places. And I happened to fasten on old houses, like hoary boulders in the inexorable flood.

We first saw this one from several blocks away, actually saw its cupola first, which rises higher than any building in sight. It rests atop a black roof so sloped it's almost a house-long steeple. The cupola is square, with a pointed roof of its own, and windows on all sides. The top panes are stained maroon.

The house overlooks a lake surrounded by eucalyptus trees. But between the house and lake runs that road with its stream of Jaguars and Impalas and Thunderbirds. So one enters from the rear, up a narrow alleyway.

From the ground it is a fortress of flaking gray-green. Along one side a wide staircase rises to the second-floor porch. Around the porch is the original front door. When we first approached, the house had been two years empty. The foot of the entry stairway was lush with high grass, untrimmed rose-bushes, and a choir of wild, white-mouthed lilies. Most of the banisters' latticed siding had fallen away, so they sagged and leaned. At the head of the stairs, beneath the porch's vast over-hang, a ragged wicker rocker nodded in the breeze that blew up from the beach and across the lake.

Peering through the heavy windows and through dust that lay like gauze over everything, we saw paneled walls of heart redwood, twelve-foot ceilings, cherrywood sideboards, and walnut chests, dark Boston rockers, chandeliers of brass, with yellow bulbs as big as streetlights.

No one had lived upstairs for two years. No one had lived downstairs for twenty. The lower floor was a warehouse for the relics of two families—the family of the candy man whose forebears had survived the Donner Party disaster of 1846, and the present owner's family, who arrived in this region soon after the Civil War and acquired the house when the candy man passed away.

In that downstairs repository we found a delicately carved chest of shelves holding hundreds of birds eggs, a room full of elderly sewing machines, another room filled with carved bedsteads, a four-foot engraving of Queen Victoria that had never been uncrated, a moth-eaten Union Army sergeant's jacket, a certificate of merit for that sergeant signed by Abraham Lincoln, a first edition of the first proceedings of the California State Legislature (1850), turn-of-the-century sepia-tones of the descendants of the Donner Party survivors, framed photos of long-gone redwood giants, back issues of the *San Francisco Chronicle* announcing the First World War through a split in the linoleum, other issues lauding Calvin Coolidge, Ramón Navarro, Rin Tin Tin.

Blending with the dust and the fumes, a spirit hung in the air above those old clothes and furnishings and documents. I knew it had drifted up to permeate the whole building. At sixty years of age, this house with its storerooms of neglected history reached that far again into the nation's past. Twice sixty years still isn't long, by Eastern or European standards, but in California it is about as far back as a non-Hispanic Caucasian can expect to reach. Unless of course you count the walls themselves, the ceilings and the door frames cut from nearby forests that grew a thousand years before the Spanish came, walls whose very touch can send one's nerve-ends probing fern layers of primeval loam.

And so we rented it, at a bargain, agreeing to help the owners restore its livability, having found, it seemed, a great deal more than a roof over our heads. Even with this wealth of continuity, however, it must be pointed out that such a house located somewhere else, say farther inland, in the Sacramento Valley or in the Mother Lode, would have held far less fascination. What appealed so is that it overlooks this stretch of coastline. It belongs to this particular beach, this curve of bay, to a fall of northern light I have spent fourteen years running to.

A lot depends on the light here. It shapes the mountains and draws a mossy green from those high meadow patches that never turn brown. Down along the river that runs through town, the light swells up under a cloud of seagulls as they rise in a swirl, between the concrete bridges. They turn, soar, dive like a shower of white sparks and descend again to their marshy, low-tide, inland island. In later afternoon the light turns the bay white. It catches eucalyptus leaves with their undersides up, like a thousand new moons.

The sea, as much as the light, gives this curve of coast its flavor. The light takes its color from the sea, sometimes seems to be emerging from it. And the sea here is ever-present. On clear days it coats the air with a transparent tinge of palest blue that salts and sharpens every detail. It's not a placid sea. This is a bend of the Pacific. Swells roll in from storm centers north and south of the equator and steadily wear away the cliffs that edge these towns. Every winter, somewhere, a wall of sandstone finally lets go and slides out from under the topsoil to be dissolved and strewn along the beaches. A few years back a block-long section of a scenic cliff-drive highway fell into the surf that had torn out its underpinnings.

So far the sea's intrusion has produced more beauty than havoc. This is the northern curve of Monterey Bay. A wooded arm of the Coast Range curves with it, embracing these lowlands. The Pacific is softened here. The worst winds are softened. The slow process of erosion has left many-colored cliffs—yellow, buff, brown, and ochre. Each striated layer reveals the pressed sand of beaches eons old. Sometimes in the low sun of an autumn afternoon they turn orange and glow like the horizon itself. Miles of these cliffs are notched with sandy coves, whose eroded walls give the beaches a wildness, a remoteness. The coves are hot and protected, yet far enough below the cliff edges that one can forget a town lies just above. Tree roots hang through the walls. Tenacious cedars and eucalyptus, like sprung umbrellas, frame the sky. Sometimes slick brown seals glide past offshore. Pelicans swoop, searching for fish. Low tides bare pocked reefs and mossy primordial worlds of anemones and chitons and her-mit crabs. From any of these coves, on most days, Monterey Peninsula, twenty miles south across the bay, seems to rise from the sea like a long-lost, velvet island.

From the water's edge one can look west toward the main part of town. There, the sand that draws its half-moon around the bay lays a final broad hot stripe along the Boardwalk, below the high-looped rollercoaster, past a long row of arches that leads to a turn-of-the-century pleasure palace called the Casino, red-domed, and of a style with the spires and turrets that cap the knolls behind it. Farther along the main beach, bearded pilings grow from the sand, anchoring a crusty pier that probes the bay for half a mile. The long beach ends at last, beyond the pier, as a final row of cliffs bend northward.

From here, two miles away and seen from the east, those cliffs are a straight line reaching out from town, a brown palisade fending off the open sea. An islet sits just beyond the palisade, thick with seals who bark and sun themselves. Atop the cliff there is a jagged stand of eucalyptus trees that never move. They have not moved in fourteen years. At sunset they are tall and black against a flaming sky. Then the seal rock is the town's last outpost. The water across the bay turns silver-white, with only the long dark pier to cut the whiteness.

I call myself a Californian. I am fascinated by everything about this state. But when it becomes an image in my mind, it is most often this town, this coast, this view. During three years in Europe not long ago (when we lived, by the way, in a four-hundred-year-old Tudor cottage), I spent two and a half of those years glad to be free of America. I actually toyed with the idea of never coming back. When I finally began to long again for the homeland, I saw nothing but a mile of orange cliffs, a slate-blue bay catching sea winds, a crusty pier. This curve of coast has been among the few constants in my life, and that is curious, in a way, because this coast is not, strictly speaking, home. I was born in San Francisco, started high school there. I came of age over the mountains in Santa Clara Valley.

The town of Santa Cruz (Holy Cross) was first a mission colony founded by Franciscans soon after the time of the

American Revolution. The mission's adobe walls have long since eroded away. Now a whitewashed and timbered replica stands on the site. Later it was a port town, and lumber town, surrounded by superb farm and ranching country. Part of it is still a fishing town. Every day a stubby fleet chugs out before dawn in search of salmon, snapper, albacore. But for as long as I have known it, this has been a beach town, first of all, a resort town and a retirement haven, with trailer courts on the outskirts, Victorian manors at the core, and interlaced with rows of summer bungalows. Around and beyond Buckhart's bleached windmill I can see them—cottages and bungalows with brick-red roofs, shingle-gray roofs, checkered roofs, shake and composition roofs, a field of roofs broken with clumps of pine and cedar and lines of eucalyptus that crisscross the town.

From here, a block back from the beach, I can see quaint streets whose houses are trellised and filigreed, slightly weathered from winter gales and salt air, painted pink or white or forest green, bedecked with driftwood or with an occasional pink plaster flamingo on the lawn, and labeled with plaques of redwood lettering: *Port-o-Call, Vista del Mar, Pair-o-Dice, The Darlingtons—Mary and Frank, This is IT, Bide-a-Wee, My Blue Haven.*

I first saw these houses and the beach and the pier and the lines of eucalyptus during my initial escape to Santa Cruz, at age sixteen, a high school junior in San Jose. It was Easter vacation and "everybody" was renting motel rooms for the week, as they still do here, to drink beer and misbehave and hopefully get arrested.

I kept returning because I liked to swim and lie in the sun and play volleyball and ride the waves, and it was easy enough to get here, thirty miles in less than an hour through wooded mountains, over good roads. One year the summer came and went and I kept coming, spending long hours alone hiking empty beaches in the fall and through the winter. I had found an unexpected fulfillment by this wide bay. The light, the sand, the glinting sea seemed to explain almost everything well enough.

In California the beach, like wine tasting, can become a way of life. My time invested served as a kind of initiation fee, admitting me to a loose fraternity of beachrats, surfers, and self-appointed exiles who found some common bond in the asocial and irresponsible womb-warmth along the coast. This was an important first, an identity not pressed upon me by family, church, or school. There followed then a series of memorable firsts that linked me to this region. I first got unmanageably drunk here, on several quarts of Lucky Lager, and vomited into that marvelous sand. I pursued my first serious love affair here, in a sleeping bag, in and out of all those wild and lovely coves. I learned what my Scoutmaster had tried in vain to teach me, how to start a fire with one match. Maybe it was the salt in the driftwood, or the extra dryness of newsprint that has baked all day in the sun. Finally, I experienced, in the presence of this sky and this reach of windworn cliff, that short-lived but overwhelming sense of unity with nature that at once dissolves and expands and defines the human soul.

Until recently I never stayed here more than a week at a time, rarely more than two or three days. Yet whenever I made that trip through the mountains I knew what to expect. Like old houses, this town with its turrets and cupolas and bungalows and fleet of fishing boats has been a refuge from change itself. And like old houses, the town is ever more archaic and out of step with the times. For many, it is becoming something of a nuisance in America's fastest growing state. And so its face, its style must soon be altered. Every weekend now the megalopolis gets closer. Between the mountains and the sea, fields vibrate, waiting for the bulldozers. Foresighted realtors have already mapped out the program of growth. Some envision a white city, agleam and curving right around the bay to connect this northern edge with Monterey. In their vision, beehive hotels will line the beaches, like Acapulco and Miami.

Evenings now I watch my favorite view, one I have come to love more than any in the world—that long arm, the palisade, capped with upright eucalyptus, the dark pier probing a silver bay—and think of the man who has promised to build a convention center there, at the edge of the farthest cliff, overlooking seal rock. He wants to tear down the trees and install a hotel in the shape of a pyramid and, next to it, an auditorium in the shape of a perfect sphere, where Lions and Oddfellows can assemble every year.

Part of me takes it for granted that this will happen because I have grown up in a state where such things happen every day. As a Californian I have learned that fourteen years is a fairly long moment to enjoy one view. Perhaps I am luckier than I care to admit. Who am I, after all? At best, a fourteen-year man in a fourteen-decade town, a thirty-year man in a two-century state. Have I any claim on a view? It is only a lucky chance that my father decided to leave Texas when he did, to settle in San Francisco before I came along. If he had not moved out in the early thirties, among the thousands in search of better jobs and better weather, I would not have been born a Native Son of the Golden West, might never have seen these cliffs and beaches. Can I begrudge the multitudes who continue to arrive, for the same reasons? Can I even begrudge the weekend quests which so clog the roads to this seaside town, little pilgrimages I myself so often made? Who do you challenge? Where do you draw the line?

Well, there is another part of me that knows you have to challenge the pyramid. That goes without saying. And you have to fight the perfect sphere. Schemes like that just have to be resisted, though you may not be able to resist the flood itself.

Each time I look out and find my view still there, intact, I feel twice-blessed, reprieved. From here, from this decaying boy's dream of a manor house I can watch it, or walk to the beach for a swim or a hike over low-tide reefs. I watch gulls soar, the seals sunning, slender leaves that turn in the wind, along the curve of coast that is the country I know and which I realize now I have always expected California to be. The knowledge that it is all a matter of time doesn't diminish the pleasure of living here. If anything, I suppose this sharpens it, like the tang of apples stolen from the yard of the mean old man. Sometimes I ask myself, If those pyramids ever began to rise, where would you go? I don't know.

It is a strange identity, to live across the street from Buckhart's bleached and vaneless windmill, to be rooted in the land of the rootless, committed to a country that seems committed to unbridled change, all the while clutching at Walt Whitman and Johnny Appleseed and Huckleberry as they grab for handholds on the last lip of the western precipice. One has little choice in such matters, of course. I have no place else to be from but here.

(1964)

The Regional Feeling

I recently met a woman in Honolulu who had returned to Hawai'i after ten years away. She had come to the mainland to go to college, then stayed to study law at the University of Santa Clara. Mililani Trask is thirty-two now, half Hawaiian, and an attorney in private practice, devoting a great deal of her time to legal aid for people of Hawaiian ancestry, while representing their complex land claims on a federal commission and before the state legislature.

"I got out of touch with my roots," she said, "during those years on the mainland. I was doing work with other groups, Chicanos, Native Americans. One day I saw that my true work was here in the islands, with my own people, in my own place. Once I came back I knew I was home, and I was here to stay."

She voiced something I hear and feel a lot these days, a feeling of renewed commitment to the places we inhabit. I keep running into people who have chosen a spot, an island, a town, a city, a desert, a cliff—the place, as Gary Snyder has said, "where you decide to stick your spear in the ground." I have talked to people about this in the Pacific Northwest, in and around Santa Fe, on the island of Oahu, in Toronto, in Vermont, and in many parts of my home state, California, which is really a large mosaic of regions, each with its singular identity and microclimate. Some of these people are active in the bioregional movement; others have yet to hear of it. Some are reclaiming places their parents or grandparents inhabited; others are starting over two thousand miles from home-of-record. What they have in common, what I believe I hear in these widespread conversations, is a new and upgraded regional feeling. It is very different from what I would call the Old Provincialism.

Provincialism implies a narrowness of perspective, a stubborn attachment to the only place one really knows. It springs, as often as not, from a fear of other places and possibilities. This new regionalism is characterized by conscious choice, together with a growing awareness of our options and what they are likely to be in the foreseeable future.

I have some back issues of a magazine called *Place* that came out of Palo Alto for a couple of years and affected me deeply when it first appeared early in 1972. It was a small-press production, featuring earthy and downhome content, in large format, with a high-gloss photo of a bearded farmhand on the cover; and that title, the moment I saw it, went through me like a beam of hot light. It illuminated something I had recently begun to sense, and which a lot of people in my part of the world were just beginning to sense. It was an extraordinary experience, as I think back, the impact of that single word.

Place is nothing new, after all. It has been a constant in human affairs from day one. How can you avoid it? You have to park somewhere and get a roof over your head, and wherever this occurs has to be a place of some kind or another. But you are not always aware of it as such, and therein lies the difference. At some point place moves into the conscious life, so that you are aware of it, begin to examine it, get in touch with it, perhaps even honor and respect it.

I don't think it was coincidence that this magazine appeared within a couple of years after the first earth photos began to circulate widely, the ones that had come back from the 1967 NASA satellite. Those photos changed forever our ways of looking at the home planet. As a result we all now know some things most of our provincial grandparents could never have known. We know how finite the earth appears from somewhere else. We have been forced to rethink its limits, and at the same time reexamine its true possibilities. In the minds of many, many people those photos triggered a rediscovery of the earth, the whole of it, as well as the various local chunks we inhabit.

A cluster of perceptions touch right here: that vision of earth from a great distance; the reawakening sense of place; the emerging environmental movement, which happened to go public soon after those photos appeared; and certain regional loyalties that have been forced out into the open, as threats to the physical world have escalated.

Everywhere you go, there is a valley under siege, where some developer wants to install a thousand new homes; or there is a mountainside under siege, where heavy industry is moving in; or there is pastureland under siege, where the Defense Department wants to install a missile site or a testing range. Most of the time someone already lives there, and these people are yelling and screaming, "Hey! Somebody already lives here!"

But in order to defend the place that is threatened, it is not enough to yell and scream. You have to become better informed than the opposition. You have to become an expert. So you study the history of the valley or the mountain range. You study the water table and the weather patterns, the fauna and the flora, the ecology and the economy and whatever else needs to be understood in order to evaluate the full impact of the intrusion being proposed. In so doing you may well rediscover a place you had been taking for granted.

It's another reason why regionalism nowadays is so different from the old provincialism. A great deal more is involved than some sentimental attachment to the view through your frontroom window, or a stubborn attachment to the way your father or your grandfather did things. It is regionalism at a higher level of awareness about the interlocking and interdependent workings of the world, and it often comes hand in hand with the knowledge that we are running out of space, running out of "other places," i.e., the ones we can move to if this place doesn't happen to work out.

I have just returned from six months in Honolulu, which feels not at all like a capital city in one of the United States but the headquarters of some tiny island republic. It was this stay in Hawai'i—being twenty-four hundred miles out in the middle of the Pacific and yet still, somehow, under the national umbrella—that started me thinking again about the regional feeling.

For the past dozen years a cultural renaissance has been in progress there. Inspired in part by the Civil Rights movement of the 1960s, people of native ancestry have been rediscovering their history and language and traditional arts and skills, as well as their deep ancestral ties to the potent land and the spectacular landscape. The expression of this is heard most effectively in the music. There are certain singers, male and female, in whose voices you hear a poignant breaking and bending of notes that is like the peak moment in flamenco singing, or in blues. It is untranslatable, a haunting sound that slides between exuberance and lament, and those bending notes themselves catch a sentiment that permeates the air above the islands. It is what Mililani Trask came home to defend in court. The locals call it *aloha aina* (love for the land).

Back here on the mainland, as I drive along the freeways of California, I hear some of this same thing coming over the country and western stations, the renewed affection for a certain place on the map, or a celebration of the life being lived there. I hear it when John Denver sings "Rocky Mountain High" or when Lynyrd Skynyrd sings "Sweet Home, Alabama." These songs validate a homeland feeling for Coloradoans and Alabamans, but they work differently than the patriotic classics, such as "My Old Kentucky Home" and "The Missouri Waltz." To my ears the place names evoke a new level of identification with those regions of America— if not a rediscovery, at least another look.

I heard something similar, in a more literary way, in a recent collection of essays by Blanche Boyd called *The Redneck Way of Knowledge*. It is about the South and about a woman (Blanche) who left her home in South Carolina at age eighteen, fleeing "Hicksville," as she called it then, and a smothering clan of relatives with their embarrassing tastes. A dozen years later, after a marriage, a divorce, two novels, seven years in the San Francisco Bay Area, and five in New York, she moved back to Charleston. She did not come back to hide from what she found in the world outside. Rather, she returned by choice, in full consciousness, and with her eyes wide open. The redneck way of knowledge, which her book explores, cannot be disentangled from those very things she ran from—the blood ties, now too strong to ignore, and the place itself, which pulled on her like an electromagnetic field.

In Honolulu I came across a proverb. It was in a collection of old sayings published by the Bishop Museum Press. I trust the translation into English because the compiler and translator, Mary Kawena Pukui, was for many years the world's reigning expert on Hawaiian lore and language. It goes like this: "One can think about life after the fish is in the canoe."

There were dozens like it in the collection. I brought this one home and have it tacked on the wall above my desk here in Santa Cruz. The more I contemplate it the more I admire the culture that could come up with such a maxim.

Does it have anything to do with regional feeling? Well, like a true old saying it can be applied in many ways. I take it to mean something along these lines: While there is no denying we have to give some attention to Life with a capital L, i.e., The Big Picture, we do not want to become so caught up in abstractions that we forget to take care of what is right in front of our eyes.

It is an old idea, to be sure, as old as Hawai'i, but an idea whose time might be coming around again, as the world shrinks, as the rate of change itself can quicken the sense of place, and sharpen the need to attend to whatever piece of earth or cityscape you love, have chosen or reclaimed.

(1983)

Loma Prieta, Part One

As California is to the nation, I have heard it said, so is Santa Cruz to the rest of this state. There is at least a little truth in this comparison. It has its own mystique and, thanks to a rare, southern-facing shoreline, its own microclimate. Off the main travel routes, even in Spanish times, it is still a place apart, a place you have to cross a mountain range to get to.

On October 17 Santa Cruz was hit with the most ruinous disaster in its history. There may have been stronger quakes in times past, but none ever did the kind of damage that has now been telecast around the world via network news. Before the mortar dust had settled on Pacific Garden Mall, before the flames had subsided and the lost lives and lost buildings had been counted, hard questions were already being asked. Would it ever be the same again? With the downtown half demolished, could the spirit of The Town survive? Or had we just witnessed the sudden end of this quirky, quasi-Mediterranean subregion of the West?

Oddly enough, these were not new questions. They'd been in the air for quite some time, and getting louder month by month, as the rate of change in this county has accelerated. Privately and publicly, many who live here have been voicing fears that the region's ambiance and special feel would soon be lost, overwhelmed by forces perhaps more formidable than a seven point one on the Richter Scale.

The first and most seismic statistic for all things Californian is the ongoing rate of population increase, which has averaged a thousand people a day, every day of every year since 1940. Given last week's events, this may slack off a bit for a month or so, although I doubt it. The state has a long history of disaster, going all the way back to the Donner Party tragedy of 1846, and so far none of it has reduced the numbers by much at all.

There are now more than 25 million people in the state, and about 80 percent of us—some 20 million—live within thirty-five miles of the shoreline, along this narrow strip at the continent's edge, from Sonoma to the Mexican border. Everyone, it seems, would like to be within an hour of the sea. So a coastal town like Santa Cruz feels this pressure in numerous ways, some of it local, some national, some international. It's a pressure that has been building for a quarter of a century, much like the pressure between the continental plates whose constant interface makes the San Andreas Fault (which closely follows the eastern portion of our county line).

We've been living here for twenty-seven years, and for most of that time the town and the county have been in a state of agitated transition. When we arrived, Santa Cruz was still what it had been for decades—a beach town, a fishing town, a resort town, a retirement haven. It was finally "discovered" in the mid-1960s, and one day stands out in my memory as the starting point, another day that shot tremors through this unsuspecting community.

It was the day the old Hip Pocket Bookstore opened its doors on Pacific Avenue, featuring Ken Kesey, his band of Merry Pranksters, and his newly published epic novel, *Sometimes a Great Notion*. They drove down what later became the mall in their notorious decorated bus. Beat generation superhero Neal Cassidy was at the wheel, and Kesey was on the roof in a red and white striped T-shirt filming his own arrival. Soon after they parked and he'd signed a few books, a scandalous piece of sculpture was unveiled. It had been mounted above the bookstore, on the front wall of the St. George Hotel, a piece from a new series by San Francisco sculptor Ron Boise. Two life-size bronze figures, a man and a woman, depicted a scene from the Kama Sutra, the Hindu pageant of erotic statuary. The street had somehow filled with gypsy girls and VW vans and bearded men in sheepskin jackets. No one knew where they'd come from, but they were there, along with Kesey and the Kama Sutra. Elderly residents at the St. George were offended, retired army colonels and their wives complained, Baptist ministers were outraged. But the counterculture had officially come to town, and Santa Cruz would never be the same again.

That was 1964. A year later, the U.C. campus opened, bringing thousands of students, faculty, and staff, along with a broad range of challenging ideas that would eventually impact local politics and public policy. A year or so after that the small craft harbor opened, and quite suddenly a transformation had begun. A slumbering resort became a New Age headquarters, a university town, and a recreation mecca for the expanding Bay Area.

Within a few more years, as the phenomenal growth of Santa Clara Valley began to ripple outward, new thousands of commuters were living here and working over the hill.

Between 1970 and 1980 the county's population increase was greater than the increase for all of Pennsylvania, which is the nation's third largest state.

Commuters have been calling for a wider Highway 17; an expansion-minded university hopes to double the size of the local campus; the tourist industry wants to attract ever greater multitudes throughout the year; and dreams of a convention center are always on someone's drawing board. There are many voices in the air. One says, This is California, where growth cannot be stopped. Another says, What's more, all growth is progress, and it's always good because it always equals money. But the boomtown mentality that accounts for so much of California's reputation has never quite prevailed in Santa Cruz, because of the kind of place it is, and because a loud chorus is always calling out the warning: Remember San Jose. Remember Orange County.

So far people have not tended to move here for professional advantage, or to accumulate great quantities of money and power. (For that you go to L.A., or Manhattan.) They want to make a living, but not necessarily a killing. Most of the people I talk to about Santa Cruz have at least one thing in common, and that is an affection for the place itself, the qualities of the place. The pressures to develop have been locked in struggle with these affections for the place, the eternal question being: how to expand and not destroy forever the features that first drew us here.

Last week's quake did two things at once. As the demands of basic survival become uppermost, it brings this ongoing debate to a temporary halt. People who have been squabbling over land-use ordinances have to let that go and join hands for the communal good, until the land itself settles down again. But as the earth relaxes, as the aftershocks subside, and with it our panic, as the lights come back on, and as the neighborhoods come back to life, as the skies clear and as our heads clear, we get a bit of distance on the damage and the loss. We have the chance now to rethink who we are, why we are here, what this region is, what it can still become.

The downtown will be rebuilt. The form it takes may not be the form it had as of Tuesday, October 17. But it can still be true to the spirit of this community. That is what survived after the destruction of San Francisco in 1906. Buildings fall, but the spirit does not die. Half the downtown is in rubble. And I grieve for what has been lost, the lives lost, the links to heritage and history that buildings can provide for us. Cooper House, once the County Courthouse, survived severe damage in 1906. It won't survive this time. Engineers say it has to be demolished, and that loss will be profoundly felt by all of us, residents and visitors alike.

But is that where you find the spirit of a place? In a row of buildings along Main Street, or in a longtime centerpiece like Cooper House? No. They can express a spirit, but the buildings themselves came later. First there was the place itself—in this case a rare mix of light and coastal curve, inland forests, and a shoreline facing south toward Monterey Peninsula, a confluence of natural features and available resources that still gives the region its look and outline and innate appeal. And then there is the dialogue that begins between the place and the people who are drawn to it, who choose it, for whatever reason choose to linger, choose to stay. I believe the spirit resides right there, in the continuing dialogue between a place and the people who inhabit it.

My friend Jeff Dunn, a third-generation native of this town, recently published a collection of essays and profiles that pays tribute to this region, to his own family, and to the range of lives lived here. He calls it *Santa Cruz Is in the Heart*. That title was a good one when the book came out last summer. It's a better title now. It reminds us, as individuals, and as a community beginning the long road to recovery, where our truest epicenter can be found.

(1989)

Coast Range Sutra

> *One night I was meditating in such perfect*
> *stillness that two mosquitoes came and sat*
> *on each of my cheekbones and stayed there*
> *a long time without biting and then went*
> *away without biting.*
> —Jack Kerouac, *The Dharma Bums*

There is a place not far from here where the final edge of America's wilderness meets Asia. Down in the deepest canyon in the wild country behind Big Sur, where boar are hunted and lions still roam, there is a zendo, a meditation hall, and a wooden gong hanging from a rope. When you hear the mallet ringing wood on wood in the pre-dawn air, you could swear you're somewhere in the mountains of Japan.

Once or twice a year we go down there, my wife and I. For each of us the trip into the Santa Lucias is a little pilgrimage to a serene and protected place that is also an emblematic place.

Because her background is Japanese, tubs of hot spring water always revive connections to her early years growing up near Inglewood, where her father farmed row crops on land now covered by the runways of L.A. International. They had an outdoor tub, a *furo*, heated from below by a wood-fueled fire. At the end of the day her family would come in off the fields and gather there to sit and sweat and talk and soak away the aches and pains.

For me these are trips into the kind of terrain my father and I used to hike through together. He was a man who kept rifles and loved to hunt, though I later realized that the chance to get out of San Francisco and wander a while in open country was at least as important for him as bringing down a deer to carry home. I never took to the killing. I'm not sure why. Maybe it was growing up a city kid. Maybe if we had truly needed the meat it would have been a different story. But thanks to him I discovered the many pleasures of the Coast Range, the wildness of the backcountry, the boot crunch of soil under still madrones, the curl of rusty bark under arid, pale blue sky.

Somehow all of these things inhabit the atmosphere of Tassajara canyon. Wild boar. Mountain lion. Temple gong. Jay squawk. Creek tumble. Black robe. Morning sutra. Steam curl in the morning fog. Madrone and oak and manzanita. Sitting buddha. Logging road.

We follow the Carmel River inland, with tawny ridges humping above condo clusters and white-railed corrals. The valley narrows to a thickly wooded corridor, and then the semirural feel gives way to dry and rolling hills. Twenty miles in we take a winding road south to the end of the pavement, where we park our car and catch the mountain shuttle van, a workhorse Ford with nine seats and four-wheel drive and many gears. They call it "The Tassajara Stage," harking back to the days a hundred years ago when a horse and wagon traveled three times a week over this same tortuous fourteen-mile track.

Heading farther south, we climb past the scars of old fires, with blackened limbs still poking through the newer growth, and here and there a tree trunk split by lightning. The dust billows out behind, while the ridges roll away in both directions, east toward the Salinas Valley, west toward the unseen ocean, and no habitat visible now, just the gorges, the ribs of granite, and slopes furred with live oak, manzanita, pine.

In low gear for the zigzag descent we drop from five thousand feet, honking on the blind curves, and arrive at last at a long dusty clearing lined with dusty cars and pickups, and pull into the canyon/oasis where it's already hot, a dry desert heat, though the canyon is green and the creek gushes through it. The heat itself slows you down, says take your time, take your time.

The cabin is simple, old redwood siding, with a double mattress on the floor, two wooden chairs, a small chest of drawers, kerosene lamps, no electricity, screens for windows, or translucent plastic tarp, so the sound of the creek, the dripping rush of it, is always there, indoors and out, all day and night, contained and amplified within the canyon's narrow, rocky walls.

We change into the robes we picked up on our trip to Japan. Yukata for me. Kimono for Jeanne. Geometrical patterns of blue on white, diagonals and diamonds, sashes at the waist. Put the shoes away and step into slippers, and shuffle along the swept path toward the bathhouse, passing other cottages like the one we've rented, survivors from the days when this was a hunting and fishing retreat. Now yellow-green bamboo rises next to some of the walls. Reed fencing lines the path, and retaining walls of fitted stone. Small settings of creek-rolled stones have been arranged next to the steps of the cottages, giving each entryway the look of a little Japanese garden. Slippers and getas have been left outside the doors.

Past the meditation hall, past the cookhouse, an arching bridge crosses the creek. An American trout stream. An Asian footbridge made of carefully crafted, curving wood. At the far side a small altar is waiting, with incense sticks, a new blossom, a figure of the Buddha. We pause and bow, which is a way of honoring that place in each of us where the universe resides, the still center that links us all. This figure has found its way to the wilderness creekside from India, by way of China, Japan, San Francisco—serene man sitting with his feet in his lap and his hands folded. Not such a bad idea, that kind of serenity. Not such a bad ideal. If you can get to it. Or close to it. If only every once in a while.

The next step is down into the heat and steam piped up from the mineral springs that have bubbled here for longer than anyone can remember, and said to be the richest springs in the United States. In these waters thirty-two minerals have been identified, among them sulfur, sodium, calcium, magnesium, potassium, iron. Drop the robe. Slide into the wide tub lined with tile. This time of day I have the Men's Side to myself. Beyond the wall I can hear women talking. Like the creek sound, their voices punctuate the stillness. Don't move too much. Moving makes currents, and the scalding currents hurt. Let the surface turn to glass. Smell rocks in the water, a faint sulfur whiff. Heat to the neck. To the chin. As long as I can stand it. Then down a rocky path to the little reservoir of cold mountain water three feet deep, backed beyond the low stone dam. Plunge in and feel the fingerlings poking at my feet and legs, tiny fishlets come to investigate, darting in the cold, cold creek.

Splash out, and head for the tubs again, for more heat.
More cold.
More heat.
More cold.

Dry off. Slow down. At the altar, we bow again to the Buddha, and the little hand-lettered sign that sums it up:

> *With all beings*
> *I wash body and mind*
> *Free of dust*
> *Pure and shining*
> *Within and without.*

Walk back along the path, under a canopy of limbs and leaves, the granite walls rising, catching light.

Blow the cabin, next to a creekside sycamore, someone has placed a battered chair, a weatherworn wooden chair that looks older than the cabins, and that is the place to sit a while and listen. No phones down here. No radio. No TV. No boombox from the guy in the next lane or from a garage across the way. No cars inside the compound. No ads. No neon. No email or internet or fax for urgent messages. Just this dry heat under oaks and sycamores, the steady tumble of the creek, the squawk of jays coming to see who's here and check for random scraps of food, with a breeze along the water from time to time to riffle leaves that send sparks of sunlight through the canyon shade. When the alder leaves quiver, a softer light splashes upward, mountain strobe light rippled by the creek god's hidden hand.

Waking early I hear the sound of water against the far wall of our cabin, like bacon sizzling on a grill. Jeanne will sleep until the chill is off the air and then head straight for the baths, to get in a soak before breakfast. I have a morning pilgrimage in mind, up to the spot where they've erected a memorial to the man who first imagined this oldtime mountain resort could be transformed into a Zen retreat and monastery.

His name was Shunryu Suzuki Roshi. Born in Japan in 1905, he came to the U.S. at age fifty-three. They say he was a small and very private fellow, both humble and forceful, instructing more by example than by words. He'd been trained in the Soto Zen tradition, and going to America was, for many years, his dream. When he was invited to become the priest at a San Francisco Buddhist temple, in 1958, he read-ily accepted. Before long he had founded the San Francisco Zen Center, which, in 1967, acquired this acreage in Tassajara Canyon. It was the first Zen monastery to be established any-where in the world outside Asia.

Four years later Suzuki Roshi passed away, having spent
the final months of his life right here, gardening, lecturing,
preparing himself and his followers for his death. In the style
and feel of what this place has become, in the very joints of
the carpentry, his example and his spirit live on.

Yesterday, in the office, I was checking through the shelf
of books and pamphlets they keep for browsers, and I heard
someone behind the counter say that after his cremation,
his ashes had been divided, with some buried here and some
buried in Japan. Though I've been to the canyon a dozen
times, I'd never heard this mentioned. It took me by surprise,
caused my forearm hairs to prickle.

"Dividing the ashes," I said, "that's quite a statement."

"He felt such strong ties to both places," this woman
replied. She wore a collarless shirt, round glasses, brown hair
cropped close.

"Do you know where in Japan?"

"Where he came from, I think. But I'm not sure about the
details. You'd have to ask someone who's been around here
longer than I have."

At this early hour the jays are quiet. Sutras spill from the
zendo in low-voiced Japanese. When the voices fade behind
me, there is only the creek. From the road I take a narrow
footpath that begins a steady climb through live oak and
bay and sycamore. A couple of switchbacks, another climb,
then I pass below an overhang into a small clearing of raked
gravel, under an umbrella of oak limbs, the kind of space that
requires you to stop and pay attention. Someone has already
been up here this morning. The tine marks look fresh. The
ground itself says walk with care.

A low retaining wall of fitted stones is built against the
farther embankment. In front of it stands a chunk of granite about four feet high, roughly triangular, with a flat side
facing out. The stone is gray with a greenish cast. From

the top, a coating of white, like thick paint or white lava, seems ready to spill. A streak of white cuts across the flat face of the stone like a vein just under the skin, or a lightning streak. Where did it come from? I wonder. There is movement in this stone, an uncarved, unaltered piece of natural sculpture that is stationary and fixed, yet somehow catches and conveys the flow and energy of life.

Around it, smaller stones make an altar, where pale green mandalas of lichen cling. On the flat place in front of these stones, a metal vase holds a bamboo stem, some wildflowers, and next to it an incense bowl.

This slightly sculpted place has the feel of the garden we saw in Japan, behind the Zen temple at Dazaifu, outside Fukuoka, though it is more surprising, somehow more remarkable, since this little space has been cleared at the very edge of raw wilderness. Here and there, young trees rise through the gravel, so that the space is open yet not empty of vegetation. With its canopy of limbs it is in fact just one step away from the rugged terrain you see beyond the trees, the steep ridges higher up with their rocky outcroppings, the empty arroyos veering off through cliffs of scrub oak and manzanita.

The centerpiece, the quietly majestic hunk of living stone, is *of* that terrain, still connected to it, though set apart now, singled out, to honor the pioneering Roshi. This shrine also honors and recognizes all that surrounds it here, the singularity of every other stone, each leaf, each life, each day, each bird trill in the morning air, each moment in the midst of the cosmic pond that has no beginning and no end.

(1995)

Clay

Pond Farm is a spread of pastoral acreage—shade oaks and yellow grass—in the hills above the Russian River, seventy miles north of San Francisco. It holds the home, workshop, and school of the master potter Marguerite Wildenhain. She spends most of each year alone at her wheel, dipping pots into syrupy vats of glaze, firing the kiln that will heat and harden the clay. For parts of each year, she teaches. And students have come from around the world to learn from her, not only about pottery but about the life she has developed through her craft.

She is a small woman, with shrewd eyes and gull-gray hair pulled back, and a mouth that smiles easily. At her wheel, you will find her dressed in faded jeans and cotton workshirt with sleeves rolled to the elbow. Her hands will be brown and wet from the clay as she plops a lump into the center and pats it into place. She kicks the lower wheel with both feet and covers the lump with her hands, pressing it, easing her thumbs into the center until a cylinder begins to rise. One hand reaches deep, pushing from inside, bulging the clay, and from this slick globe a slender neck sprouts, then flattens at the top to a lip. She kicks the wheel again, hands barely wet with brown water as she shapes the bottle, trimming, smoothing. "Imagine," she says, "that you are breathing into the bottle or pitcher or bowl, and when you can breathe no more air into it, when it is full, then it is finished."

With a copper wire, she cuts the bottle from her wheel, lifts it, sets it in a row with others, then throws a new lump onto the wheel and begins to pull from the brown clay another pot—a jar this time, or a footed bowl—as she has been doing for over forty years.

This wheel is at the center of her world. From it radiate the glazed and figured vases, platters, bottles, and jugs that have earned her an international reputation for inspired craftsmanship and artistic integrity. Today her work stands in galleries and museums from Munich to Dallas, from Pasadena to Stoke-on-Trent. Marguerite Wildenhain was trained in Germany at the famous Bauhaus of the old Weimar Republic in the years after World War One. Her work continues the tradition she inherited there—a sureness of touch, a mastery of form, a classic simplicity.

Whatever she breathes into her work has somehow permeated the land, the buildings, the garden of succulents around her cottage. And in the summer when her workshop becomes a classroom, when the students come to study her ceramic techniques, it's not just pottery she offers but an attitude toward one's work, as well as a style of living—all derived from the tradition she was trained in, transplanted to northern California's hills in a way that makes Pond Farm a world of its own.

It's a modest empire she designed herself and has maintained for more than two decades. A few years ago, the State of California decided to extend the boundaries of a state park to include her land. It meant the end of Pond Farm—until potters, artists, teachers, admirers, and former students from all parts of the country deluged Sacramento with pleas on her behalf. They succeeded. She is still there, on a lease that allows her to continue her work as long as she lives.

To reach this world, you head north from the resort town of Guerneville, then enter a lush grove of redwoods, a state park of shaggy trunks and deep-forest ferns. You emerge on a mountain road that curls up through slick hills of summer grass until you reach a wooden gate, where a sign says "Pond Farm Pottery," and below that a hand-lettered footnote, "There is no duck pond, trout farm, or fish hatchery."

The farm takes its name from a marshy hollow, fed by a natural spring, in a depression between three hills. Above the pond, atop one of these hills, set among oaks, palms, bay, and walnut trees, stands a peak-roofed redwood building—a combination pottery, display room, and school—with a firing kiln and twenty-one potting wheels arranged along aisles where, during July and August, she bustles from student to student, commenting on everything from lid width to logic.

Twenty-five years ago, this building was a wind-eaten barn of a style still common in northern California—a long center room, high-peaked for hay storage, and flanked by two sloping side sheds where animals or vehicles were housed. The back end was extended, a fourth room was added to the front, and all became workrooms. The pottery floor still slopes a little, following the original pitch. Above it now, in the central room, frosted panes fill the pottery with light but no glare. Along the smaller, slant-roofed side rooms, the windows are framed with roses and look north toward wooded hills or south over the Russian River Valley. Because the farm is some seven hundred feet above sea level, the air is almost always clear. Mornings, the valley below is filled with fog that drifts in from the ocean fifteen miles west. In the summer when the class starts work at eight, the fog is a white lake beneath steep ridges of the Coast Range.

Inside, the fittings are almost entirely of wood. She designed it that way. Nothing glitters, nothing gleams except the pots when they're glazed. Everything is tinged with a faint tan chalkiness from the years and tons of clay that potters have kneaded, fondled, and spun. Along each aisle runs a narrow plank, where the students, like bakers with heaps of brown dough, wedge and pound their clay into loaves.

The wheels, too, are wooden and turned by foot-power. While working clay on an upper wheel, the potter keeps it spinning by kicking a wheel near the floor and fixed to the same shaft. She prefers this to a motored wheel.

She pushes her arms into a deep, imaginary bowl and begins to pull an invisible pot. "As you begin to open the clay, you kick hard and take a breath. When you are working well, just when you need another breath, you have raised the clay to a point where you naturally want the wheel to move slower. And it will have slowed down some by then." Her elbows jut as her hands depict the breathing point. "So you take another breath and kick the wheel, and your hands and feet and lungs are all working together making the pot. There is a rhythm in your body, you see, that no motor can duplicate."

Between these wheels lie planks that intersect the aisle-long shelf. As each student finishes a piece, he places it on the plank in front of him. When one is full, lined with tan jars and jugs and pitchers, he carries it outside to dry in the sun. When the pots are leather-hard, some may be decorated, painted, or etched with a thin knife.

Most will be smashed. Because what she offers, in this onetime hay barn, on this isolated hillside, in this quietly efficient Arcadia, is a course as demanding as an American potter is likely to find. She emphasizes first a mastery of forms. When you've shown that you can center and open a lump of clay—and not every student can do this properly at first, even after a year or two of potting elsewhere—you then make a simple flowerpot. You throw ten flowerpots, maybe fifteen, until you can control that particular form. You break them up, drop them into a heap of shards that later will be reprocessed into usable clay. And you progress to the next form, a simple dish the students call a "doggy dish," of which you throw ten, or twenty. In this way, moving at your own pace, in terms of your own skill and experience, you study the bellied coffee mug, you add a handle, you make a mug narrow at the top and wide at the bottom, and so on until you've faced spouted pitchers, footed bowls, cups, plates, and teapots—in all, some twenty basic forms. Each grows from the previous one in an orderly sequence, and all are classic, fundamental to the potter's craft.

The reason for this approach, she says, is simple. "It's a matter of starting at the beginning. Too many teachers put a student on a wheel and turn him loose, saying, 'Express yourself.' Well, self-expression is fine, but first you must master fundamentals. It is purely a matter of knowing what you are doing. You ask a carpenter what he is making. He can tell you. It will be a door or a window or a wall. You ask some potters what they are making. Today too many say, 'I don't know. We'll see how it turns out.' I don't believe you can make a good pot that way. You have to know what you are making."

Emphasis on control is but the first step. Form is the springboard. Through its discipline one arrives at the fullest freedom of expression. "When you know how to throw well," she says, "all the plates, pitchers, and bowls, when you can produce decent teapots with spouts that pour and lids that fit, then is the time to try more consciously for personal forms, for more imaginative pots, for wider experimenting."

When they arrive at Pond Farm, the students have been throwing pots for from one to ten years. From among some fifty applicants each year, she chooses twenty-one. Some are gifted college students, some are arts and crafts instructors with master's degrees in ceramics, some are already professional potters. Each year, five or six are former students back for advanced work. Recently she accepted an electronics engineer who decided in midlife to leave the weapons industry and pursue full-time what had long been a hobby. Hopeful potters have come to her from every state in the Union, as well as from Canada, China, India, and Lebanon. They rent cabins or camp somewhere along the river and drive the winding road each day to spend six hours at their wheels.

After two months' work, during which a student throws four or five hundred pieces, five or six may be saved, glazed, and fired in the kiln. Some students fire nothing. "There's no use," she says, "wasting glaze and kiln space on a poorly made pot." On the other hand, a talented student may end up with a dozen pieces worth keeping.

While the class works, the teacher moves from wheel to wheel, from room to room. When she speaks, her accent is not quite French though she was born in France, not quite German though she studied and lived in Germany for many years, not quite Dutch though she worked in Holland before coming to California. Still, her voice is distinctly European and persuasive with the soft certainty of one who has devoted a lifetime to her art.

A willowy, freckled girl with slender hands is molding a pitcher with a short neck and a pouring lip. The teacher stops near the wheel, narrows her eyes. "These look too much like plastic, like rubber. You see? The curve is too fast from the bowl to the neck. You want to curve not so fast." And she weaves her hands like a man describing a woman's hips. Her hands and wrists are chalky brown where clay has dried.

The girl says, "Yes. Yes, I see what you mean." She squashes the pitcher into a wrinkled glob and begins again.

Behind her sits a husky, bearded man—intent, shaping a jug and kicking his wheel ferociously. The teacher's eyes crinkle with an amused severity. "Kick more gently, otherwise you loosen the screws in the wheel. Then they must be tightened. And you know who has to crawl under all those planks with a screwdriver."

At the third wheel, a blonde woman of about thirty is trimming a footed bowl. To a potter, the "foot" is everything beneath the bowl itself, and this one is too high for the bowl's size. "It is a matter of proportion," the teacher says. "To have a foot this high on a bowl this wide, you need handles on both sides, for balance, for form. But that depends, then, on what the bowl is used for. On a doggy dish you don't want a high foot and wide handles. Too elaborate, don't you think? Not appropriate."

Her voice grows louder and her dark eyes crinkle again. Other students, still hunched over their wheels, listen to a digression meant for all.

"I once threw some funeral urns and they came out very small, because you know the box that holds the ashes is always small. About this big. I decided I had to do something about that urn. So I put it on a high foot, and I made a fancy lid, and big handles on each side, and it became a noble piece. It had dignity, suited to the function. But you don't want to do that with a doggy dish."

Her voice stops. Once more she glances at the footed bowl, then smiles at the woman who has already begun to raise another, and she steps through the low doorway, out of sight into the next room. The work goes on. New bowls and pitchers gradually fill the planks, as wheels spin, as each student works harder to erase the rubbery look or find the right balance of all the parts.

Each morning at ten, the class stops for coffee. On the yellow mat of footworn grass in front of the pottery, they lounge in the sun or under the peach tree. Some mornings she reads aloud from Stravinsky or Van Gogh or T. S. Eliot or Ben Shahn, while nearby stands the previous day's potting—high jars with lids, bowls with graceful handles, narrow-necked bottles. All are chalky tan, drying in the sun, delicately etched or painted earthy reds and browns and sinuous with a purity of line that grows from the basic forms.

This particular morning she reads about the migration of eels. It's a story by Rachel Carson, describing how young eels, spawned in mid-Atlantic, leave their birthplace near the Sargasso Sea and head for America's eastern coast, then swim upstream against the current to inland lakes which eons ago were part of the Atlantic and which, if geologists are correct, will become so once again.

What has this to do with pottery? Nothing perhaps—or everything. The eels typify that urge toward origins, which for man, in one sense, is the clay. Also they appeal to this teacher's lifelong fascinations with the forms and movements of nature. "Observe how nature solves its many problems and you will learn more about pottery, more about form than I can ever teach you."

For this reason, the class moves outdoors one day each week. Next to the pottery stands a broad walnut tree, and in its shade a low, roughhewn table with benches. The students spread out there and try to sketch a stone; on another day, a flower; on another, apples, leaves, the trees themselves.

"Look closely at that oak. Every thrust, every line has its reason. Exactly how does it grow out of the earth? Where do the large branches start? How again do the small ones fork, at what angle, and in what proportion? What does the bark look like? And the leaves, how are they arranged? What is the movement of the total tree, definitely upward as in the pine, or drooping as in the willow? If you look closely, you will discover the oak's particular tension. It comes from inside pushing out. And in a few lines you should be able to capture it."

Toward the end of her course, they attempt the human figure, and the motive is the same. Under the walnut tree they spend an afternoon sketching one another, while the teacher moves from drawing to drawing. The willowy, freckled girl is lying on her side; and across the circle, the bearded man who kicks his wheel so violently is sketching her now, with rapid strokes.

The teacher squats near him. "Have you looked closely at that girl?"

In the pottery he sits right behind her. He grins. "As a matter of fact, I have."

When the rest of the class begins to laugh, the teacher smiles broadly. "For about six hours a day, yes?"

Their laughter swells, then trickles into silence, and she continues, "Well, look once more. See how she leans on her elbow? The whole weight of the body seems to push on her arm. That is the line of tension that will give your drawing strength. With the others, who sit or lean in another way, the line is somewhere else, and with each person it is different, though they may take the same pose. Always look for that line of tension."

She shows them masterpieces from her own collection. In a workroom she displays the drawings she has collected— by Picasso, Feininger, and Gerhard Marcks, the German painter and sculptor she studied with at the Bauhaus. She has over a hundred of his works, spanning half a century. Above the cluster of heads there rises the study of a nude, and the teacher remarks, "See the lines. There are not many. But each one is sure and certain. Notice this single stroke that makes the leg. All of us can learn much from such a man, about how to shape a pot, how to control its contour, and how to decorate it."

She's sitting on a low stool, in her tennis shoes, workshirt, and jeans. Gently she sets the drawing down. Inclining toward the stack, she reaches for another and adds what might be— were it not for the intensity of her gaze—just an afterthought. "It is finally a matter, you see, of working from within, from within the subject and from within yourself. Rodin said it in his *Testament*. 'All life surges from the center, then grows and blossoms from the inside toward the outside.'"

Marguerite Wildenhain talks a great deal, but she does not preach. She simply offers what she knows. And her students listen because masters are rare these days. One quickly senses in her voice, her manner, the strength of her hard-won authority.

She began as a sculptress, studying first in Berlin. Later she worked as a designer in a porcelain factory but soon gave that up and apprenticed herself in pottery at the Bauhaus in Weimar, in 1919, the year it opened, led by the architect Walter Gropius, together with such men as Gerhard Marcks, Paul Klee, and Kandinsky. For seven years she worked with Marcks and the potter Max Krehan. Her training included a prolonged study of traditional European potting technique as well as the newest concepts of form and style.

When she left Weimar she was a master potter. For several years she headed the ceramics department of an arts and crafts school in Halle/Saale. Meanwhile, she worked again designing porcelain. When the Nazis came to power, she moved to Holland, where she set up her own pottery and continued to design porcelain for a Dutch manufacturer. Just before the Nazis invaded Holland in 1940, she moved again, this time to the United States.

In Holland she had met an American, Gordon Herr, who talked about starting a crafts center in northern California, near Guerneville, and it was there she settled in 1941. The crafts center never materialized, but she remained, having found an ideal place to work and live.

During her first two years in California she taught at the College of Arts and Crafts in Oakland. But she decided she would rather try to survive as an independent potter. She had two thousand dollars saved, and one weathered barn on a hill above a marsh. With Herr's assistance she started work on the side room once used for stalling horses. She shoveled out manure, tore down rickety partitions, installed shelves, a kiln, and four kick wheels.

She invested a thousand dollars in equipment, leaving another thousand to live on until her pots began to sell, or until students began to arrive.

They weren't long in seeking her out. Her reputation had followed her. From many parts of the country came requests for instruction. At first she took two or three at a time, for a few months, sometimes for a year. By 1948 she could afford to add ten more wheels. Soon she began to offer her two-month course. In time she was able to buy the land, remodel the rest of her barn, and add seven more wheels, making twenty-one, the number of students she now accepts.

For twenty-five years she has remained free, professionally and economically, from institutions and foundations, living almost entirely by her work and her classes. And because she is a potter first and a teacher second, her students receive a rare kind of instruction. "I actually invite them to my home, you see, where I work and where I live. So they see not only how I make pots but what the life of at least one potter is like. That is something you don't get in many schools these days."

Her students agree. They get no piece of paper when they leave, no credential or diploma. But as she points out, "They *can* throw pots. If we must set a precise goal, I would rather see a potter work toward a master*piece* instead of a master's *thesis*."

She sums up her theories on craft, education, art, and life in her book, *Pottery: Form and Expression*. It's not a ceramics manual with kiln temperatures and glaze formulas, but rather one potter's statement of belief. It begins like this:

Technique alone, without any moral and ethical point of departure or aim, has brought us to the very edge of a universal catastrophe that we have in no way overcome.

To achieve this necessary future victory over ourselves and the terrifying world that we have created, we will need to find again a synthesis between technical knowledge and spiritual content. It is not a question of the crafts only, the problem is as wide as the whole of human civilization.

Down the grassy slope from her workshop-classroom stands the redwood cottage she designed and built. Outside the door her patio is spotted with shards set in concrete, rims of broken bowls, jagged sides of jars and pitchers glazed green or mottled blue or ebony. Above these fragments, a grape arbor sifts the sun that showers down with Mediterranean insistence. On summer afternoons when a day's session is finished, she may invite a few students to her patio for a glass of wine. And this leafy world of warm breezy shade is her salon.

Around the house and patio grows her garden of cactus and succulents—over thirty varieties originally fertilized with the manure from in and around the horse stalls she renovated. "One hundred and forty wheelbarrows of manure I carried down here, and I remember every barrow." Her eyelids close above a grim smile, then snap open brightly. "But it made a lovely garden, I think."

She points to a plant with flat, thick leaves and a broccoli-like blossom at the end of a long stem. "You see that cactus? I have watched it for many weeks. I sit here and watch how it gradually crosses the pattern of those trees back there and the yellow field. Every day the shape is a little different against the background, and every day it is beautiful in a slightly different way. Here, you know, there is time to observe such things."

Everyone turns to look at the plant. "That's why I live in the country. There is time to think, time to watch things grow. In the city there is no time, everything happens too fast. I go to the city sometimes because I must, but I'm thrown completely out of balance. Out here I always know

where I am, and who I am. Do you know the Greek legend of
Heracles and Antaeus? Antaeus was that giant Heracles had
to kill. It was one of his labors. But he could only kill him if
Antaeus' feet left the ground. As long as his feet were on the
ground, no one could harm him. Well, I am like Antaeus."
And she grins. "Not that I am a giant. But..." She raises her
small feet, where she is sitting, and plants them solidly on
her patio. "Out here my feet are on the ground."

(1968)

Loma Prieta, Part Two

week after the earthquake I had a call from an editor in New York who wanted to know if our house was still standing and were we okay and was the town okay. He'd been trying to get through for days. He'd been out here a couple of times and had a particular affection for Santa Cruz, the bay, the local ambiance. All he'd seen on television was what the world had by then seen many times over—flames rising from the wreckage of a main street eight miles from the epicenter.

"We're all right," I told him. "Everything that used to be on a shelf is now on the floor. The chimney cracked and will have to come down. But we'll survive."

"My heart goes out to you people," he said.

"It was bad. But not as bad as it looked on the news. They always show you the worst part."

"Anybody pulling out?" he asked with a nervous chuckle. "You people thinking of moving to safer ground?"

"We've talked about it," I said, which was true, but after two days of terror, followed by two days of despair, then two days of paralyzed apathy, I had finally come around to the longer view. "I guess every place people live has its hazard. Carolina has its hurricane. Texas has its tornado. Minnesota has its blizzard. Kaua'i has its tidal wave."

"None of that sounds as bad to me as an earthquake," he said. "That is the worst of the worst. And yet"—here his voice dropped, seemed to get lonesome with what sounded like regret—"and yet when I think about your life out there on the coast, I realize that in between the quakes what you people have is the best of the best."

"I don't know if I would go that far."

"Believe me, I look out the window here—sometimes it feels like everything is simply falling apart."

I should point out that this editor was about to lose his job in the wake of yet another corporate merger. For him the Big Apple had recently lost most of its polish. But what struck me was the sound of longing as he continued to talk about "the coast"—a place where something else seemed possible, some alternative to whatever his life had become. What I heard in his voice was yet another version of the Legend that never seems to die, somehow survives in spite of all reports to the contrary, in spite of a seven point one on the Richter Scale.

Where does it come from, this legend, this vision that glows and shimmers out here along the continent's Pacific shore? This editor friend of mine, he was not remembering twilight congestion on the Nimitz. He was not seeing the chemical spill that puts ten thousand cars on hold for an hour or two or three. He was not remembering the yellowish cloud larger than Lake Tahoe that hangs over the L.A. basin much of the time, nor was he thinking of the disappearing aquifers under San Jose. From his midtown office, over-whelmed by career crisis and gazing west, he was remembering other things.

He was remembering the look of San Francisco as you cross the Bay Bridge in late afternoon, when light rising off the water gives the city its own aura, and Tamalpais is rimmed with violet against the western sky. He was remembering the look of Highway 1 as you head south from Pacifica, from urban sprawl to the sudden and dazzling wildness of the shoreline cliffs. He was remembering trim fields of brussels sprouts covering the benchlands outside Davenport, and then, coming around the coastal curve, the look of the Monterey Peninsula as seen from the north. From across the water, on a clear day, it appears to be a large and mountainous offshore island, the island you will one day have all to yourself, the cloud-bordered island of your dreams.

The legend of California takes many shapes. Financial gain is always part of it. Long before the Gold Rush men dreamed of an El Dorado out there at the farthest edge of the unknown world. Opportunity is part of it, the legend of a place you can travel to in order to change your life or your luck, to take the risk, to start again, or play the final card. And setting has been part of it too. This region's natural endowments—the extraordinary mix of climate, resources, and scenic grandeur—have been as central to the legend as Barbary Coast or Hollywood or the perfect '57 Thunderbird.

I am continually amazed that so many of these endowments are still available to us, given the rate of growth, the rate of consumption. No matter where you live, no matter what traffic jam is driving you crazy, you are never more than an hour or two from some stretch of spectacular coastline or open country and the essential nourishment—call it food for the soul—these places offer us.

Wilderness is still within reach, often within view. Here in Santa Cruz, where twenty-five thousand people now commute daily over Highway 17 into Silicon Valley and then commute back home again, the through-county traffic at rush hour along

Highway 1 is not much different from Marin County or Santa Monica. Yet if you stay on Highway 1, heading south, you will soon arrive at Mal Paso Creek, trickling through the first of what Robinson Jeffers called "the many canyons the great sea-wall of coast is notched with."

It's another example of a sudden and startling shift in terrain. From the Monterey / Carmel coastline—a bulge of points and beaches and sandy knolls that is essentially Mediterranean in character—you enter an entirely different realm, with its own brand of loveliness, bold and stark and monumental. For as far as you can see, the headlands of Big Sur are rising to the south. If you are in the mood to set foot to a hiking trail, within about ninety minutes from Santa Cruz, or two hours from Silicon Valley, you can be climbing past one of those headlands and into the Los Padres National Forest.

Who dares predict how long such transitions will be possible? One of the large California ironies is the way its very virtues seem fated to bring about the state's undoing. According to recent projections from the Bank of America, we can expect six million more people in the next decade. The rate of growth statewide now runs about fourteen hundred to fifteen hundred people *per day*, every day of every week, along with the more alarming fact that the number of vehicles grows at a rate greater than the human population. The pressure on resources and open space, which already seems enormous, can only increase. All the more reason that these natural blessings—the shorelines, the beaches, the headlands, the wetlands, the parks, the peaks, the buttes, the groves, the desert vistas, the surviving whitewater rapids, the surviving stands of first-growth redwoods—should be revered and attended to.

I use the word "revered" by design. Not long after the earthquake I had another conversation about California, with a man who sees it not from without, not from afar, but from within, a man so deeply rooted you can almost think the western earth is speaking through him.

His name is Frank LaPena, stocky and brown-skinned, with a silver beard and silver hair receding from his smooth forehead. He lives in Sacramento, where he heads the Native American studies program at the state university campus. He grew up farther north, in a region bounded by the McCloud River, Redding, and Mount Shasta, traditionally the home region of his people, the Wintu.

We talked about Mount Shasta, which dominates the landscape in Wintu country. For him this fourteen-thousand-foot volcanic peak is much more than a dramatic landmark and a photographer's delight, much more than a challenge for climbers and skiers. It is a holy place he approaches with respect and reverence. For him the mountain can be a kind of mentor.

"If you sit still and listen to it," he says quietly, "it can teach you a lot."

He described a sacred spring, one you reach via an old trail not marked or shown on any map. "I used to get water there to take as a gift to my uncle, who was an elder living on the Clear Creek Reservation. It was the best gift I could take him, because he knew where it came from, that it came from the mountain and was blessed. You have different kinds of springs up there, you see. Some are sulfur. Some are hot. This was a soda spring, with cleansing and purifying powers. You offer a prayer when you take the water. And all this would be carried in the jar that I brought to my uncle."

Layered with generations of family memory, Shasta also serves as a chapel and a sanctuary. He talked about a pilgrimage he had made to the mountain when another uncle passed away. He went on foot and left behind a lock of his own hair, as he expressed his grief and prayed for safe passage. For the Wintu, who call themselves the mountain/river people, Shasta is your final point of contact with this world, and your gateway to the next.

As I heard these stories I envied Frank. I envied this kind of tie to a feature of the California landscape. He is linked to a majestic place by bonds both ancient and ancestral. No matter how much we may claim to care about the state or some part of it, few of us nowadays have been here long enough to have an ancestral sense for the region. Two generations is a lot. Seven is about the longest pedigree you hear anyone claim, if some forebear happened to be with the Portolá or De Anza party. Half a generation is closer to the norm.

I call myself a native, since I was born in San Francisco. Early in life I was following my Texas father along trout streams in Mendocino County and tent-camping in the Yolla Bolly mountains above Ukiah. So I have come to love the ridges and the valleys of the long Coast Range, the part of the world I look upon as my natural habitat. Can you measure that against the earth-tied ancestry of a man whose people have inhabited the upper Sacramento Valley for thousands of years and countless generations? Of course, you can't. There is no comparison. But maybe there is a lesson to be learned. Maybe we can learn something from the people who have been here the longest. Now, more than ever, some reverence would help, to leaven the speed and the greed.

I told Frank that after the Loma Prieta quake, with its epicenter just eight miles away, I'd been filled with fear and runaway anxiety and, for a while, a sense of betrayal. I told him I'd longed then for a place I could go and stand and voice my fear and release my anxiety and make some kind of peace with the powers residing in the earth.

"As you tell me about your pilgrimage to the mountain, I realize what a yearning I have in my own life for that kind of ritual or for that kind of relationship. I wish my culture provided me with more guidance in this area. But it doesn't."

I was astounded by his reply. "You don't have to deprive yourself of that," he said. "It is really up to you. It is always

available. You can awaken that aspect of a place, if you make
your own connection with it."

It is really up to you.

What a liberating idea—that I could awaken the sacred
aspect of a place, or at least open the way to such a possibility. What it means is being awakened to that place in myself,
that possibility in myself, and allowing the openness to such
a dialogue.

Frank had reminded me of things my body and my nervous system tend to forget, spending, as I do, too much time
in the world we've created for ourselves, the world of concrete and credit cards. It is sometimes convenient to forget
that our strongest ties are not with the asphalt but with what
lies just a foot or so beneath it. Maybe this is the upside of
a 7.1 on the Richter. During those thirty seconds when the
ground wobbled and this house rolled like a ship at sea, I was
forced to acknowledge, in another way, our oldest and most
primal bond. The earth itself is always in charge. We are here
by grace, as lucky guests, and we really have no choice but
to honor and respect and revere its many cycles and its many
wondrous forms.

(1990)

PART TWO

KINSHIP

Oh, Susannah,
Don't you cry for me,
For I come from Alabama
With my banjo on my knee.
　　—Stephen Foster

Ancestors

In 1809 my great-great-great-great-grandfather left Buncombe County, North Carolina, and crossed over the Appalachians into central Tennessee. I have thought a lot about that trip. Of the numerous trips it has taken to bring my family—that is, the handful of us scattered along this coastline—from the eastern edge of the continent to the western edge, that one looms largest in my imagination. I cannot say it looms large in memory. No one now living knows much at all about it, nor have I heard it talked about or seen anything written about it, apart from the dates and the names of counties, and the prices he paid for a couple of pieces of land, and the name of his wife, Temperance, the names of their four sons, Gideon, Louis, Reuben, Nathan, and their one daughter, Elinder.

His name was Noble Bouldin, a churchgoing farmer who came from a long line of farmers, as far back as lineage can be traced. The first Bouldin to cross the Atlantic, they say, was a fellow named Thomas, a Warwickshire yeoman who landed at Jamestown in 1610 and quickly acquired some land along the James River. Perhaps he was the original immigrant ancestor. If not, there was another Bouldin, sooner or later, very much like him, who carried the seed, and Virginia was the homeland for almost two hundred years, until after the Revolutionary War, when the West began to beckon, the West, at the turn of that century, being Ohio, Kentucky, Tennessee.

In those days nothing happened suddenly. A family on the move might stop a while along the trail, set up a cabin and clear a piece of land, as Noble did, in 1803 or thereabouts. He paid a hundred dollars for fifty acres, between the Blue Ridge Mountains and the Great Smokies, and worked it for a couple of years, no doubt picking up scraps of information here and there about what lay beyond the peaks in the distance.

Perhaps he made the next trip alone, the first time, scouting ahead before bringing his family farther than most white Americans had ever traveled and into territory few had ever seen. Perhaps it took a couple of weeks, or a month, with long days of solitary riding, during which he missed his wife and children, but also savored the solitude and the daily discovery of new terrain. On one such morning he may have gotten an early start and reached a ridge top just as the sun rose behind him, adding sudden clarity and sharp shadows to the rippling landscape, causing his heart to swell and his skin to prickle and his blood to run. He may have shouted something then, one long syllable of exultation.

Or perhaps not. Perhaps he was a born slob, unmoved by natural wonders, insensitive to color and light, and concerned only with grabbing the best piece of land he could find before someone else got hold of it. Maybe he was an ignorant, stubborn, hotheaded redneck, a rifle-toting hillbilly racist from North Carolina. But I prefer not to remember him that way. I prefer to dwell on his name—Noble—and to look in his farmer's heart for signs of noble character. I prefer to see him

on the ridge top at dawn, like a wolf in the wilderness, celebrating with his voice, celebrating the miracle of his own life.

However it happened, he must have liked what he saw or
had heard about. According to courthouse records, he sold
his Buncombe County acreage for a two-hundred-dollar
profit. Then he packed up his family and all their worldly
goods and continued west. There were tools to carry, a
plough, knives and rifles, a Bible or two, a fiddle. Noble was
in his thirties then, halfway through the Appalachians and
halfway through his life. I see him wearing a hat like the one
Walt Whitman wore for the frontispiece to *Leaves of Grass*,
a dark and wide-brimmed hat, tipped back. No one knows
what he looked like. He passed away before cameras came
along. I can only speculate, and hope, that he resembled
Whitman, with that kind of questioning eye, the trimmed
beard showing some gray, and the top button of his long
johns showing underneath the open-neck shirt.

He would be walking in front of a horse, and Temperance
would be riding, in order to hold and nurse the newborn
daughter. There were other horses, perhaps a wagon or two,
perhaps not. It was spring, and the ground was cool and
damp, but no longer muddy, and by the summer of 1809 they
had staked out a Tennessee homestead, in Warren County,
near the banks of the Collins River.

After that, one thing led to another. Noble had already
begat Gideon, who was thirteen when they made this journey. Gideon eventually built a house right on the county line,
making it possible, so I have heard, to leave Warren County
and cross over into Van Buren County just by stepping from
the parlor into the kitchen.

In 1831 Gideon begat Montesque, the fifth of his ten children
and my great-great-grandfather, naming him after the eigh-
teenth-century French philosopher. I will defend the moun-
tainized spelling of this name the way George Hearst once
defended himself at the California Democratic Convention.

The rambunctious, self-made millionaire father of William Randolph Hearst, George was hoping to be nominated for governor. One of his opponents had accused him of being so ignorant he had spelled the word bird, b-u-r-d. "If b-u-r-d does not spell bird," Hearst asked his fellow delegates, "just what in the hell *does* it spell?"

If M-o-n-t-e-s-q-u-e does not spell Montesquieu, what else in the world *could* it spell?

This fellow did two things that linger in the family memory. 1. Sometime before the Civil War he left the flat farmlands his grandfather and father had settled and worked, and he moved up onto the nearby Cumberland Plateau. In a region called Pleasant Hill he built a two-story house out of axe-hewn logs and began to raise his family. 2. When the war came along he did not fight for the South, as several of his brothers did. Montesque fought for the North. Or so goes the official version of that era—the official version being what I first heard from my grandmother, as she passed her memories on, during the years when I was growing up in San Francisco. Back in 1969, however, when I made my one and only pilgrimage into the Cumberlands to look up some of the surviving relatives, looking for the granddads and great-granddads I might have known, I heard another version, and one that appealed to me a lot more.

One of Montesque's grandsons was still alive, an aging cousin thrice removed, who had spent his whole life in those mountains, farming mostly. At eighty he was erect and spry and vigorous, wore a twill shirt, coveralls. He felt a special bond with Montesque, since he was the only one in the family, or in the entire world, for that matter, to inherit the name. I should say he *almost* inherited the name. When it crossed the Atlantic, from Paris to Van Buren County, in the 1830s, two letters had fallen out, like teeth. And somewhere between the generations, a consonant had disappeared, so that this eighty-year-old cousin of mine had ended up with a name that is surely unique in the long history of French-speakers taking liberties with English, and English-speakers getting even by taking liberties with French. His given name was *Montacue*.

We were in the frontroom of his old frame house in the little town of Spencer, Tennessee, sitting in two straight-backed chairs, when I asked him about this spelling. He shook his silvered head in true wonder.

"It's always mystified me," he said, "how a whole letter could get lost like that. When I was born, granddad was still alive and sure must a knowed how to say his own name. It ain't like people up here got somethin so big caught between their teeth, they're afraid to let some air through. I guess that ol *S* just dropped out of sight about like the way granddad did during the war."

"Which war was that?"

"*The* war," he said.

"I heard somewhere that he fought for the North."

"Nope. He never fought for the North. Not my granddad. Not Montesque Bouldin."

"That means he must have fought for the South."

"Nope."

Again he shook his head, not with wonder now, but with purpose and what looked like the beginning of a grin. "He didn't fight for the South neither."

"Well then, what did he do during the war?"

The craggy face opened. The eyes gleamed with pleasure. "Far as I know, he didn't fight for nobody. He just hid out til the whole thing was over."

"Hid out?"

"Hunted. Kept to himself. Stayed off the roads. Wasn't nobody goin to find a person up here who didn't want to be found. Wasn't nobody goin to come lookin for him anyhow. In these mountains. A hunderd years ago. There's places I could show you right now, you could have all to yourself for six or seven months. You take where I grew up, over there toward Pleasant Hill, where granddad built his log house. You can't even git in there now. I don't know if I could show you how to *start* gittin in there, it's all so growed over."

As he talked I was thinking, That guy sounds like my kind of ancestor. Not only was he named for an eminent man of letters, he seemed to have a mind of his own. There are some, I suppose—other cousins, on other branches of the family tree—who would call it sloth and cowardice, not to have fought for one side or the other, when his own brothers were out there somewhere slogging through the mud and gunsmoke of the 1860s. But Montesque's grandson obviously didn't see it that way. Nor did I, the great-great-grandson, dreaming of hideouts.

As we sat there, grinning about this forerunner we had in common, and the memory of his independent spirit, I began to dwell on the episode, as I had long dwelled upon the trans-Appalachian passage. I began to see those mountains from high altitude, as if hovering in a hot-air balloon, and high enough to observe uncountable puffs of smoke rising from invisible rifle barrels far to the north and far to the south, a wide circle of silent puffs and cannon clouds. In the center, surrounded by forest, there is a softer puff, a misty cloud rising at the base of a mountain waterfall, and Montesque is standing there in his boots and his heavy trousers.

Next to him stands a little girl. She is six years old, already lean and tough-limbed, tough as hickory, the way she will be throughout her life. Her name is Arminda, though he calls her Mindy, his oldest and favorite daughter, who has just hiked two miles through the trees to bring him a pail of food. The pail is sitting on a rock, and she is looking at it because the hike has made her hungry, hungrier than usual. She is hungry all the time. She says, "You gonna eat pretty soon, pa?" And he says, "Fore long." And she says, "When you comin home?" And he says, "You miss me, darlin?"

"Mama says to tell you the soldiers come and gone and they didn't git near our place."

"Did you see em?"

"Mama says they look so sick and raggedy she doesn't believe they'll ever hike through these woods again. Or any other woods."

"Well, that's real good news, darlin. Now what we got to eat in that bucket?"

"It's only cornbread, pa. Mama says she just about run out of everything else."

"You tell your mama there is a bear likes to wander down to the far end of this here pool every evenin about sundown, and it won't be long fore he takes his last drink of water."

"You gonna shoot him, pa?"

"I might. Or I might just sneak up behind him and catch him by the neck and stick his head under the waterfall just like I'm gonna do you," grabbing her lightly then, lifting her under the skinny arms to swing her out over the pool, while she squeals with fearful delight.

Later, while they are hunkered down in the grass, breaking off chunks of cornbread, she says, "Pa?"

Through his mouthful he grunts, "Yunnh?"

"Can I stay here with you?"

He chews a while and looks at her and looks away and says, "No darlin. Mama needs you back home. And I'll be back home fore you know it. You tell her I said that too."

And much later, while she trots through the twilight forest, to make it home before dark, she is already remembering that lift over the water as if it happened long long ago, the ecstasy of it, as the man in her life, the one she loves more than any other, lifts her up and swings her around and out, toward misty plumes and the plummeting rush of white. It seems to last forever. And yet it ends too soon, too soon...

Or maybe this little meeting of the father and the daughter did not register deeply at all. Maybe it was just another day in the long months of days when he was lying low. I am only guessing here, a grandson-at-large searching for his past, making it up as I go along, searching for some way to account for the look in her eyes in the earliest photo of Arminda I have seen, taken right at the turn of the century. Forty years and nine children later, her stern and weathered face says, "Nothing lasts forever," and "Everything lasts too long."

Yes, Noble begat Gideon. And Gideon begat Montesque. And Montesque begat seven sons and daughters, among them Arminda, who was my great-grandmother, born in that two-story house at Pleasant Hill. Around the age of twenty-two she married into another mountain clan, Irish in origin, if you trace it back far enough, another line of farmers and smalltime landholders who had arrived in Tennessee by way of North Carolina. Her husband's name was James Wiley Gulley. He too is in that turn-of-the-century photo, slouched next to her, and I am sure he contributed something to the look on Arminda's face, as husbands always do. She was well past forty by that time. She looks past sixty, sitting up straight, with her knees together, underneath the full-length, neck-to-shoetops dress. Her lips are pressed tight, her hair is pulled tight against her temples. Her eyes are formidable, challenging, as if this camera is not to be trusted.

Her husband's eyes are slant-browed, seemingly at ease. He is leaning on the chair arm, with knees apart, wearing jacket and vest, but no tie. His hair is uncombed. Perhaps he has been drinking. It has always looked that way to me. This was their first and only family portrait. If he'd had a couple of quick ones while they were setting up the shot, I wouldn't have held it against him, being the father of nine children, in those times, which were hard times all across the land and particularly in the South. Behind him stands his oldest daughter, who has just turned twenty. On his knee he holds a son who looks to be about three, while Arminda holds their youngest, a girl not yet a year old.

It must have been a madhouse getting everyone dressed and in position for this picture, which represents about ten seconds in their combined years on earth. The camera clicks, and a moment later the faces unfreeze, a chair scoots back, the talk begins, as the son-in-law standing in the back row rips loose the chafing, high starched collar, and as great-grandma breaks out the corncob pipe she smoked. What I wish for here is a movie of the day they took this portrait, an hour before and an hour afterward, with all the grunts and belches and the curling smoke. And yet this frozen moment captures something essential, bearing out everything else I have heard about these two great-grandparents of mine. Unbending, severe, Arminda was the stronger, the family rudder, and J. W. was the lovable ne'er-do-well, a singer, a joker, a man "with a long streak of fun in him," as I heard one old nephew say.

Perhaps it was the inclination of Arminda, the oldest daughter, to take command of things, and the inclination of James Wiley, who had older brothers, to let her do just that. Or perhaps it was something about the characters of their two clans. The Bouldins tend to be built like trees, ramrod straight, both men and women, and among themselves they make remarks about the Gulleys, as people do—families, clans, tribes, nations—who have intermingled through the years. The remarks are made lightly, in intimate jest. The receding chins of certain Gulley men, I have heard it said, suggest uncertainty of purpose. In a friendly and kidding sort of way someone will point to a small, fenced and long-untended graveyard where Gulleys were buried, until it was abruptly closed back in 1912. The last grave dug there was filling up with water faster than the gravediggers could bail it out—a sign of the high water table at that particular spot, and also an example of the unfortunate choices Gulleys tend to make.

On the other hand, it may be that my grandmother was right when she said the Union Army left on her father a lasting mark, and that this is somehow the key to his character. She grew up listening to his tirades about Yankees. She often said he had re-fought the Civil War every day of his adult life. Too young to enlist, he was old enough to remember the day a detachment of Union soldiers appeared in their yard. He was ten at the time. His father and older brothers were off somewhere fighting on the Confederate side and had left young Jim behind to take care of his mama and be the man of the family. She was in labor, so the story goes, when these barbarian Northerners arrived at the farm, like locusts, and left with every live animal and every scrap of food, including a stash of turnips and potatoes Jim had buried.

He never forgave them for what they did that day, stripping the farm while his mother lay there crying out with labor pains. The *them* he never forgave included that small band of soldiers, together with all officers and enlisted men in the entire Union Army, and every man, woman, and child who happened to live north of the Mason-Dixon line. In later years some of his grandchildren would deliberately take the northern side in the endless debate, just to get him started. They would prod him to tell that story again, hoping he would follow it with other tales of Yankee treachery and deceit and end up singing "Dixie," his favorite song (he did not know and so was never troubled by the strange irony that this Confederate call to battle had been written in New York City by a composer from Ohio):

> Then I wish I was in Dixie. Hooray! Hooray!
> In Dixieland I'll take my stand
> To live and die in Dixie...

That is how my grandmother liked to remember him, sitting on the front porch in Huntsville, Alabama, singing gospel songs or patriotic songs about the South.

Maybe this is why he chose to move his family out of the mountains and into a mill town in another state—to put a hundred and fifty more miles between himself and the hated North. Or maybe it was that decade's depression, and the near worthlessness of cash crops, that decided him to give up trying to scrape a living from his fifty acres outside Spencer. Or maybe it was some old restlessness in the blood that sent him in search of traveling money, when he agreed to team up with a brother-in-law and pick a large orchard somewhere down the hillside, on Bouldin land. These two men moved their families into a house near the orchard, for a month of picking and peeling and slicing and drying. They built two drying kilns right there and came up with sixteen hundred pounds of produce, which netted Jim Gulley about forty-eight dollars. With that and a covered wagon, he and Arminda and their eight kids set out for Alabama. They kept fifty pounds of dried apples to eat along the way and carried fifty pounds of fresh apples to trade for other food. It took them a week to make the trip, which is not quite as fast as a person on foot could have walked it.

I see Jim in his coveralls, hunched above the reins. He does not hear the squabble breaking out amongst the kids crammed in behind him, nor does he notice the line of brown spittle staining his beard. He is chewing tobacco and thinking of their next stop, when he can step behind the widest tree and take a pull from the flask he has hidden somewhere on board, and he is dreaming the dream you always dream when you pull up stakes, of another start, or an easier life, or at the very least another way of doing things.

His family had been in Tennessee about sixty years. Arminda's had been there for ninety. In our patchwork legend, this wagonload of kids rolling south over rocky roads at the speed of three miles per hour is remembered as a kind of exodus from the homeland, the wagon pulled by donkeys and covered with bedsheets stretched over curving hickory staves.

Their destination, their Mecca, their Jerusalem, their Silicon Valley, was the Huntsville of the 1890s, a town which had recently become a new industrial center, fueled with Yankee money and drawing country people from all directions, to work in the textile mills. The shifts were long, and the pay was low (fifty cents a night, my grandmother told me). But the work was steady, and a man with a big family was considered a lucky man indeed, in those pre-child-labor-law days, when anyone ten years and older was employable.

Jim Gulley soon had five of his children drawing wages, though he himself never did go to work in the mills. He took odd jobs around town, when the spirit moved him, and delivered lunches to his breadwinning crew, then tended to hang around the mill, ostensibly to make sure they behaved themselves. More likely he was hanging out with his cronies, other fathers-on-the-loose with other lunches to deliver. He was in his mid-forties then, at a time when the average lifespan was about forty-two. Maybe he figured he had already outlived his generation and paid his dues and earned a rest, and what were children for anyhow, if not to comfort and sustain a man through his autumn years. Or maybe it was true, what his ancient nephews cackled about when I met them in Tennessee in 1969.

"Don't you know that's why he went on down to Huntsville in the first place?" one of them told me with a wink. "If I'd a had that many young-uns, I'd a done the same. Ol Jim, he was lazy, but wasn't dumb. And he never wore a long face neither. Wasn't nothin could get him down. I remember the time him and Bud Bouldin picked that orchard clean and dried all them apples. Jim was working overtime there for a spell, but he already knew he was on his way offa this mountain, ya see. He was whistlin all day long and singin so loud you could hear him clear to Memphis."

That formal family portrait was taken on the front porch in Huntsville, four or five years after they had settled in. It hangs now in my living room here in Santa Cruz, where I pass it several times a day, a portal, an opening into a long-gone world. I think of it as a door that swings two ways, into the past and into the future. The year was 1901, the threshold of the twentieth century. These great-grandparents, Jim and Arminda, could be any of the ancestors of the previous two hundred years. Their faces, their body angles, their clothes are of an older time. But that young girl at the far right, the one with the dark hair piled high, rolled and shining, with the thoughtful and sadly burdened eyes, she is my grandmother, Nora Alda Belle Gulley. Of the dozen people in this photo she will be the only one to continue the journey to the continent's farthest edge.

She is thirteen here but, like her mother, she looks much older. She is not a schoolgirl and never will be. She has already put in three years of ten-hour shifts at the cotton mill. She has her mother's long limbs and wears the same kind of dress, sleeves to the wrist, collar to the chin, hem to the floor, everything covered but the hands and the head.

She has her father's slant-browed eyes, and at thirteen she is showing at least one of his traits: she is not cooperating. In this photo she is the only one not gazing at the camera. She has glanced away. Perhaps a young man on horseback has just trotted around the corner, though I doubt it. The eyes don't seem aimed at anything specific. While her body sits on the porch, her mind is elsewhere. Knowing how her life turned out, I can read into her look the wistful foreknowledge of the man who will one day entice her, and father her children, and then disappear, the reluctant husband, the main man in her life, and a man in mine too, though I never met him, the grandfather who covered his tracks.

This is what I see in those young/old eyes. Already she is watching him walk away.

His name was Eddie Wilson, a young mill hand from Danville, Virginia, or so he claimed, who moved into their neighborhood in 1909 or 1910. So little is known about this fellow I call him Elusive Eddie. He had black hair and blue eyes, and like Jim Gulley he was a sometime singer who appreciated good singing when he heard it. Sixty years later I met a woman in Huntsville who said she once had a crush on Eddie. A few years younger than my grandmother, she evidently had watched their courtship with teenage jealousy.

"In the evenin, after work," she told me, "if it was warm, Nora would sit out there on the porch with her guitar and sing 'Red River Valley,' and Eddie would yell across the street, 'You'd break the heart of any boy in Alabama!'"

Eddie too played guitar, and mentioned once that he had some Cherokee blood. He also liked to pick clover on the way to the mill and make up songs about it.

Or so I've been told.

Everything is vague, except the marriage date, 1910, and the fact that he was gone by the time my mother was born, and the huge silence that later surrounded his memory. Though family meant more to Nora than anything but heaven itself, she would never talk about this man who was the only man she married and the only man she dated after the age of twenty-two. Eventually he wrote and told her he had joined the army. A while later she sent him a photo of their baby girl. He then wrote from Griffin, Georgia, begging to come back. It was the only letter of his she kept, and she kept it hidden from the world until she was almost eighty.

"My dearest little wife…" it begins.

Three years after he had disappeared, he returned to Huntsville, and in due time my uncle was born. But by then, Elusive Eddie was gone again, heading to Virginia, he said as he left, to borrow some money to put down on their house.

One of Nora's younger sisters witnessed this farewell and remembered her parting words to him.

"Eddie," Nora said, "as sure as we're standin on the ground, I am never gonna see you again."

"I'm comin back as quick as I can," said Eddie. "I swear it."

She may have heard from him after that, but she burned all the letters. No photos have survived, and no information at all after 1923, which was the last time anyone remembers hearing he might have been spotted. It was near Danville. Many years later the brother of a friend of the family recalled seeing him in a cotton mill. "How you doin, Eddie?" he called out, "Long time no see." But this fellow in his thirties who resembled Eddie and moved like Eddie and was back at Eddie's original line of work told this brother of a friend of the family that he must be mistaken. The next day he had checked out of the mill, whoever he was, moving on. Where to? No one knows. Where from? We can only guess. Any relatives? None to speak of. A letter he had supposedly written to a sister, before he married Nora, came back to Huntsville unopened. Forty-five years later a phonebook poll of all the Wilsons in the Danville area turned up no leads. Once or twice Nora asked him to tell her the story of his life, but he never got around to it. In that one letter she saved, he wrote:

> You said tell you what I had bin doing these long yeares well darling you no that would fill a common size book and I will tell you all about it when I come...

She was seventy-nine when she finally dug out these pages and showed them to me, the grandson with a taste for history, pressing for evidence. Though she knew exactly where the letter was, she had not looked at it for decades. She put on her glasses and read it aloud, while color rose into her cheeks. She began to cry. My mother was there, and she too began to cry at the sound of this message from the long-lost father. We all cried at the words rising out of his fifty-year silence. For me, it was the first real proof of his existence. Until then I'd had nothing to validate him, nothing as solid as a letter written by hand, on folded and fragile paper, in purple ink. Now his words, the voice of the missing grandfather, were coming from her throat, like the disembodied words a medium pulls out of thin air.

With money saved from her years of paychecks, Nora went ahead and bought a house in Huntsville, by that time knowing two things for sure: she wanted to make a home for her kids, and she did not want them growing up in the mills. When an older brother moved to Texas, in search of a drier climate for his wife's lungs, Nora soon followed, sold her house, put the equity into a quarter-section of the Texas panhandle, and went back to the farming life she'd known as a young girl in Tennessee. Before long half her family had made this move, other brothers and sisters, and Jim and Arminda, who spent their final years out there.

On her deathbed, in 1926, Arminda summoned her grandchildren one at a time. My mother was fifteen then and remembers the last words she heard from this fierce-eyed woman born in a log house before the Civil War.

"Loretta," she said, "don't you never go ridin alone in a car with a man."

"I sure won't, grandma," my mother said, thinking, *Not if I can help it anyway*. And she may actually have tried, for a while, to follow this advice. But by that time, as we know, the world was filling up with cars. A few years later she was riding alone in one with my father, as they left Texas together, heading west and bound for California.

Nora eventually leased the farm and followed her daughter. She lived with us or near us, in San Francisco and later in Santa Clara Valley, for the rest of her life. She always considered herself a widow and tended to dress that way. In her view, Eddie was dead and gone. Yet she kept his name, and that in itself gave him a ghostly presence during the years of my growing up.

She had come west without a man, but I realize now how many she brought with her. She was a channel for all the

Southern names and places. She talked about life "up on the mountain," as if the mountain were rising right outside the window, between our house and Golden Gate Park. She sang songs her dad learned when he was young, and some of them were playful, like "The Crawdad Song":

> Yonder come a man with a sack on his back, honey.
> Yonder come a man with a sack on his back, babe.
> Yonder come a man with a sack on his back,
> Got more crawdads than he can pack,
> Honey, baby mine.

Others had a haunting and medieval sound, and years later I would learn, via the F. J. Child collection of *English and Scottish Popular Ballads,* that she was puttering around our kitchen humming versions of tunes that had crossed the Atlantic two hundred years earlier, to be carried into the Cumberlands along with the rifles and the plough:

> There were three crows up in a tree,
> and they were as black as black could be.
> *With a humble bumble snigger-eye grinner*
> *snooze-eye rinktum boozer.*
> One of those crows said to his mate,
> "What we gonna do for grub to eat?"
> *With a humble bumble snigger-eye grinner*
> *snooze-eye rinktum boozer.*

She was the channel for ballads, for voices, for all these ancestral details that otherwise might have been lost to me. She also passed on a way of thinking about ancestry that is essentially Biblical, and patriarchal. She studied the Bible every day. Wanting to transmit the best of what she knew and believed, Nora would read aloud at night from the Old Testament. The stories in Genesis had a special appeal for her. With that soft, grandmotherly, mountain voice she often read aloud from Genesis:

And Enoch lived sixty-five years
and begat Methusaleh...
And Methusaleh lived a hundred and
eighty-seven years and begat Lamech...
And Lamech lived a hundred and eighty-two
years and begat a son, and he called
his name Noah...
And Noah was five hundred years old, and
he begat Shem, Ham and Japheth...

The elegant ring of the King James Version itself can work a spell on you. It seeps into your blood and into your way of measuring time and charting a family's path. Maybe this is why the missing grandfather came to preoccupy me. There was a place in the genealogy and in the nervous system crying out to be filled. And maybe this is why I traveled back to the homelands in 1969, in search of patriarchs.

Or maybe it was simpler than that. I had lived with both my grandmothers. They both came west to spend time with us. Having known them and their unconditional love, I had no need to go looking for replacements. But the grandfathers were both out of reach. Elusive Eddie had closed the door behind him, while the granddad on my father's side had passed away in Texas before I was old enough to make that kind of trip. I see now how consistently I have been drawn to elderly men. I never went looking for a father figure, because my dad was always there. He came home every night. But I have sought out grandfatherly men, elders who seem to carry in their eyes and in their faces some knowledge of ancient times.

Among the numerous old Bouldins and Gulleys I met during that pilgrimage to Tennessee and Alabama, one drew me more than all the others. He seemed to be the elder I had come searching for. It was old Montacue, my great-grandmother's nephew, my grandmother's first cousin, a man of her age, who had never left Van Buren County. He

welcomed me as if we'd known each other for a lifetime.
Perhaps we had. I recognized him instantly and recognized
someone in myself, the subsistence farmer I might have been,
or could have been.

He led me to the shed outside his house where all the
canned goods were stored on shelves, sealed Mason jars filled
with fruits and vegetables. He handed me a quart of applesauce, just like Nora would have done if I'd come visiting,
pressing it on me, and then a quart of string beans striped
with sliced pimentos. As he was reaching toward a pint of
chutney, I protested. I was flying, I told him, and my carry-on
luggage was already crammed full. He refused to hear this
remark. Pushing the third jar into my arms, he nodded toward
the string beans and looked at me with a kind of relentless,
stubborn generosity. "Them Kentucky Wonders'll surprise ya,
I guarantee it. They're gonna taste mighty good when you
git home."

We walked out into his small orchard, where the last yellow
leaves of autumn hung on the apple trees. I have a photo of
the two of us standing among the leaves, beyond his white
frame house. Gazing at it now I see that he looked exactly the
way I always wanted a granddad to look, in his coveralls, his
twill shirt, his ruddy cheeks, his silvered hair. He was taller
than I am, and that too felt good, to have a granddad you can
physically look up to, even at age eighty.

I idealize him, of course. I idealize them all. Having met him
and some others of his generation only once, I can fill in most
of the rest myself, create my own ancestry. We have to do a
lot of that, in any event. We get some names and dates, if we
are lucky, whatever trickles toward our own time. But most of
it is lost. The number of teeth old Montacue had at sixty; what
he thought at age twenty-five walking alone behind his mule;
what he used to say when he made love, or what he failed to
say—these are the details you have to fill in for yourself. It

makes you wonder if there is any real difference between
the making of your family's past and the making of fiction.
In either case a process of very careful selection is at work.

In the paragraph above, for instance, I mention his coveralls and his ruddy cheeks. I left out his arthritic knuckles.
Why? Maybe I forgot. Maybe I didn't want to go into it.
Maybe I am superstitious, afraid that mentioning a cousin's
arthritis will have an effect on my own knuckles later on.

That is just one example. The process of selection is a
process of invention. Take Montesque Bouldin, and the
two extant versions of his allegiance during the Civil War.
Not only do I choose to believe what his grandson told me,
I choose to see his non-combat record as honorable behav-
ior, another form of heroism. Or take Noble, a fellow from
Virginia, who passed through North Carolina on his way to
Tennessee. Why start with him? Somewhere back there I
had thirty-one other great-great-great-great-grandfathers of
more or less his age. Any one of them could serve as progeni-
tor. But who were they? What were their names, their jobs,
their passions? Some were Scots, some were German, some
were Cherokee, some were Louisiana French, with maybe
a little Cajun blending in. But who knows how much? What
role models might they have offered, what identity supports?
I'll never find out. They are invisible now, or receding fast,
whereas Noble is remembered because the Bouldins happened to be ardent record keepers and bearers of the family
flame, and because Nora came West with her memories, and
because she liked to talk.

My father's mother didn't talk as much, or know as much.
On his side the family memory gets very dim around 1900.
And I don't really mind. Thirty-two great-great-great-great-
grandfathers is probably more than I could deal with. One
is plenty, although in truth I could have let Noble join the
others. I could have chosen to forget him. He just happens
to appeal to me. He is a gift from my grandmother, one I

happily accept. So it is with all these ancestors. They create me. I create them. We give each other life.

Take Elusive Eddie, the man who passed through Huntsville on his way to who knows where. I will never be able to let him go. I still try to picture him, and when I do the picture is not black-and-white. The years before the First World War were lemon-tinted years, and grandmother's long dress touches the grass, with her hair piled high and her waist cinched tight, as her beau departs, moving off into thick sunlight. They are in a park in Alabama, beside a pavilion where a brass band plays. I see light glinting off the tuba, the trombone, playing background music for a distant voice, a young woman's plaintive voice, half humming, half singing.

Her arm lifts to shade her eyes, taffeta crinkling at the elbow. It is her one good dress saved for rare occasions, for this Saturday stroll, only to find herself watching him leave, his slow-motion exit across the shimmering grass, his reckless boater tipped, his custard trousers lost in the glare off the lake, while she hums and sings:

> Man fell down and bust that sack, honey.
> Man fell down and bust that sack, babe.
> Man fell down and bust that sack,
> Just watch them crawdads backin back...

She watches with eyes that were shaped at birth to expect this and every other burden, and yet in all these years he has not gone twenty paces, light so thick and luminous how can anyone escape.

(1986)

The Dangerous Uncle Returns

I have never been able to keep track of all my cousins. They are scattered across Texas and Alabama and Arkansas and Tennessee, dozens, perhaps hundreds of cousins, and I have lived my life here on the coast, where my father settled in the early 1930s. In those pre-jet and pre-power-steering days it was a huge and risky move for anyone to make, a young man's move, an immigrant's move, to a new world and a fresh start. Though he did not cross a national boundary to get here, he crossed a desert and two mountain ranges and left behind a clan, three or four generations of relatives I would otherwise have grown up among. As it was, I grew up with an immigrant's sense for the homeland—east Texas, to be exact—as the place my father departed from, a distant place that would send us relatives now and again, other continental travelers on missions of kinship, always keeping one or another of the family ties stitched together.

Since he passed away, twenty years ago, there has been less and less of this. He had been the link to the old country, while I had been doing more and more of the kinship work you do in California, where the blood relatives tend to be few and far between, building up the spirit family, the cousins and brothers and sisters of the heart. So it took me by surprise when the phone rang one night at dinnertime and I heard the voice of my cousin Hoyt calling from Firebaugh, over in the Central Valley, about a hundred miles from here. I should say, it took me by the throat.

I didn't mind that he was calling from Firebaugh. This part seemed just about right, since it is a farm town surrounded by many square miles of croplands. In style and terrain Firebaugh is much closer to east Texas than it is to this seaside resort town. Hoyt's voice could have been a Central Valley voice. There was a country edge to it, high and nasal, and ordinarily that's a sound I like to hear. It is the sound of the homeland. It is why the voices of Willie Nelson and Roy Acuff and George Jones always comfort me, the voices themselves, quite apart from the words being sung.

When the phone rang and I heard someone say, "You'll never guess who this is," the voice had humor, a hint of comradeship. It was the name that triggered my alarm. I did not know Hoyt at all. But I had known his father, and this was enough to put me on double alert. His father had been the wild one, the demon uncle, the loose cannon on the family deck, the man everyone feared would come for the weekend and stay for a month, which he often did.

Our paths had crossed once before, Hoyt said, at a family reunion sometime around the end of World War Two. Now he was retired, after forty years of construction work. He had fitted out an RV for cross-country travel, and he and his wife were driving around the western states.

I remembered the reunion. I remembered the year because we had made the trip in a brand-new 1947 Buick Roadmaster with white sidewalls and swept-back fenders. I still have a picture of my father standing next to that car. It was his proof to the folks back home, and to himself, that he had done all right in California. He had eight brothers and sisters and they all had kids by that time, and the older ones already had wives or sweethearts. Relatives were spilling out of the house, into the driveway and both yards, the biggest family gathering I would ever attend. I met fifty or sixty people that day. Maybe Hoyt was one of them. I didn't remember him. It didn't make any difference. When he called I really had no choice. Blood is blood. We were first cousins, and he was seventeen hundred miles from home.

"Sure," I said. "How about tomorrow? You come by the house and we'll get caught up."

He called again from the big Sears store just past the freeway off-ramp.

"Jim," he said and paused for a light cough, a raggedy clearing of the throat. "Jim, it's Hoyt. I found the exit, then figured I might get turned around."

"You sit tight. I'll be there as quick as I can."

"I figured Sears would be a good place to call from."

"It is, Hoyt. It's perfect. Where are you, which side of the building? Shade or sun?"

"I'm standing here in the shade, right by the main window."

Driving over there I was thinking of the first time I had seen Hoyt's father. I might have been eight. We were living in San Francisco then. It was a Sunday morning. I was the first one up and looking for the comics, looking for the cartoon couple called Maggie and Jiggs, whose antics always decorated the outside of the *San Francisco Sunday Examiner.* I opened the front door and found Maggie and Jiggs cradled in the arms of a man sprawled across the entry porch of our second-story flat. He was unconscious, unshaven, reeking of vomit and stale cigarettes. In the driveway below, a dusty pickup was parked at an angle, stacked with crates of spoiled tomatoes.

While I helped my father drag him inside I said, "Who is it, dad?"

"It's your uncle Anderson."

"Is he sick? Is he dead?"

"He's been drinking, son. He's probably been drinking for about a week."

He slept for six hours. When he had sobered up enough to talk, my father tried to find out where the tomatoes had come from and who owned the truck. It had Arizona plates. Anderson shook his head, helpless with regret. He could not remember if he had bought it or stolen it or borrowed it or found it by the side of the road.

This time he slept for sixteen hours. The next day he woke up talking. "You children," he said to my sister and me, "you come in here and say hello to your Uncle Andy. Has your daddy told you anything about me? If he hasn't he sure should have. How old you gittin to be, Jimbo? Fourteen? Fifteen?"

"I'm eight, Uncle Andy."

"Eight! Shoot! Big as you are I thought you'd already be in high school! Well, I want you to watch what I'm about to do here. Your daddy ever tell you I was double-jointed?"

We watched him bend back a hand until his thumb touched his forearm. From that moment on, he had us. He could do hand tricks, coin tricks, voice tricks. Pretty soon we were sitting on the bed and he was telling us stories, long ridiculous stories—something my father never seemed to have the time to do. That afternoon Andy took us both for a walk in Golden Gate Park while my father called the DMV, to locate the owner of the pickup, and pondered how to get rid of a ton of oozing tomatoes before the neighbors called the health department.

Much later I would learn that it had always been this way. They had come of age together, Anderson and Dudley, two years apart. They had played and fought together, slept in the same bed, and weeded cotton rows together in the heat of

summer. Though different from each other in almost every
way, they had in common an early restlessness that put them
both on the road to the coast, Dudley first, then Anderson.

I had seen a lot of him, growing up, because my dad could
never turn his back on this prodigal brother. It was classic.
Dudley was the steady one, the family man who put his
money in the bank and kept the windows puttied. He went
into house painting, got his contractor's license, and that was
his career. Anderson drifted from woman to woman, from
job to job, the charmer, the rascal who always left a mess
behind, the bronco brother no one could tame. Between
women, between jobs, between binges, he would turn up on
our doorstep—my father's lifetime test and trial.

For me he was always the most dangerous and the most
exotic uncle, the one who made you laugh the longest. He
had been a nephew's great pal, and his own worst enemy.

If I were meeting Anderson I would have expected to see him
slumped against the building with his chin on his chest, or
out in the parking lot trying to sell someone a battery he had
just discovered behind the Sears Automotive Center. Easing
past the rows of cars, I was prepared for just about anything
but what I found. Hoyt was standing right where he said he'd
be, alert and chipper, in the shade, by the window, not more
than three paces from the phone.

I pulled up to the curb, climbed out, and watched him
smile a slow Texas smile. He flicked his head sideways. "Forty
years is quite a while," he said, "but I believe I'd recognize
you anywhere."

As we shook hands he was searching my face the way I
searched his, looking at the temples, at the nose, the mouth,
the jaw for signs of family history, signs of lineage. In his
eyes I was looking for some of the wildness I used to see,
the devil's glint that said, "Whatever you can think of, son,
I wouldn't mind giving it a try at least once." It wasn't there.

These eyes were blinking, watching, waiting, not at all the eyes of Anderson. These were someone else's eyes.

"Where's your RV parked?" I said.

"Still in Firebaugh."

"How'd you get way over here?"

"I've got my van," he said, with a crafty little grin. "I haul it around on a trailer hitch. Once I get the RV parked, I'm traveling light. My wife has people in Firebaugh so she stayed over there too."

I saw then who he reminded me of. These were Dudley's, my father's eyes. His laconic delivery was like my father's, as well as this double-rigged mode of travel. Anderson would never have thought of that. And Hoyt's grin was very much like my father's grin, tight and careful, as if his leathery skin had only so much give. His clothes were what my father would have worn, a brown-plaid, long-sleeve shirt, from Sears perhaps, or Penney's, and plain slacks of a darker brown. His hands had the same long fingers, a guitar picker's fingers, the skin mottled and darkened as my father's had been when he was about Hoyt's age.

It was my first signal that this was going to be a day of resurrection. All at once this stranger/cousin was no stranger at all. It seemed miraculous, the little miracle of family resonance, as if uncanny forces had been at work, re-carving this one in that one's image.

Twenty years after my father passed away, here he was looking at me again, and as I was about to discover, Hoyt hoped I could do something similar for him—that is, provide some version of Anderson. He was not here to invade a cousin's household, as I had feared. He was on a pilgrimage. He was reassembling Anderson piece by piece. The long-gone trickster had left for California when this man was seven years old. Now Hoyt was sixty-six, with his own family raised, yet he was still the son searching for the father he had never known. There was something youthful and unfinished in his eyes. They were full of questions.

In the back of his van a cardboard box held the pieces he had assembled so far. After he followed me home and parked, he lifted out the box and let the van door slam. "I guess I'll bring this on inside."

My wife was gone for the day. We had the house to ourselves. It was just me and Hoyt and the ancestors already gathering as we sat down. He did not want a cup of coffee or a soft drink or a beer. He wanted to talk and show me what was in the box, run his hands through its heap of old letters and clippings and scraps of paper with lists of names and phone numbers, and brown-edged photographs.

He pulled out a snapshot of his mother at around twenty-five, Andy's first wife, another relative I'd heard about but never met, my aunt-for-a-while, a slender woman sitting on the ground somewhere in east Texas in the 1920s, with her hair parted off-center and hot-curling down over both ears. In the fierce sun her eyes are caught between a smile and a frowning squint.

"She's the one raised my brother and me. When Andy took off they'd been together seven, eight years. Between the day he left and the time I was grown, I only saw him twice. Maybe a year later he drove from L.A. to Texas in a brand-new Ford. And he showed up again about ten years after that. But for all intents and purposes he was gone...as of nine-teen-twen-ty-eight." He stretched out those words. "They had married young, of course. Probably too young."

I didn't hear any blame in his voice. Whatever Hoyt had lived with in his younger years, whatever bitterness or weight of rejection he had to carry, he had let it go. It was too late for blame.

He had an older photo showing Anderson and Dudley in front of the family barn and blacksmith shop when they were very young, barefooted, wearing hats and rolled-up trousers. "This was probably taken around 1910," he said. "That's your dad, and my dad right next to him. They were always real close, from what I've heard."

"That's true. Seems like Andy was around our place a lot."

"They say he was always quite a character."

My earliest memory seemed too bleak to start with. We both knew Andy had drunk himself to death. There was no need to dwell on that. The fact is, in his later years he had returned again to Texas and Hoyt had been with him at the end. He had made his peace with Andy's death. Andy's life was what he had to talk about.

I told him what a raconteur his father was, and what a contrast to Dudley, who had never been a talker. I told him they were like W. C. Fields and Gary Cooper, yet they both had learned from our granddad how to work with every form of tool, and Andy, if he chose to, could build a fence or mend a roof or tune a car. Then I remembered something that had happened after we moved south from San Francisco into Santa Clara Valley, in the days when it was still called the world's largest orchard.

My father knew a rancher who had thirty acres of apricots. One summer this rancher's foreman went into the hospital. It happened to be a summer when Anderson was drying out, paying us room and board whenever he came into a little money. He took over the apricots at the height of the season and got those thirty acres picked in time to catch the peak of the market. I remembered this well because I was on his crew, at age fifteen, picking for twenty cents a box. I can still see Andy underneath the trees working twice as hard as anyone else, feverish, obsessed. He was lean and wiry, and once he had focused on a task he was like Ahab. He could pull you along in the wake of his own frenzy and kinetic will.

"He would be down on his knees scooping up windfall apricots," I told Hoyt, "then hauling a ladder between the rows. He'd be running from tree to tree."

Hoyt smiled his broadest smile. He seemed to like this, though it was hard to tell. "Did you say running?"

"Almost like somebody was chasing him."

"That sounds about right. He must have been the world's most restless man."

"He did such a good job he got a bonus. And that was the last we saw of him for eight months or a year. The day he got paid he was wearing my dad's favorite pants and shoes, which was the part dad remembered. He knew Andy would be back, but he knew the pants and the shoes were gone for good."

Hoyt almost laughed that time, a hesitant, distracted laugh, then he nodded, as if this story confirmed something. "I can tell you saw a whole lot more of him than I ever did."

"I suppose that's true, if he took off when you were seven."

"I always knew he spent a lot of time out here. I should have made this trip myself long ago, but you know what it's like. I just never could tear myself loose." He jerked his head sideways again, exactly the way my father used to do, a kind of cowboy's punctuation mark, signaling both amazement and melancholy. "Picking them apricots…that's real vivid."

Something wistful had come into his face, and I saw then the irony of our two boyhoods. I knew things about Anderson Hoyt could never know. The brother who had been my father's curse had given me things he was never able to give his own sons—time, comradeship, rambling stories, momentary lessons in how to shuffle cards or use the knee to lift a shovelful of dirt. As if I had stolen something that should have gone to Hoyt, I felt an unexpected rush of guilt, and I wanted to say that he wasn't alone, that both these brothers had been elusive men, elusive fathers. Hoyt, I wanted to say, Andy left when you were seven, Dudley stayed home almost every night, and yet he still eluded me, he slipped away before I ever got to know him, being such an inward man, so much inside himself, so reluctant to speak, to touch, to reach. He was in every way the opposite of Anderson, who carried his heart on his sleeve, who could laugh from the belly, could weep in public, would grab you by the shoulders and tell you his life story three or four times a day.

I didn't say any of that, though, imagining what Hoyt would think: You had them both, a father in the flesh, the uncle too.

"You probably know about his hairdresser days in Los Angeles," Hoyt said.

"He had the gift of gab, I know that much. He had talked certain people into believing he was from Paris, France, instead of Paris, Texas."

"Then you probably know about his other wife."

"Not much," I said, "except that he left her too, pretty early on. Wasn't that it?"

Hoyt dug into his box again and found a map of L.A. and a midlife portrait, a framed 8x10 studio portrait from the late 1930s, when Andy's hair was full and wavy. The sharp jaw made me think of Errol Flynn. This was how he looked around the time he walked away from his second family. Hoyt knew where they had lived, because he had stopped there once, during a troop transfer at the end of the Second World War, hoping to meet Andy's two West Coast sons. But they were away at boarding school, and the mother did not much like to talk about Anderson. So Hoyt continued on to Texas, and the decades slipped by, and he had not returned until just this year, when he finally visited L.A. again.

A trip to the county courthouse yielded a forty-year-old divorce decree with the full names of the two sons. Back in the old neighborhood he started knocking on doors. A woman across the street remembered the family and thought she knew of someone down the block who might know someone else with a lead. Before long there was a phone number. The fellow who took the call was understandably cautious. He had never heard of Hoyt. He was in the entertainment business and wary of anyone claiming kinship. But in the end he agreed to meet.

As Hoyt told me this story I saw his van swing onto another freeway exit ramp, heading out along another Sears-lined boulevard in search of a man he hoped would be his younger half-brother, a man he hoped might flesh out the void of Andy's time in southern California, as I was now fleshing out the void of Andy's time up north.

He had come armed with names and dates and photographs, scraps of history and small details of family lore no one could have invented. "The next thing I knew," Hoyt told me, "I was meeting his kids, who were Andy's grandkids, which meant I was their uncle, or maybe half-uncle."

From the box he pulled out color prints of his newfound half-brother, the half-nephews and half-nieces, and the other half-brother, who was already gone, along with a sketch of this tangled genealogy. As I studied the two scribbled clusters branching out from Anderson, it occurred to me that someone locating ancestors usually heads back toward the roots. To trace the history of this father who was always on the run, Hoyt had to leave the old country for a while and come out here to what they call the land of the rootless and poke around among the farthest branches of the family tree.

"It's the strangest thing," he said, "him having two separate families and neither one knew much at all about the other. Andy wasn't really trying to keep one woman from knowing what he'd done with another. He just plain ran out on all of us. And both those women were so fed up, neither one would so much as talk about him to their own kids."

Hoyt was not passing judgment. He had uncovered a whole subworld of previously invisible relatives, and he loved it. After sixty years he had nothing to lose and a lot to gain by letting them occupy the space Andy's long-ago exit had created. He was filled with wonder, and I was glad for him. Yet his story made me lonesome. I felt the loss of all those years he'd been cut off from his half-brothers in L.A. I may have felt this more than Hoyt did, because he grew up with a brother, and I did not and have often longed for one and used to dream of meeting a brother somewhere. I was feeling warmth and loss together, and then anger came welling up. Andy angered me, for what he had put these sons and mothers through. The careless uncle. The selfish uncle. For the first time I saw his monumental recklessness the way Dudley must have seen it.

We went on swapping stories, since that's what Hoyt seemed to crave—Andy's army years, his days as a circus roustabout, the time he showed up with that truckload of rotten tomatoes, his hand tricks, his coin tricks. But now my memories were colored by the fact that Hoyt was there in front of me, evoking them, Hoyt the elder from the distant clan, the father, the nephew, the near-brother first cousin, and still the son whose early days should rightly have contained some of Andy's voice and raucous style and underside of tenderness, but never did.

Eventually we went out for hamburgers, then it was time for him to start back. We were standing by his van when he reached into a second box and handed me a big pink grapefruit. "These come from down toward the Rio Grande." He handed me another, and another, until I was juggling half a dozen.

"Whoa. That's plenty."

"See these words right here? Texas Sun? That means they're going to be as sweet as anything you ever tasted."

His eyes were searching mine again, on the edge of a smile, as if six loose grapefruit were faintly amusing. It was a tentative, deferential look I had seen in my father's eyes a thousand times, and something began to come clear to me then. I was still pondering how a man who could not face fatherhood could have been the uncle a nephew missed the most once he was gone. I saw that every time Anderson departed, Dudley had been relieved, while I had been disappointed; the fun and entertainment was leaving the house, and only my father remained. Anderson's presence had always exposed what Dudley was not: spontaneous, unpredictable, expansive, absurd. Now here came Hoyt holding them up to another light, one brother defining the other, as night defines day.

He had been sent, I knew, to remind me of the kind of man my father was—soft-spoken, steady, unswerving, unpretentious, trying to stay honest and get through life as best he could. It is one of the mysterious blessings of kinship, the way a family resemblance can open such a window. Hoyt and I were linked by blood, but not in that most primal way. In him I could see qualities I'd forgotten or never quite acknowledged when the air was charged with all the father-son intensities. His search for Anderson had brought us both closer to who these brothers had been, and the search itself was an act of forgiveness. By the time he drove away I knew he had long ago forgiven Andy his many sins. That was not what I would have to do. In those few moments we stood there I forgave myself for having so long expected Dudley to be someone he could never be.

I wanted to communicate this, thank Hoyt somehow, but couldn't, didn't have the words for it yet. Or perhaps, at parting, I became again my father's son, reverting to a Gary Cooper style I had learned from him, hoping Hoyt could tell by the firm handshake and a look in my eyes that I meant more than what I was saying. "Really good to see you, Hoyt. Wish you could stay a while."

"Can't hardly do it," he said, with a sideways head-flick. "Told the wife I'd be home for dinner."

"Next time then."

"Yes sir. Next time it is. Meanwhile you be good."

With a wink and half a smile he climbed into the van, and away he went, bound for Firebaugh, then back to the homeland, south and east toward Texas.

(1988)

Words and Music
Notes Toward an Autobiography

i. This Long Wrinkle

Not long ago I was up in Round Valley, north of San Francisco, visiting some friends. It's a bowl of mountains surrounding what used to be a lake bed. In midsummer the sky turns light around five, and I was out walking very early, along the graveled road that cuts through their acreage. On a nearby hillside sprinkled with oak and madrone I saw some movement. A buck bounded into the open, evidently stirred by my approach. When I stopped, the buck stood his ground watching me, his head turned, waiting, a two-point buck in elegant profile against the tawny summer grass.

For two minutes, at least, we watched each other, while my mind wheeled back forty years and more to the days when I had come into this valley, and into others like it, with my father, in search of animals just like that one. I was thinking how such a sight, for my father, in those days, would have filled him with the huntsman's excitement and erotic rush. To see such a creature poised, with the chest exposed, the buff coat glowing, almost shining, as if polished, this was completion, this was fulfillment, this was what gave meaning to life. He would have raised his rifle, and he would have aimed just behind the shoulder, hoping to penetrate the heart and see the buck drop where it stood.

He had grown up the son of a cotton sharecropper and itinerant blacksmith. By the time I am describing here, the years right after World War Two, we were living in San Francisco, where I'd been born. He had found work painting houses, and now he was an independent contractor with a couple of pickup trucks and usually a crew of three or four men to manage. These trips into the northern counties were his way of getting some relief from the paint and the thinner and the dropcloths and the ladders and the city.

We would head across the Golden Gate Bridge, through Marin County, which was still mostly dairy country then, on toward Petaluma, which called itself "The Egg Basket of the World." ("I'd just as soon not have to drive across a basket full of eggs," he would say. "Once them shells start breakin, you're gonna have nothin but a mess, the way that egg yolk will get up around your axles and your tie rods.") Beyond Willits we'd bear right, heading inland, and follow the Eel River over twenty miles or so of dirt road and find our spot and park and set up camp with the other men who had come along, other contractors, or journeymen painters my dad had hired, sometimes my Uncle Jay, who was also from Texas and managed a Union Oil station—working men taking a few days off to roam the backcountry.

There would be steaks and potatoes and beer and whiskey, but not too much whiskey, not the first night, at any rate. We would sleep in sleeping bags, in a tent if the weather turned bad, and be up at dawn for more food, sausage and eggs and bitter coffee and toast half burned over the grate. Then we

would load the rifles and move out in pairs, in search of fresh
tracks and droppings.

"You head over that way, Jimbo, along that draw, up
toward them trees. See the ones I'm talkin' about? I'll head
over yonder, across that clearing, and maybe we'll scare
something up. They've been through here already, but they're
not far off. I believe we're gonna get us one or two before the
day is out. I just feel like this is gonna be our day. The thing
is, don't get jumpy. And don't yell or do nothin' sudden. Just
take your time…"

We would split up, stepping quietly, watching out for anything that might snap or crackle, using hand signals. I'd walk
and squat a while, sweat and wait, look to see where dad was.
I can see him still, across the draw, his jeans belted high, his
red billcap, his twill shirt patched with sweat, hunched like a
soldier on patrol. He loved it out there. It was his passion.

Do I mean the killing was his passion? Or do I mean all
the rest of the things you did to reach the moment when you
pulled the trigger—the driving and the joking and the beers
and the open-fire cooking with the shadows sliding toward
you down the darkly burnished slopes, and the knowledge
that these hills and groves went on for miles and the land you
had entered was as thick with wildness and roaming creatures
as the late-night sky was thick with stars?

In his case I think he needed them both, the wildness, and
the rifle that would give him some piece of it to bring back
home, antlers, the side of venison, a glossy hide. In my case,
it was something like the New Testament, which has been my
mother's passion. I had never liked the Sunday morning meetings much, the sermons that went on forever, and clothes I
didn't want to wear. And yet I inherited the words to three or
four hundred gospel songs, and learned to love the language of
the King James Version of the Bible, and after many years of
downgrading Jesus and the irrational notion that anyone could
be resurrected from the dead, I rediscovered the wisdom of his

teaching and came to appreciate the many ways there are to die and somehow return to life.

I guess I was ten when dad gave me my first rifle, a .22. It was the first year he took me hunting, which was also the first time I watched an animal die at close range. Not a major animal, just a gray squirrel I took a shot at because I wanted to please him. It fell from a pine limb into the blanket of needles beneath the tree and twitched a few times. Watching the blood trickle, I knew I was supposed to feel strong and proud. This was what I had been practicing for. This was why he had bought me the rifle. As dad hunkered to inspect the hole, I felt no pride. I felt shame and loneliness. He said it was not a bad shot at all and said we should keep the tail, which we did. It hung on the wall of my room for years—for him the emblem of someone he hoped I would become, for me the emblem of something I hoped I'd never have to do again.

Forty years later, as I stood transfixed in the cool morning air of Round Valley, it occurred to me that this deer I'd been watching was surely a descendant or distant relative of one my father had shot, or shot at. Silently I asked the buck for forgiveness. In the same moment I gave thanks that my father had brought me out to places like this at the time in life when whatever is presented to you leaves its mark, its indelible and ineradicable imprint.

In search of game we traveled north and south of San Francisco, as I have continued to do throughout my life, exploring this region I call my natural habitat. And by habitat, I do not mean California. Not all of it, from border to border, from Berkeley to Tahoe. As a subject, or as a vast network of interlocking subjects, California can give you a lifetime of things to think about, and write about, and wrestle with and brood about. But as somewhere to call home, it's just too big. There is too much to grasp. Our nervous systems are not designed to identify with something as large and diverse and contradictory as the State of California. Its population is greater than Canada's. In square miles it's larger than Japan. Along the eastern seaboard it would encompass everything from Boston to Cape Hatteras. It would include the Adirondacks and parts of Appalachia.

The Coast Range itself is various enough; yet in this long wrinkle bordering the continent's western edge there is a continuity of terrain and vegetation and weather that has helped me stay located, both physically and spiritually. It is a subregion of the far West, stretching from Eureka in the north to Point Conception in the south, including the ridges and ranges between the Pacific shoreline and the western foothills of the Central Valley. The mountain chains are called Yolla Bolly, Diablo, Santa Lucia, Gavilan. Between the ranges there are long fertile valleys called Anderson and Napa and Sonoma and Santa Clara and Salinas. There are the mineral-rich mudbaths at Calistoga, and the wilderness Zen center at Tassajara Hot Springs down inside a gorge behind the drop-off cliffs at Big Sur, and the old mission towns of San Juan Bautista and San Miguel. A couple of missions still stand out there by themselves, among the foothills and the oaks—San Antonio de Padua, La Purisima—restored adobe relics from the days when this stretch of California was the farthest outpost of the Spanish empire. And there are the cities built on hills and slopes and sprawling across the onetime fields and dunes—San Francisco, my birthplace; San Jose, where I finished high school and went to college and met my wife; the city/state called Stanford; and Santa Cruz, where we have settled and raised our three children.

I have lived other places and traveled around quite a bit—in Europe, in Asia, in Mexico, and among the Pacific Islands. But I have always come back to this region I call my place, this long string of places. Again I thank my father, and my mother too, for the choices they made that brought us here and kept us here. Given the general ebb and flow and slippery temporariness that accounts for so much of life along the western shore, I consider myself lucky to have anywhere at all to feel connected to.

These places, in turn, have connected me to certain travelers and storytellers and poets who have touched me in a very visceral way. I think first of the chanters and legend-makers from the coastal tribe whose creation story begins like this:

> Water covered all, they say.
> Only peaks remained, they say.
> Here eagle and hummingbird and coyote took refuge,
>   they say.

I think of Fray Juan Crespi whose *Diaries* describe the trailblazing overland expedition north to San Francisco Bay, led by Captain Portolá in 1769; and of Robert Louis Stevenson, who passed by here in the 1880s, wrote for the papers in Monterey, later traveled through what is now known as "the wine country," and left us *The Silverado Squatters*. There is Jaime de Angulo, and Robinson Jeffers, and William Everson, and Lew Welch, and most immediately John Steinbeck. In their works I have felt a compelling territorial kinship.

Nowadays I can walk down to the sandstone bluffs a block from where we live and, across the waters of Monterey Bay, I can see the outlines of the region they call "Steinbeck Country." Did I have such a view in mind when we chose to live here thirty years ago? Not at all. Not consciously. But as it happens, he *was* the first novelist who caught me and really held me. And as it happens, on almost any day of the year I can see the low place in the shoreline, the broad delta where the Salinas River spreads out and meets the bay. I can see the mountain ranges he describes in the early pages of *East of Eden*, representing for him the polarities of light and shadow, the sunny Gavilans to the east of his home valley, and to the west the Santa Lucias, shaded in the afternoon, less knowable, more foreboding.

I was seventeen, just starting college, when I came upon *Tortilla Flat*, then *Cannery Row*, then *Of Mice and Men*. By that time we had moved south from San Francisco into Santa Clara Valley, which could still claim to be the world's largest orchard—6 million fruit trees, their springtime blossoms adding to the lower end of San Francisco Bay an inland sea of pink and white. As I read his books it did not occur to me that the Salinas Valley, another hour south by car, was also framed by parallel ranges and opened onto a bay. It did not occur to me that the hills and mountains hovering around his stories were parts of this continuous terrain I'd inhabited all my life. At no point did I think or say aloud, "I *know* this place. I *know* these people." Yet that was how his stories affected me—at that level of implicit recognition. As I read *The Long Valley* and *The Pastures of Heaven* and *In Dubious Battle*, these were the valleys where I'd already spent summers picking apples and apricots and peaches. These working stiffs were the men who had worked with my dad before and after World War Two.

Am I saying Steinbeck has been an influence on my work and way of seeing? I've never been comfortable with that use of the word "influence." The most you can say is that you have your favorites. There are writers you admire, for the skill or for the art or for the level of inventiveness or for the professionalism of a career well spent. And there are writers—sometimes the same ones, sometimes not—to whom you are powerfully attracted, for reasons that may or may not have something to do with literature and literary values. They speak to you, or speak for you, sometimes with a voice that could almost be your own. Often there is one writer in particular who awakens you, who is like the teacher they say you will meet when you are ready for the lesson. In my case it was John Steinbeck. He spoke to me from a landscape and a history that I knew before I knew *about* it.

ii. The Yin and the Yang

In an interview someone once asked a well-known novelist why he had chosen this particular career. "It allows me to use the word *work*," he said, "to describe my greatest pleasure in life."

"You mean writing," the interviewer said.

"No, I mean brooding, and pacing back and forth, and staring out the window."

Soon after I'd finished graduate school at Stanford and we'd moved from Menlo Park over the hill to the coast, I was doing just that, brooding, and pacing back and forth, trying to finish a short story I had started during my Air Force time in England, some four or five years earlier. As I paused to stare out the window I noticed a candy store that stood on a corner about a block away, on the far side of a large open lot, empty except for a few neglected fruit trees. We'd been living in this house for a couple of years, and I'd been visiting the town of Santa Cruz off and on since high school, so I had seen this candy store a hundred times, perhaps a thousand times. Yet I had not-seen it. I had never looked at it—a fixture in my daily life, so familiar it had gone entirely unnoticed. As I studied the details—the whitewashed walls, the corny Dutch windmill—something began to buzz, the tingling across my scalp that I now refer to as the literary buzz, a little signal from the top of my head that there is some mystery here, or some unrevealed linkage that will have to be explored with words.

I sat down at my machine and began to describe the candy store. By the time I finished, fifteen pages later, I had described the stream of cars along the coastline road that runs through the neighborhood, I had described the town, and where I thought it fit into the larger patterns of northern California, and I had begun to examine, as well, why I chose the town and this stretch of coast and the windblown house we still occupy.

The result was an essay both regional and personal. In terms of my perception of myself as a writer and what I could write about, it was a small but crucial turning point. It was my first attempt to write not only *about* this part of the world, but to write *from* this part of the world. This was also the first piece I sold to a national magazine—it came out in the now-defunct *Holiday*—and the first piece that earned anything like a significant amount of money, six hundred dollars, which was a decent fee for an essay, back in the mid-1960s, and a bonanza for us, in the days when four hundred was our monthly budget.

A few years later I saw something else for the first time. Like the candy store, this too had been waiting outside the window. I had of course heard the legends of the San Andreas Fault. I had drunk from the reservoirs of water stored in long depressions created by the movements of the continental plates. I had crossed the rift zone countless times in my travels up and down the coast. So in one sense I had been seeing it all my life. Yet I had not-seen it, not until I read an article in *Scientific American* about a recently verified theory called "Continental Drift." This astounding vision of global geology was just then going public. In the air for decades, as a theory, it had not been universally accepted by geology professionals until the late 1960s—which had given rise to a spate of articles such as the one I'd come across. I was electrified. Here was one of the most influential natural features of the western American landscape. I had lived within a few miles of it since birth, yet it had been virtually invisible to me, a legend, a folktale, an elaborate rumor.

I had to know more. I called my friend Gary Griggs, a professor of earth sciences at U.C. Santa Cruz. He had studied these things. For one of his courses he had already designed a fault-line field trip. A week later we were climbing into his pickup truck, with a six-pack of beer and some country-western music on the radio, heading south from Santa Cruz toward Watsonville, then following the Pajaro River along Highway 129.

The river has carved a trough through that fold of the Coast Range, a trough called Chittenden Pass. It's a place where the river crosses the San Andreas, which in turn marks the zone where two pieces of the earth's crust meet and grind together, the Pacific Plate and the North American Plate. Thanks to deep cuts by road crews in the 1930s, we could stand there and see these two massive slabs spread before us like an open-faced sandwich—on one side, a chunky wall of granite, overgrown with brush and eucalyptus; on the other, a brighter wall of buff-colored shale, stratified at a steep angle pointing up and west, as if the granite sides were nosing in under the shale. Above this layering there was a dip in the ridge, the kind of low spot that makes the trace line visible from high altitude.

We followed the fault line for fifty more miles, past sag ponds, and little avalanches, and displaced creek beds. In Hollister Gary turned onto a side street lined with Victorian cottages and farm-town houses. Down the center of this street we could observe the tar line, which was offset about eight inches. Hollister sits right in the rift zone, as does the La Cienega branch of the Almaden Winery, a few miles farther south. The winery was being gradually torn in two. For students of ground flow it is a historic site. It is where the fault line's pattern of steady creep was first identified, back in 1958.

By the end of this day I felt as if I'd flown a light plane from Mendocino to Tehachapi. I was imagining the long crease, a diagonal seam through the north/south flow of ridges. I saw how all the places I had known and cared about were in some crazy, fearful, and fascinating way stitched together along this seam. And I had begun to see how the forces that came pushing up against the continent to make the lovely and inspirational mountain ranges, and to shape the valleys between the ranges—these same forces also accounted for the rift zone that had triggered so much damage in 1906 and in 1928 and 1968, and could jump and jolt again at any moment. The sources of creation and the sources of destruction, or rather, the ongoing threat of massive upheaval, were one and the same, and had been coexisting in the earth for a long long time.

That day I felt again the tingling cross my scalp. Not long afterward I began to enter the lives and histories of the fictitious Doyle family, whose inherited acreage happens to border the notorious fault line. I had embarked upon a long exploration of the yin and the yang of coastal geology, which you might say continues to this day, since the Coast Range has its place on the so-called Ring of Fire that encircles the Pacific. This Ring, sometimes called a Rim, is seismic and economic and political and multicultural and mythological, and sacred too, with sacred craters here and there around the huge circumference, and shrines of every type.

The day I made that trip with Gary Griggs I began to feel a tension pulling. I could not then have put it into words. Indeed if I had been able to, I doubt that I would have plunged into the making of a story that became the novel *Continental Drift*. But looking back I believe it might be described as a tension between the fertile and abundant and essentially pastoral landscape of my youth, and the continuous presence of an unpredictable subterranean power. It was of course tempting to regard this in the Biblical way, as some version of the tension between good and evil. Many were already doing so. In those days it was fashionable to predict that the San Andreas Fault would sooner or later crack wide open and everything west of it would drop into the ocean. Such an event would not simply be a geological misfortune, it would somehow be fit punishment for accumulated sins. But sin and retribution did not interest me nearly so much as what this famous fault line can tell us about the great wheel of earthly cycles and the coexistence of opposites.

iii. *Where Strangers Meet*

Now I see that I must start again, go back again to San Francisco and start at a different place, since it all begins there.

When they packed up their suitcases and left west Texas behind, my mom and dad were fugitives from farming and ranching country where the land was wearing thin. The community they joined had a lot in common with the one they'd left, composed mostly of transplanted Southerners and Southwesterners, Anglo and Protestant, who had all come west in the 1930s, or soon after the outbreak of World War Two, when the Bay Area's shipyards started working double and triple shifts seven days a week. They all clung together, as immigrants usually do. Not until I entered high school did I begin to see beyond this community and to grasp the range of histories that had shaped the city of my birth. These histories were shaping me too, but in ways I would not understand until many more years had passed.

Lowell was the city's high school for the college bound. It was located about midway between Ocean Beach to the west and the Embarcadero to the east, the long row of shipping docks that poked out into the bay. A four-story red brick building, vintage 1912, Lowell drew students from all parts of town. It cut across district lines, which meant it also cut across culture lines and ghetto lines. Suddenly I found myself sitting in classrooms with Japanese kids and Hispanic kids and Jewish kids and Italian kids. I recently glanced through the yearbook from 1949, the year I left Lowell. I see the photo of a kid who had just transferred in from Teheran.

For the first time I was watching and admiring athletes who were Asian American. One of the lightweight basketball teams had a very good season, according to the yearbook—thirteen wins and four losses, "paced by forwards John Chin and Yukio Isoye." They were graceful and quick, and during the warm-up games, before the varsity took the floor at Kezar Pavilion, they were counted among the heroes.

I remember a husky fellow named Allen Gan, president of the scholarship society, who also threw discus on the championship track and field team. I remember Rudy Suarez, soft-spoken and swarthy, a loping right end, as well as a varsity basketball sharpshooter. If he had not graduated at midyear he would have made All-City. I remember that the student body president in 1949 was a track star named Jim Plessas, listed in the yearbook's "Hall of Fame" as the All-American Greek. He broke two city records that year, in the low hurdles and the broad jump, ran the relay anchor lap, and was generally regarded as the man who led the track team to its fourth straight city title.

I don't mean to suggest that Lowell High in the late forties was a model of cross-cultural harmony. It was a mid-city American high school with in-crowds and out-crowds, nerds and prima donnas and rivalries and status symbols and graffiti in the locker rooms and fights in the park two blocks away. But looking back I see that it had a profound effect on the way I would come to perceive the world. Though I usually entered the old brick building full of teenage fears and doubts, I nonetheless took it for granted that a high school could have a Japanese forward, a Chinese discus thrower, a Jewish halfback, an Italian quarterback, a Greek student body president. For a couple of formative years I had the chance to walk the hallways of a little city-within-a-city where people with all these histories had found a way, at least part of the time, to get along.

I had to leave California to find out how rare Lowell was for that day and age. I was midway through my junior year when my family moved south to Santa Clara Valley, where I finished high school. From there I was sent to Texas for a short-lived football career at a small Christian college. This was a family idea. My mom and dad wanted me to get to know the old country, to see the skies and listen to the winds of their younger days. And we had a cousin who had the ear of a coach, who wangled me a scholarship.

I have a yearbook from that campus too. It is fascinating to scan the faces. This happened to be a school where almost everyone came from Texas or Oklahoma. They were all white, all Protestant. In short, they all looked much like me and my relatives, a yearbook full of almost-kinfolk. Texas was my almost-homeland, and this was my natural tribe. Yet something was missing. I would not have been able to say quite what. Not back then. I was a freshman, running on hormones. But now, looking back, I see that the monocultural climate already seemed as odd to me as the arctic.

I made some friends there, met up with uncles and half-cousins I might otherwise never have known. But a year later I was back on the coast. I had transferred to San Jose State, where I soon met the woman I would eventually marry. Her father had grown up near Hiroshima. Her mother's parents were immigrants from Niigata, in northern Japan. Jeanne herself was born in southern California, and her parents had moved north from Long Beach a few years after the World War Two internment.

We arrived at that campus on the same day, with the same major, journalism, and the same minor, Spanish. It was a much smaller place than it is today, about one fifth the size. In 1952 there were six thousand students, and we were the only two with this particular major/minor combination. During the first quarter we had five classes together. Everywhere I went I saw this radiant young woman of Asian descent. Call it coincidence. Call it luck. Call it destiny. In any event, once we started going together, we did not see ourselves in sociological terms. She was Jeanne and I was Jim, and we could not stay away from each other. It was much later when someone would say, "What was it like to be dating an Asian American?" or "There couldn't have been many interracial couples back then..." Only later did I begin to think about the sequence.

If I had been born in Texas, or if I had stayed there, chances are much slimmer that I would have stepped across such a border. But in the mid-1950s Santa Clara Valley, like San Francisco, was already a multicultural region, and I had already come to think of the world as a place where cultures could intermingle.

To cross this border, of course, was to enter a realm I knew almost nothing about. I was very innocent back then. My view of cultural intermingling was very narrow. This view began to change on the day I met Jeanne's father, a man I only saw once. We were never introduced. She was afraid for me to meet him, knowing how deeply he would disapprove. She too had taken a border-crossing step, the first in her family to do so. There were ten brothers and sisters. She was the youngest, and she was the renegade.

Soon after we started dating, I drove out to her family's house, south of San Jose. It was a Saturday afternoon. She had said she'd meet me in town, but for some reason I insisted on picking her up. Maybe I saw this as the chivalrous thing to do. Or maybe I knew this was the only way I'd ever have a chance to look him in the eye.

Her father was working strawberries then. The house was off to the side of his field, among some outbuildings. As I pulled into the yard, he appeared on the porch, in jeans, an old felt hat. I was driving a 1938 Chevy sedan. He looked first at the car, with grave doubt, then at me. He had a thin black moustache and a weathered, aristocratic face. When I told him why I was there, he shook his head and seemed to cough. He stepped down off the porch, stood with his feet planted and his hands on his hips, holding me with his gaze in a way that forced me to look at him.

In that brief exchange, at the edge of his acres of immaculately tended strawberry furrows, I saw a man, or felt the spirit of a kind of man previously unknown to me, a man from Asia, a man from Japan. I would later learn that he had lost most of his relatives in the bombing of Hiroshima. Thirty years before I was born he had immigrated to the United States, to work, to live, to make a fresh start. He and my father had at least that much in common. His home region was in a deep depression when he left Japan, at age seventeen, heading east on a steamship bound for the Land of Promise. He had worked as a lumberjack, a cook, a farmer, and eventually as a fisherman based at San Pedro. After the attack on Pearl Harbor he was arrested by the FBI, falsely charged with delivering fuel to enemy submarines off the coast of California. He lost his boat and he lost a career sitting out the war inside a fenced internment camp. He'd been so scarred by that experience, he stopped speaking to Caucasians. It was a point of honor. Now, into his yard had come a suntanned Anglo fledgling with scales on his eyes and lust in his heart, driving a neglected '38 Chevy and looking for his daughter, the youngest, the first to go away to college.

All this was in his face. Though I could not have known it, I must have felt it. I felt something coming from him, and it was not hatred or bitterness. What he projected was the hard-won toughness of a man who had survived everything America and Japan had thrown at him, who had preserved his dignity and found a way to continue.

That was 1953. It was almost twenty years later when Jeanne and I began taping her recollections and the vivid childhood memories that would become *Farewell to Manzanar*, the story of her family's experience during and after World War Two. Three decades after they'd all been loaded onto busses in downtown Los Angeles and ferried north to Owens Valley in the lee of Mount Whitney, she finally reached a point where she wanted to talk about what had happened there. She needed to talk about the events—the evacuation, the details of life inside the camp, as she remembered them from age seven and eight and nine. More importantly, she was ready to give voice to her deepest level of feeling and emotional knowledge. For each of us, for our different reasons, writing that book, getting that story told, was a way of paying tribute to her father and her mother, to their lives and the remarkable spirit that carried them through those years.

After that meeting next to his strawberry field, I never saw him again. The year before we were married he passed away. But as I came to know the clan he'd left behind—Jeanne's nine brothers and sisters and their families—and as I learned to be the new uncle to thirty-six nieces and nephews, and heard the many family stories, I continued to think about that afternoon and this man who is the grandfather of our three children. For me it was a moment of awakening, the beginning of an education that continues to this day. A window had been opened, for the first small glimpse of another world, another way of being in America, another way of seeing the white world I had, until then, pretty much taken for granted.

iv. My Father's Passion, My Mother's Voice

In our family my mother was the reader and the singer. She had a bell-like alto voice, and she could carry a tune because she'd grown up among people who entertained one another with singing. She sang in church—always sitting down close to the front, so she could make eye-contact and harmony-contact with the songleader—and she sang around the house. This was before we had TV sets going day and night. Maybe she sang to fill the spaces we now fill up with talk shows and daytime serials. She sang gospel tunes—"Rock of Ages" and "When the Roll Is Called Up Yonder." She sang western swing tunes like the ones made famous by Bob Wills and His Texas Playboys. She sang old favorites such as "You Are My Sunshine" and "Oh Susannah" and "Camptown Races." These and much older tunes she had learned from my grandmother who, in her day, had been a singer too and who still knew some of the ballads she'd grown up with as a girl in the Cumberlands.

My mother provided the lyrics, you might say, while the accompaniment was provided by my dad. He was not a singer. But he was a devoted picker, practicing every time he had an hour or so to spare. His main instrument was the steel guitar, which he had learned to play while he was in the Navy during the 1920s. He joined right out of high school, looking for a way to see somewhere else in the world besides east Texas. The next thing he knew he was in the Hawaiian Islands, stationed at Pearl Harbor with a submarine crew, where he spent three years.

I can't say for sure what happened to him there. He never talked about it much, partly because he never talked about anything much. But something had made those years important for him, given them a shine. My guess is they were magic years. The islands have quite a bit of magic, even now, in spite of the crowds and the prices and the traffic. Hawai'i is still the northern point of the Polynesian triangle. From a cobalt sea the emerald mountains still rise to cut their jagged edge against a technicolor sky. Imagine what it was like before statehood, before tourism, before the mega-hotels went up, before planes had started crisscrossing the Pacific. He was eighteen, nineteen, twenty. The steel guitar was a new instrument then, invented by Hawaiians, and introduced to the world not too long before he got there. He fell in love with the picks and the strings and the sliding steel bar and the sweet music they could make.

In one of my earliest memories he is down on his knees in front of the radio. We had one of those oldtime radios made of dark carved wood, with a curving top and cloth over the speaker, a piece of furniture large enough to dominate the room. Set against a wall by itself, it had a strangely compelling presence. When three or four of us were gathered in front of it gazing at the speaker and listening to one of the evening programs—"One Man's Family" or "Suspense"—you might think it was an altar to the Deities of Sound.

Kneeling there alone on a weekend afternoon he would hold his ear up close to the cloth and fool with the dials, trying to bring in a show known as "Hawai'i Calls" that used to be broadcast live from the lanai of the Moana Hotel. This was when the Moana and the Royal Hawaiian were the only two hotels at Waikiki. The M.C. was Webley Edwards, and he would always find a way to remind you of the climate you were missing out on. With a mike down close to the shore-lapping surf, he would say seductively, "Temperature of the air here at Waikiki is seventy-six, temperature of the water is seventy-four." The musical director was Al "Kealoha" Perry. Sometimes Lena Machado would sing (known as "Hawai'i's Song Bird"), and sometimes the great falsetto artist, George Kainapau.

My father would wait all week for this. Some Saturdays the shortwave signal would be so faint it was nothing more than a thin and lonesome trickle struggling to make it across twenty-four hundred miles of open water. Every once in a while, if the weather was right, you could hear the songs and the voices loud and clear, the ukes, the rhythm guitars, and somewhere behind the music the lapping surf. Then my father would set back on his heels and listen reverently.

That is what I remember. Anything that brings your father to his knees is going to make an impression on you, and this was what could do it: the sound, or the very hope of hearing the sound, of "Hawai'i Calls."

When the show was over he would plug in his amp and hook up his steel and spend an hour working on one of his big production numbers, such as "On the Beach at Waikiki," or "The Hilo March," upbeat, full of slides and chimes. His fingerpicks would flash, and the strings would whine, and at these times you did not interrupt him. If you tried to get his attention—"Hey Dad, Mom says dinner is almost on the table…"—he would show no sign that he had heard you, as if he were in another room, or on his own private island. If you tried again, "Hey Dad...," you might get a scowl, but not a glance, since he would not lift his eyes from the strings and the picks.

Why the scowl? He was practicing. What was he practicing for? He had a band, he would tell you later, and in a couple of days they were going to be rehearsing again. But it was more than that, much more. I know now that the tunes kept him connected to a time and a place in his life he always dreamed of getting back to and never could, except via the radio and the transporting powers of the music itself.

He always had a band when I was growing up. They didn't play for money, they just played for the pleasure of it, and for parties now and again. They practiced in our living room because he had speakers and a couple of mikes and the most space. These were all men from Texas and Oklahoma, bringing along their Gibson guitars, a fiddle, a banjo, or a mandolin. It was mainly a western band, with an island flavor contributed by my dad and his amplified steel. His all-time favorite tunes were "The Hilo March," which he delivered with bravado and many flourishes, and "The Steel Guitar Rag." Running a close third was "The San Antonio Rose," usually sung by my mother. She had carrot-colored hair and fair skin that would turn pink with tearful happiness as she stood by his speaker and sang this song from the homeland they had left behind, a song of yearning for those "lips so sweet and tender / like petals fallin' apart..."

As I kid I resisted the sounds of their repertoire. To my ears then, it was cornball music. But maybe it all goes back to nights such as those, and to the three kinds of music I grew up with—gospel, and country, and Hawaiian.

I have written a novel called *Love Life*, about a woman who is guided by the voice of Hank Williams and has a not-so-secret desire to be a country singer. I have also played in a lot of bands myself over the years—dance bands, bluegrass bands, jazz combos, and in piano bars—and I wrote another novel, called *Gig*, about the night club world as seen from a musician's point of view. And something about those island tunes my father played and loved and listened to—and listened for—has sent me across the water time and time again, to live a while, to write a while, to listen. After numerous essays and articles, video documentaries, and the novels I have located there, I still have not had my fill of the place.

The Coast Range is my base. I have come to see Hawai'i as a heartland, some form of older spirit-home. And why should that be so? I am still not entirely sure. Jeanne and I like the multicultural mix—that is part of it—the faces and the voices and the foods and the races that gather there from all parts of the Pacific region. In the histories of our two families the islands stand as some kind of meeting ground or crossroads. They hold a position, both geographical and symbolic, out there in the middle of the ocean midway between California and Japan. Jeanne's grandparents came to Hawai'i as contract laborers, and her mother was born on a Kaua'i sugar plantation in 1895. Her father spent time in Honolulu on his trip across the Pacific in 1904. We were married in Honolulu in 1957 and spent our honeymoon hitchhiking around the outer islands, visiting the craters and old temple sites and ghostly valleys, meeting people who have become lifelong friends.

At the time I'd already been out there for about six months. After graduation from college I had some open space in front of me. I saved enough money for a one-way ticket, thinking then this was an original idea for an expedition. I was so busy setting out on my own I had not stopped to remember the sound of his guitar or where he had learned to play it. But I hear it now—"The Hilo March"—and I am wondering if he himself ever got to Hilo. He could have, though he never mentioned it. There's no way to know for sure. There were so many things he never mentioned. Maybe this song was in the air. Most Hawaiian songs pay tribute to a specific place, a bay, a mountain, a point of land, a town. Maybe he had heard the 1920s recording that first made it famous, a steel guitar version by Pale K. Lua. Maybe he just heard it, and it worked on him the way it has worked on me.

My first trip took fourteen hours from San Francisco. En route I was dreaming of beaches. But I soon found myself drawn inland, toward the mountains, and the chain of craters that bear witness to Hawai'i's volcanic origins. Like a chain of stop-time photographs, they chart the history of the earth, from Kaua'i in the north, the oldest island, with its razor cliffs worn down by wind and endless rain, to Hawai'i in the south, the Big Island, the youngest and still growing, each time new lava steams into the sea, spilling outward from the region Hawaiians call "The Navel of the World."

This is the island I prefer to visit now. Hilo is its principal town, a port town on the windward side. The Big Island has produced many talented musicians and composers, some great dancers and chanters. The best slack-key guitar players have come from there. I like to go into the high country and sit for a while among the plains and heaps of old dark lava and listen to the stillness of the craters and then come down into town and listen to the music, always listening for some note I must have heard once, or more than once, or maybe something in between the notes he was picking on the silvery strings that held him captivated after he had switched off the radio and sat down to practice on those long-ago Saturday afternoons.

(1992)

PART THREE

THE
WRITING
LIFE

In the beginning was the Word...
—John 1:1

A Portrait of the Artist

From his lips smoke spurts like steam from a locomotive's wheel rods, curls from the pipe bowl, and billows up to filter light from the stark bulb above his easel. Tobacco whiff swirls with pungency of burnt umber while he squints at what he claims will be me. He daubs. He glances at the real me, widening for an instant his blue eyes to catch who knows what detail—perhaps the very glint of the eye that watches him.

The pipe hangs half-clenched from lips accustomed to it, lips that give with the pressure of the slanting stem. Below the mouth grows a chin-wide goatee, not tailored, not waxy, but whiskery and rough like the beard of an old man, while around the chin a whiskery shadow spreads from the goatee up the cheeks and down the neck almost to the chest hair creeping above his shirt. Above the eyes, above dark brows that link in a wrinkle when he squints, the forehead rises into realms his hair has abandoned, rises brown from the sun, brown from squinting into the sea's glare. And above it all,

between the smoke and the blue eyes, his wild hair is parted
far to one side, and to conceal recession it is combed across
his head like a Scandinavian's—like a Scandinavian sailor
who has spent a day bucking the Baltic in a sixty-mile gale.
His hair looks as if a gale blew forever through his studio.
Yet in here it is still and humid.

This Nordic head half-turns to look at me, but the rest of
the artist, squatting on a tattered canvas camp chair, is immo-
bile—long legs bent, back straight, broad shoulders steady,
toes spread and paint-spattered. Only the head moves, and
the magic arm.

The arm moves, it seems, of its own volition. A color
finds its complement so quickly that the arm, the hand itself
must surely make the decision. The hand wields the brush
with a magic rhythm, holds it like a drummer holds his stick,
and the quick mixing, the skip from gob of azure to blob of
ochre, the momentary blending stir is the painter's paradiddle
before the brush leaps again for the canvas—its touch then,
the climax of each roll.

At last, out of the billows, the burnt umber, the pipe-
clenched squinting, the paradiddles, and the endless wiping
of brush-ends in an ever-held paint-thick rag, the hand trans-
forms a palette of oily globs into a human face. The artist
rises from his rickety canvas perch, steps back, and invites me
around to his side of the easel.

He puffs a moment and asks, "What do you think? Hon-
estly now, tell me exactly what you think."

I see a figure dressed in coat, tie, and vest, seated in a
straight chair, gazing pensively sideways with a bemused seriousness. Behind him a wall of books is vaguely suggested.
The whole is dark, shadowy, somber.

"I don't think it looks much like me."

"Waddya mean?"

"Of course, that's a hard thing to evaluate," I say. "I guess
nobody really knows what he looks like."

"True."

He lifts it from the easel and sets it against an apple box across the room. We study it from this new perspective.

"It's a caricature," he says.

"Doesn't a caricature exaggerate prominent features?"

"Yeah."

"What's exaggerated? Head size? Ears?"

"It's not a physical caricature." He puffs. "It's the essence I try to exaggerate."

"Can we call it a caricature then?"

"Maybe not. Maybe it's just a portrait."

I keep studying the painting and he pours out two glasses of burgundy from a jug. "I've been thinking about this painting all week," he says, "ever since I asked you to sit. I didn't want it to be just another portrait. I wanted to say something important, about you. And I got this idea. You may not agree with it. You may not feel at all the way I want the painting to feel. But I suspect that you do feel the same way. You see, that's supposed to be a picture of a creative personality—in your case, a writer—who has things to say, but who lives with the difficulty of communicating what he feels, a writer who sees the gap, who sees himself in the gap between conception and execution, but who still accepts this condition as inevitable. He's chosen this path, and he's discovered some of the pitfalls, but he's on it and he accepts it all."

I quote Eliot: "Between the idea and the reality falls the shadow."

He sits up suddenly, spilling wine on the floor. "Yeah. Exactly. That guy on the canvas is in the shadow, but he knows it, and he stays there by choice." He looks at me penitently. "Now, maybe you don't feel that way about writing. I'm pretty sure you do, though. I mean, I feel like we have that in common. I know I feel that way about painting, I feel that way all the time."

"Sure I feel that way."

"Do you see it in the painting? Do you think it comes across?"

"It's a possibility; I doubt that every viewer would see it like that, though. The guy obviously has something heavy on his mind. But exactly what it is would depend, I suppose, on the viewer. On a painting like that, everyone throws his own shadow."

"I don't care what anybody else thinks. I just want to know if you see that particular shadow in there."

"Sure I see it."

"What about the electric chair idea? That's why I have him sitting in that straight-back chair, with his hands holding the chair arms, not clutching, but sort of rigid. I don't want it to be too obvious, but it's there, don't you think?"

"It's there all right, but I don't agree with it. I mean, I don't think it's like being in an electric chair at all."

"Oh yes, it's exactly like that. I feel that way all the time."

"Well, I don't feel that way. It's supposed to be a portrait of me, isn't it?"

He puffs in silence, studying his work. We sip wine and shift the painting from place to place to cut the glare and get new angles, not talking. Sitting on his low bench, we finish the jug, watching the portrait.

(1965)

How Words Sink In

Words are the basic tools, if you are a writer. But why? Why do you choose one set of tools rather than another?

Over the years I have played quite a bit of music, acoustic guitar and upright bass, a little piano. I've made some money at it too, from time to time, and could have made much more. Why didn't I choose music as my main line of work? Why did I choose words instead of notes?

Why didn't I choose sound?

Or stone?

Why not a hammer and a chisel?

Why not paint?

Why not the brushes and the stepladders and the drop-cloths of the painting contractor, to follow in the footsteps of my father?

When these questions first rose to the surface, I had been reading a lot about the lives of writers, and I had made what was, for me, a fascinating discovery. I was struck by how often there has been a minister or a preacher or a rabbi or a priest somewhere in the immediate family. I had begun to keep a list, which now is rather long and includes, to name a few—the father of Jane Austen, the father of James Baldwin, the father of Isaac Bashevis Singer, the father of W. S. Merwin, the father of E. E. Cummings, the father of Robinson Jeffers, the grandfather of William Burroughs, the grandfather of Joy Harjo, the father and grandfather of short story writer Joy Williams, the father, grandfather, and great-grandfather of Ralph Waldo Emerson, the father and two brothers of Harriet Beecher Stowe, the father of Amy Tan. In other families, where there had been no minister nearby, there would sometimes be a devout and Bible-reading mother, such as the mother of Herman Melville, who wrote articles for a Methodist journal…

As my list grew, it started me thinking about possible links between the literary urge and the role or presence of scripture in one's life or general vicinity. Needless to say, there are numerous ways to account for a literary urge. But in my case the presence of scripture seemed to be a key. As I pondered this, I eventually came to understand the influence of the church I happened to grow up in, which was New Testament Christian, congregational in style, and fundamentalist. This was not, by any measure, a literary or intellectual world. In fact, it was the opposite. Yet in this world language had exceptional power, since all our devotional activities and efforts to communicate with God consisted primarily of words.

Both my parents came from what is sometimes called the Bible Belt. Born in Oklahoma, my dad met my mother one summer while he was doing fieldwork in the Texas panhandle. After they settled in San Francisco their habits did not change. They ate the same foods they'd eaten back home, blackeyed peas, cornbread and buttermilk, porkchops and applesauce, white-flour biscuits and red-eye gravy. They

listened to the same country-western music—the Grand Ole
Opry, Roy Acuff doing "Wabash Cannonball" and "The Great
Speckled Bird," the Spade Cooley Band doing "Shame, Shame
on You." They built their Sundays around the same Bible
classes and sermons.

Coming of age on the West Coast I was often ashamed of
my parents and resisted their down-home ways. In my view
then they were "Okies," and I was not an Okie. I was born
in the city by the Golden Gate, where you saved your paper-
route money to buy cashmere sweaters. I spent a good part of
my youth looking down upon the things they tried to offer me
and looking for ways to distance myself from what I thought
they were. It took me quite a while to recognize the many
gifts hidden right alongside what I had so earnestly rejected.
It took me quite a while to see how the very desire to be a
writer began in those Sunday morning services that had been
transported from the Bible Belt to the far Pacific shore.

Fundamentalist means you look to the letter of the Old and
New Testaments for guidance, and nowhere else. We were so
fundamental that almost everything had been stripped away
from the place of worship. Think of the role words can play
when all other enticements and sensual attractions are gone.

The meeting halls of my boyhood were deliberately under-
adorned. Light drifted in through long panes of plain translucent glass. The walls were bare. Rows of wooden pews faced
an open stage, a pulpit, a single cross above the curtained
baptistery. Sometimes a bouquet of flowers would appear,
but nothing else to beguile the eyes, no statuary, no incense
to entertain the nostrils. There were no robes or hats or scep-
ters, no gleaming pendants or rich brocade to appeal to your
sense of theatre, no bells or chimes or gongs or drums, not
even a piano or an organ to help the spirit soar.

According to the logic of our Elders, the New Testament
makes no mention of stained glass or carved statues or upright
pianos, and if it was not right there on the page in front of you

in God's own words, you'd better not presume to dress up a worship service just because it seemed like a good idea.

God's written word was the measure. And if you hold to the letter of the New Testament, you do not have much left *but* words to express the longings of the human spirit:

Words in the form of scripture readings from the pulpit.

Words in the form of prayer, both public and personal.

Words as they form the sermons and exhortations and invitations to come forward and be baptized in the name of The Father and The Son and The Holy Ghost.

The fact that all our preachers and deacons and elders had come from somewhere south and east seemed to give the words more weight and more zeal. They all had ties to Texas or Oklahoma or Arkansas or Alabama or Tennessee. The voices carried a mix of drawl and old-fashioned oratory that somehow sharpened the effect of the King James Version, when it was quoted or read aloud. They savored the archaic terms, as if it were a private language that belonged to them. Belonged to *us*. Words you never heard anyone else use, they would utter with special relish, words like "viper" and "begat" and "smite thine enemies," and "raiment" that could be "girded about the loins."

Even at meal times, the words came first. Give thanks to God with your voice, *then* eat.

And sometime after dinner, in my earlier years, one of the women's voices would begin to read from the New Testament, or from the Old. Sometimes it would be my mother's mother, born in the Cumberland Mountain region of Tennessee in 1888, a seamstress by trade, who had followed her daughter out to the coast. After three elementary grades she'd had no further schooling. Church work was the center of her life. The Bible was her solace and her reference and her daily inspiration.

You could hear this in her voice, carried across the continent from the mountains of eastern Tennessee and into our frontroom there in the Sunset District of San Francisco, as we listened to her read aloud the stories of David and Goliath, Jacob and Esau, Joseph and the Pharaoh, Paul and Silas, the parable of the Prodigal Son.

"Bring hither the fatted calf," she would read, "and kill it. And let us eat, and be merry, for this my son was dead, and is alive again. He was lost, and is found..."

Sometimes it would be my mother doing the reading. She was born in Huntsville, Alabama, raised on a Texas farm. She always did the best she knew how, passing on to me and my sister whatever she had learned from her mother to share with her kids, and how can you not listen to your mother's voice when she is reading to you from Genesis, from the Psalms, reading how flames appeared upon the heads of the apostles on the first day of Pentecost after Jesus ascended, and how they spoke in tongues, with miraculous command of new and unknown languages.

Eight or ten years of this, when you're young and impressionable, can have a profound effect. It all sinks in. The words sink in, their very sounds and, at some level, the potent message they carry. In the Gospel According to St. John one sentence spells it out:

> In the beginning was The Word,
> and The Word was with God,
> and The Word was God.

Quote a verse like that and you run the risk of sounding self-congratulatory, as if you have hit upon some true path to salvation via the sacred calling of prose or poetry. I would not want to go nearly that far. Nor do I wish to suggest that writing can become another form of religion. This is more personal. This is about what you can internalize growing up in the presence of scripture.

An abiding belief in the power of words has been part of my inheritance. But when I first started writing, for the high school paper, that was the furthest thing from my conscious mind. For quite some time the motive was simply to get a story told, hoping to see it in print, and later, hoping to get some money for the effort. As the years went by, writing turned out to be a good deal more than that. In Zen terms you might call it a form of Practice. The daily struggle to pursue a line of meaning becomes a kind of path that allows you to travel both outward and inward.

There are a million paths (as Don Juan once said to Carlos Castenada). Mine happens to be made of words, and there is no mystery now about why I chose it. Long after I left home, at age seventeen, and left the family church behind, the role and the appeal of words stayed with me, the idea that they might provide access to a higher power, whatever name you choose to give it, the idea that words themselves might somehow save you.

(1998)

Beginner's Mind

A while back I received a call from the travel editor of the *San Francisco Examiner,* wondering if I could contribute something to a special issue he had in mind.

"What's the theme?"

"Sacred places," he said.

"Give me an example."

"Give *me* an example. Have you been anywhere recently that really felt like it had a sacred dimension or spiritual power?"

"Did you say this is for the Travel section?"

"I'm tired of package fares and wine lists. We have to move off in a new direction."

I had just returned to California from an extended stay on the Big Island of Hawai'i. I'd already started working on a piece about an old temple site that had affected me profoundly, called Mo'okini, over on the northern shore. It stands by itself on a windswept point, with a spectacular view across the channel toward Maui, where the dormant volcano Haleakala comes rising from the water like Mount Fuji. In the presence of the ancient stones heaped there I had felt something that held me in an unexpected way. It started me thinking how certain places can be selected or designated or recognized as sacred. I was writing the piece because I had to, and had not thought much about where to send it. Before this call I would certainly not have regarded it as a "travel" piece. But eventually that's where it first appeared, along with half a dozen other articles that shared some similar concerns.

Judging by numerous letters this editor received, the issue was a huge success, the kind of thing many of his readers had been hungering for. And that issue is emblematic of something we've been seeing more and more of in recent years, as editors and writers and travelers begin to reexamine our motives for venturing forth, when we do, and to look again at this shrinking world.

I say "look again" because in some ways contemporary travel writing has started to resemble certain works written one hundred fifty and two hundred years ago. For centuries travel writing was synonymous with the discovery of new places—I should say, places that were new for the traveler as well as for the reader. The writers weren't Writers with a capital W, who held M.A.s in journalism from Columbia. They were explorers, ships' officers, soldiers, geographers, missionaries—people who had other jobs besides writing about their trips and voyages. They kept logs or journals or wrote books and extended reports on the regions they'd encountered, the terrain, the daily life.

The works that endure, that stand the test of time, usually involve something more than mere diary-keeping or description. The essay or the book will be about a country, a city, a mountain range, an archipelago. It will also be about the effect of that place upon the traveler. Between the place and the person some form of dialogue is going on. Along with the outward journey, there is often an inward journey.

Several years before Melville wrote *Moby Dick*, he wrote the books that made him famous. They were instant hits, which continue to be read as examples of this classic type of travel narrative. *Typee* (1846) and *Omoo* (1847) emerged from his years as a common seaman in the Pacific whaling fleet. Somewhere between autobiography and fiction, these books about the Marquesas and Tahiti provided readers of that day with vicarious trips to remote corners of the globe few of them would ever have the slightest chance of visiting. They were also about Herman Melville the young American wanderer and cultural observer, whose romantic imagination was being tested, and who himself had embarked upon a personal journey of discovery. His first sojourn on a Polynesian island was not only an encounter with an improbably exotic landscape; it also enlarged his worldview. Toward the end of *Typee* he writes,

> ...entering their valley, as I did, under the most erroneous impressions of their character, I was soon led to exclaim in amazement: "Are these the ferocious savages, the bloodthirsty cannibals of whom I have heard such frightful tales? They deal more kindly with each other, and are more humane, than many who study essays on virtue and benevolence..." I will frankly declare that after passing a few months in this valley of the Marquesas I formed a higher estimate of human nature than I had ever before entertained.

Not long after these books appeared, the nature of travel began to change, as well as the nature of *who* could travel. It was a change brought about by the enormous technological advances during the nineteenth century, which gave us steamships and railroads, ultimately automobiles and aircraft. New transportation options gradually gave rise to what came to be called "tourism" and a tourist industry geared to ever faster and more available modes of movement for ever larger numbers of travelers. In time another kind of travel writing developed, designed to serve this burgeoning industry. Call it "Travel Promotion," something little known when Melville was sailing the Pacific.

In 1872 Harper Brothers published *California: For Health, Pleasure, and Profit*. Written by Charles Nordhoff (grandfather of a later Charles Nordhoff, who co-authored *Mutiny on the Bounty*), it was an illustrated guidebook to a new land that was healthful, pleasurable, profitable, and safe. Here is a typical passage:

> It is generally acknowledged that some very respectable people live in California; but we who live on the Atlantic side of the continent are sorry for them, and do not doubt in our hearts that they would be only too glad to come over to us. Very few suspect that the Californians have the best of us, and that, so far from living in a kind of rude exile, they enjoy, in fact, the finest climate, the most fertile soil, the loveliest skies, the mildest winters, the most healthful region of the whole United States.

This book was financed entirely by the Southern Pacific Company, whose recently completed rail system linked the east and west coasts. In its day the book was a bestseller, one of the biggest books of the late nineteenth century, and had a tremendous influence on transcontinental travel, as well as upon the influx of people into California, which, in the 1870s, was a region yet to be promoted in a big way—a legend, but not yet a commodity.

Nordhoff's book was a harbinger of things to come. Eventually travel writing, in the minds of a great many readers, would be synonymous with just that: travel promotion, travel advertisement. Thus we now have Sunday supplements of the type my friend at the *Examiner* was hoping to avoid, indeed whole magazines concerned primarily with overseas shopping opportunities, package deals, hotel fixtures, pool temperatures, and jetski rental rates. The articles are not about journeys or discoveries. Rather, they emphasize the various pleasures that await you once you reach Acapulco or Singapore or Lahaina.

This kind of writing is not going to go away. As long as tourism booms, it will continue to proliferate. But meanwhile the great wheel turns, and in recent years we've witnessed a resurgence of the kind of travel writing we used to see in the days before travel itself became a commodity. It's part of a broader pattern of rethinking who we are and what we are doing with the fragile systems of this planet we call home.

Strange as it may seem, even though every square mile of land and sea has long ago been mapped and charted, the travel writer may actually have more than ever to write about, as we rediscover or perhaps discover for the first time the irreplaceable value of historic sites, nature's forms, the indigenous cultures. While geographical exploration has just about run its course, cultural exploration is far from over. One of the great tasks before us all is learning how to move back and forth across borders that have been barriers for far too long. I for one welcome the traveler who can help me see across a border, see another culture with clearer eyes.

These changing times, of course, make the writer's role ever more complex. The technology of movement is so sophisticated now, no peak or forest or isolated atoll is immune to an influx of visitors. As the global population thickens, the volume of travel and numbers of travelers escalate from year to year. In heavily trafficked regions like California, Hawai'i, Bali, Nepal, travel is both a blessing and a curse, bringing welcome money into local economies, but at an alarming cost, impacting the environment, the resources, the roadways. And how then do you proceed without contributing to the overkill?

I know that many of my own expectations have been shaped by what I've read or seen in photographs and on film. My expectations, in turn, can have quite an effect on what I look for or fail to look for, what I see, or fail to see. For any of us who work, either full-time or part-time, in these expectation-shaping media—print, photography, TV, film—there's a responsibility and an opportunity to be attentive to the spirit of any place one presumes to write about or attempts to depict. We need to look for ways to convey a sense of respect for the sacred, for the cultural life and its traditions, for the very delicate ecologies of a Hawaiian island, or any other island, the great Earth Island from which we all have sprung.

If readers are told that Hawai'i is a golf course with a mai tai waiting at the nineteenth hole, that may be all they ever expect to find. If they are told that hula is older than ballet and has a high ritual role in Polynesian cultural history, going back a thousand years and more, they may come to the islands looking for something else, and they might find it and be affected by it.

To write well and persuasively about any journey, you have to know where you've been; you have to get the facts right, do your homework. But as a fundamental way of proceeding, I find the respectful approach to be essential, along with a willingness to be vulnerable, to be instructed, to let my own assumptions and preconceptions be tested and challenged, to be in what Suzuki Roshi calls the beginner's mind. "In the beginner's mind," he says, "there are many possibilities; in the expert's mind there are few."

(1999)

How Selling a Car Can
Almost Get You to Nigeria

I t started in the Safeway parking lot on Stevens Creek
Boulevard in San Jose. That's where I sold the car to the
medical student from Shanghai. It was my mother's car,
a nice-looking Ford Tempo, and this Chinese fellow wanted
his cousin, who spoke no English, to look it over. While they
were driving away, the idea for a short story came to me. Two
months later I wrote it. After the PEN Syndicated Fiction
Project decided to include it in their 1989 series, I figured that
made a pretty good life for one story, since it not only went
around to twenty-five daily papers, it was also broadcast over
National Public Radio.

I'd moved on to other tales and other projects, and a year
had gone by, when someone called from Washington, D.C.,
where the PEN Project and NPR have their offices. Three
stories from each year's series are chosen to be read aloud at
a gathering at the Library of Congress, and would I fly back
there to read "A Family Resemblance" and attend a reception?

The Library of Congress. All I really knew about it was what you read on the copyright page, on the backside of the title page of whatever book you're flipping through, where it says "Library of Congress Cataloging-in-Publication Data." Nearby there will be a number, such as 90-30094—which I had taken to mean that somewhere on the other side of the continent in a vast and formidable building lined with corridors and shelves, the thirty thousand and ninety-fourth title for the year 1990 had been duly recorded and stored. My vision was of a monolithic bin, the ultimate library, its endless basement heaped with manuscripts, while mega-scholars sat hunched in dome-like reading rooms, somehow sealed from the outside world. Would they actually take time from their researches to listen to my account of a bilingual car deal?

There was only one way to find out.

I flew into Dulles, where I was met by Alan Cheuse, a novelist who co-edits the PEN Project and is also a book commentator for NPR's "All Things Considered." My plane was late, so we headed straight for the reading. In late November the trees along the boulevards were mostly stripped bare, with a few patches of color remaining, yellow, orange, rust, and leaves piled everywhere. We came up to Capitol Hill via Independence Avenue just as the moon edged into a magenta sky.

Where Independence meets First, you can see the three main buildings, each occupying most of a city block. The oldest, finished in 1897, is named for Thomas Jefferson, who offered all sixty-five hundred volumes of his personal library to seed the collection back in 1815. The Jefferson Building is the one you most often see in photos—ornate, built of stone, in the Italian Renaissance style, with many Greco-Roman pillars, a balustrade along the roofline, its greening copper dome soaking up the twilight.

The Adams Building (art deco, 1939) stands right behind it. We were headed for the Madison Building, the newest, a six-story fortress of utilitarian white marble, said to be one of the largest library structures in the world. When it was completed in 1980, it doubled the library's carrying capacity.

That is the most obvious difference between this and other libraries—the size, the scale. The Library of Congress holds over 86 million items—books, maps, periodicals, songs, scripts, prints, photographs, software—and the listings increase at the rate of ten per minute. As the nation's library, it is filled with exhibits, some permanent, some rotating, all having to do with words, language, documents, and information. Inside the Madison Building I stole a couple of minutes to check out a lobby exhibit called "A World of Names," celebrating the origins and variety of geographic names around the nation. There were elderly maps and modern maps, etymologies, a wall of song sheets featuring place names in the titles, and a wall full of T-shirts that said

INTERCOURSE, PENNSYLVANIA

JERSEY DEVIL TAVERN
PLEASANTVILLE, N.J.

THERE IS NO LIFE EAST OF
CALIFORNIA INTERSTATE 5

We took the elevator to the sixth floor and stepped out into another lobby, where glass cases displayed pages of Arabic script—an exhibit called "The Book in the Islamic World." From there we followed signs down a carpeted and silent corridor of doorways, took a turn into another long corridor, then another turn, and I was having the déjà vu feeling: we were going nowhere in the federal labyrinth of my dreams. And this is exactly what happened. One more turn and we found ourselves back in the lobby full of curlicue Arabic texts, none of which could tell us what we needed to know.

A man and a woman stepped out of the elevator, and she said, "Let's follow those two fellows. They look like they know where they're going."

"You're taking a great risk," said Alan. "But at least they can't start until we get there."

We set off again, took a different turn into yet another labyrinth. But this time it was the right one, and eventually we found ourselves in front of a mural photo of Montpelier, the colonial-style Virginia home of James Madison, for whom this building was named. The room where I would be reading was called the Montpelier Room. The other readers were already there, running mike tests for the audio and video recordings— Laura Furman, a former Guggenheim fellow, from the University of Texas, Austin; and David Michael Kaplan, from Chicago, who recently had a story in the O. Henry Prize Collection.

Waiting my turn with the audio engineer, I looked around. It was quite a room, worth the twists it took to get there— wall-to-wall carpeting, upholstered chairs for the audience now flowing in, a small stage, a podium, and full picture windows, so that the glittering lights of the city came at you from two sides. In Washington, D.C., where no building can be taller than the Capitol, six floors is about as tall as they come. To the south there was the dark curve of the Potomac. To the west you looked out upon the Cannon Building, directly across the street, where our congressman had his office. The Capitol's night-lit dome was a block away.

Black Elk, the great Sioux holy man, once said, from his stronghold in South Dakota, that "anywhere is the center of the world." Which is true. But D.C. seems to be more central than most places. A room like the Montpelier Room could go to your head. From there the Supreme Court is right around the corner. The Copyright offices are right down-stairs—half a million items registered every year.

The reading itself went very well—that is, the sound was good, the stage didn't squeak, none of us had a coughing fit, and at that altitude there were no dogs or children to contend with. It was a good crowd, a diverse and enthusiastic crowd. The event was open to the public. At the white wine reception I had a chance to find out who attended—and there did not seem to be one hunched or bleary-eyed researcher among them.

In addition to the head of the library's Poetry and Literature Center and the director of the PEN Project, there was the "Book World" editor from the *Washington Post*, some previous winners of PEN story awards, an attorney from Manhattan, a physician in town for the National Kidney Foundation annual meeting, some graduate students in writing from George Mason University, a professor of something who said he loved my story but wanted to suggest another ending, and a warm-spirited woman from the U.S. Information Agency who asked if I would like to travel to Africa on a lecture for their Arts America program.

"Which part of Africa?"

"My territory is the sub-Sahara."

"How sub?"

"Do you speak French?"

"I used to."

"Nigeria is one place I'm thinking of."

"I'm a Pacific Rim guy," I said. "I sort of keep my eyes on Asia, the South Pacific. I haven't thought much about going to Nigeria."

"It's just one possibility," she said. "There are others."

Interesting, I thought. No. More than interesting. As I stood there with my glass of sauvignon blanc, the gob of pâté on my pumpernickel wafer, catching a glimpse of the Washington Monument down at the far end of the Mall, I was thinking, This is pretty wild. You start out trying to get rid of a car in the Safeway parking lot on Stevens Creek Boulevard, you fly three thousand miles to the Montpelier Room of the Library of Congress, and you could end up on a plane to Lagos.

I told her to send me the details. But I knew I wasn't going anywhere else just yet. Before I flew home, I would stay right where I was a while longer, and savor the heady view.

(1990)

The Days with Ray

I first met Ray Carver at a collating party in San Francisco back in 1969. This was when George Hitchcock was editing and publishing *Kayak*, the quirky and influential poetry magazine, out of his house on Laguna Street. I had just come back from two months in Mexico and had to think twice about climbing into a car again to drive the eighty miles from Santa Cruz to the city. But it was considered something of an honor to be invited to one of these gatherings, a little nod of recognition from George, the small-press impresario. And I had been told that Ray would be there. His stories were showing up in literary magazines and quarterlies, and I had been wanting to meet him.

He was living on the Peninsula then and already writing the tales that would make his reputation, haunting stories of contemporary suburban and small-town life, in spare and stripped-down prose. But who could have foreseen the impact they would have on a generation of American writing? His first collection, *Will You Please Be Quiet, Please* (1976), was still years away. So was the review in the London *Times Literary Supplement* hailing Ray as "The American Chekhov." By the time he died, in 1988, at age fifty, he would publish eleven volumes of poetry and short fiction, among them *Furious Seasons, What We Talk About When We Talk About Love, Cathedral*, and *Where I'm Calling From*. His work would be translated into more than twenty languages, while in this country he would become the single most emulated storyteller since Ernest Hemingway.

But as of the summer of 1969 all this was yet to happen. He had shown up at the *Kayak* collating party because Hitchcock was about to bring out *Winter Insomnia*, Ray's second book of poems. In his low-keyed way he had an immediate effect on me. Among other things, I was struck by his clothing—a plain white long-sleeve shirt and dark slacks. I liked that.

The late sixties was the height of the counterculture, which had its world headquarters right there in San Francisco. The streets were teeming with headbands and broad-brim hats, turquoise pendants, amulets, moccasins, roman sandals, shirts covered with hand-sewn embroidery, and leather fringe hanging from every vest and jacket. But the Bay Area scene did not interest Ray much at all. He was not affecting the look of a hippie or a cowboy or a Buddhist or a trail guide or a lumberjack. Oblivious to the costumery of the times, he was a man of the West who dressed in a sort of Midwestern way, conservative, though not entirely respectable, since the white shirt was wrinkled and the slacks were rumpled as if he might have spent the night in these clothes.

After an hour or so of snacks and drinks, George put everyone to work on his literary assembly line, someone to collate the pages, someone to add the cover, someone to trim the edges, to staple, to fold, to stack, and so on. I was assigned to the stapling gun. Ray ended up next to me, working the trimmer with its guillotine blade.

Neither of us was mechanically inclined. We had already
talked about various forms of car trouble that had bewil-
dered and defeated us. We wondered if our participation that
afternoon would have any effect upon sales. That is, we wondered if readers would buy a poetry magazine spotted with
the drops of blood that would inevitably fall upon its pages
once we touched the machines we'd been asked to operate.
We wondered if Hitchcock might get sued, the way angry
consumers will sue a food processor when a loose fingernail
turns up inside the can of stewed tomatoes.

Then the joking subsided. We bent to our tasks. What
I remember most about that day is standing next to him for
the next hour or so, not talking much, standing shoulder
to shoulder, stapling, trimming, stapling, trimming, as we
worked along with George and the others to put this issue
of the magazine together.

Ray was an easy and comfortable man to be with, to stand
next to, or to sit with for long periods of time. He had a ready
wit, and an infectious laugh, and no pretensions about him, no
attitude. In every way he was unassuming. From the first meeting I felt a strong kinship, and I realize now that it was due, at
least in part, to our similar origins. Years later we would finally
talk about how both our fathers had come west during the early
1930s looking for any kind of work, his from Arkansas into the
state of Washington, mine from Texas to the California coast.

There was something else about Ray that I found enor-
mously appealing. I think of it as a priestly quality. I never
imagined I would be making such a statement about him,
but as I look back I believe it's true. He could be very brotherly. He often seemed filled with wonder. And you knew he
would never judge you for your sins, whatever they might
be. That was my experience, at any rate. In later years he had
the capacity for genuine forgiveness.

He also had a brotherly demon in him, and this was
appealing in another kind of way. Ray could talk you into

things, cajole you or seduce you into things you were not per-haps ready for: a pied piper on the prose and poetry circuit.

One afternoon stands out in my memory. This must have been six years later. I was upstairs working on something, I can't remember what, when I heard footsteps down below. Our attic had been converted into a writing space, which was private yet still not entirely cut off because the old wooden building is so poorly insulated. Rising toward me came the sound of large and deliberate footsteps, too heavy to be those of my wife or one of our kids. I listened until the foot-steps stopped, in the room directly below me. A voice called my name.

I didn't answer. I didn't care who it was. I didn't want to see anybody just then or get into a conversation. It was about three in the afternoon.

Whoever this was had now moved to the doorway at the bottom of the attic stairs.

"Houston, you sonofabitch, I know you're up there."

Again I didn't speak.

"Answer me!" he shouted.

I knew this voice, but I said, "Who is it?"

"It's Carver."

"What do you want?"

"Goddam it, come down here and say hello to some people."

"I'm busy. I'm working."

"Of course you're working. We're all working. We're busy as bees. Do you want to come down or shall we come up?"

"I'll be there in a minute."

He was traveling with Bill Kittredge and a big, red-bearded fellow named John, recently arrived from Alaska—all large men, large and thick. The four of us completely filled my living room. Ray was carrying two bottles, a gallon of vodka, and a half-gallon of grapefruit juice, which he carefully set upon the rug. From a plastic bag he withdrew a plastic cup and began to fill it.

With his rascal grin he said, "You tell me when," though he paid no attention to my reply. They had been at it since lunch, or earlier. Ray was living in Palo Alto at the time. On and off he'd been teaching here at U.C. Santa Cruz. He had them on a kind of sightseeing tour with no clear agenda, making it up as they went along. I surrendered to the inevitable and began to quench my thirst with the drink he had prepared, which ran forty-sixty in favor of the vodka.

I don't remember all that we talked about. Kittredge was down from Montana as a Stegner Fellow at Stanford, so we must have talked about that. Ray's first book of stories, *Will You Please Be Quiet, Please*, had been put together, so we must have talked about that. It was a rambling conversation about books and writers and schemes and plans, that grew noisier as I caught up with them, as we sat and sipped and argued and laughed, and while Ray, self-appointed host, refilled and refilled the plastic cup.

I guess an hour had passed when someone mentioned starting back.

"What do you mean?" said Ray.

"Who can drive?" said Kittredge.

"My God, you're right," said Ray. It was his car. "Who's going to do it?"

This led to a long debate over who was most qualified to navigate Highway 17, the curving mountain speedway that connects Santa Cruz to Santa Clara Valley and the Peninsula.

"Maybe Houston should," said Ray, at one point, "while he can still see."

"Gladly," I said, "though there is a problem with that. Once we got to your place, I would need a ride over the hill."

He leaned toward me with a raspy and infectious giggle. "Well, it goes without saying. One good turn deserves another. We'd just have to give you a lift back home."

The next thing I knew they were lunging through the house, down the hallway, out the back door and into the yard.

While they piled into the car we shouted our goodbyes. It was a big, unkempt American car, a car from a Ray Carver story, with low tires and a rumbling exhaust. It lurched a couple of times, kicking up dust. Ray took the corner without braking. The rear end swung wide, he gunned it, and they were gone.

There was no wind. The sky was clear, ordinarily a great time to be outdoors. But my head was throbbing. I was alone in a sudden stillness. In those days my driveway wasn't paved. It had not rained in a month or so. Dust hung in the slanting light of late afternoon and slowly settled around me, and I stood there wondering what I was now supposed to do, stunned with drink at quarter to five and abandoned in my own driveway.

Later on we would talk about that trip and others like it, and Ray would always laugh the hardest, hearing his escapades repeated. But it doesn't seem so funny now. It fills me with sadness, thinking back on the turmoil of those mid-1970s days, when he was always on the run. I prefer to remember him as he was in the years after the running ended, after the drinking stopped.

The last time I saw him was in February 1987, maybe six months before he learned about the cancer in his lungs. By that time he had gone back home to Washington. He and Tess Gallagher were living in Port Angeles. He had come down to the Bay Area to spend a few days as the Lane Lecturer at Stanford, which included a public reading at Kresge Auditorium. It was a triumphant return to the campus and to the region where he had honed his writing style. To a packed house he read "Elephant," which had recently appeared in the *New Yorker*, and got a standing ovation. Ray had a hulking, self-effacing way of receiving praise. At the podium he looked a bit surprised. He also looked genuinely prosperous. He was wearing an elegant suit, light beige, almost cream colored. It had an Italian look, single-breasted, with narrow lapels.

As I stood there applauding with all the others I was thinking about a time I had flown to Tucson, fall of 1979, on my
way home from a trip to Albuquerque. Tess had a one-year
appointment at the University of Arizona, and Ray was on
a Guggenheim. He'd been moving around so much I hadn't
seen him for a while. I'd heard about the big changes in his
life, from him, and from others, but I wasn't quite sure what
this meant, until we went out that night for Mexican food.
"You have whatever you want," Ray said, when it came time
to order the beverages, "I'm sticking with the iced tea."

As we began to talk I saw that the crazy restlessness had
gone out of his body. He had lost some weight. He was calmer,
clearer, his laugh was softer. He had spiraled all the way down,
he told me, drunk himself into the final coma, which he
described as being at the dark bottom of a very deep well.

"I was almost a goner, I see that now. I was ready to go out.
I could have. I was ready to. But I saw this pinpoint of light,
so far up there it seemed an impossible distance. It seemed
completely beyond my reach, and yet something told me I had
to try and reach it. Somehow I had to climb up toward that
last tiny glimmer. And by God, I managed to do that. What
do you call it? The survival instinct? I climbed out of that hole
and I realized how close I had come and that was it. I haven't
had a drop from that day to this, and I've never felt better in
my life."

He had always had the will to write, no matter what. Now
he had joined that with the will to live. It made a powerful
combination. You can see the effects in his later stories, and
you could see it in his face the night he read at Stanford.

After the reception that followed the reading, we found
some time to chat, catch up on things, old times, new times—
a chat which turned out to be our last, face to face. I had never
seen him so happy. There was a lot of light around him, the
kind of light given off by a man who feels good about himself
and his work, a light enhanced by the ivory-tinted cloth of his

tailored suit. Ray had quite a bit of money tied up in that suit, and he liked it. That is, he liked the *idea* of it, though my guess is he was not entirely comfortable wearing it.

He had a way of leaning in and lowering his voice, even when no one else was around, as if what he was about to say should not be overheard or repeated. "I have to tell you something," he said. "Every day I feel blessed. Every day I give thanks. Every day I am simply amazed at the way things have turned out. All you have to do is look at what I'm wearing. Look at this suit…"

He laughed his high, light, conspiratorial laugh. "Can you imagine me wearing anything like this? It's just astounding!"

(1992)

Remembering Wallace Stegner

He was the steadiest man I've ever known, steady in his habits, steady in his tastes, in his view of the world. I met him in 1961, last saw him in February 1993, just weeks before he passed away, and in all those years the essential things about him had not changed. He knew his mind. He answered his mail. He got his work done in a way that generated the unflagging admiration of any writer who knew the depth of his commitment to the task itself, the daily task. In his eyes there was always a look that matched the effect of his stories—probing, unswerving, humane. Like so many of his characters, Wally Stegner looked straight at the physical and social world and did not flinch at what he saw.

A few years back I had the chance to visit him in his studio, in the wooded hills above Los Altos. I was there to do a profile for the *Los Angeles Times*, whose editors were about to inaugurate their annual literary awards and had chosen Wally to receive their first Book Prize for Lifetime Achievement.

A wrought iron fireplace stood in one corner. Outside, a cottony cloud cover, somewhere between fog and impending rain, had crept over the closest ridge, chilling the air. He brought in an armload of wood from the porch. When the blaze was crackling he settled into his armchair, facing the view, and we talked about this Western world he'd spent his life exploring.

When he started writing in the mid-1930s, he didn't see it as something he had set out to explore. He saw himself then as a Westerner, but not necessarily a Western writer. He was drawn to realistic fiction, and he happened to come from a certain part of the country, which in turn became the setting for several early stories and novels. But he'd written half a dozen books before it occurred to him that his work had a regional identity.

"I want to write about what I know best," he said. "That became clearer and clearer. And there is some kind of torque that works on your life. You get pushed into accentuating, developing further on what you know. By the time I'd written *Beyond the Hundredth Meridian* I was up to my waist in Western history. By the time I'd done a couple of books on Mormonism, I was farther in. It all happens to be Western because one thing leads to another. One hand washes the other."

Stegner had a ground-wire that ran deep and kept him anchored to the earth and to the earthy places that were important to him. In his day-to-day living, and in all his books, whether fiction or non-fiction, the sense of place has been essential to an understanding of the life. One such place was East End, Saskatchewan, where he spent several boyhood years, a town he often circled back to—in *On a Darkling Plain* (1940), and in his first big success, *The Big Rock Candy Mountain* (1943), and in *Wolf Willow* (1962). Another is Salt Lake City, where he grew up and went to college, locale for his 1979 novel, *Recapitulation*, wherein a man returns to his hometown, plays the past against the present, and brings his life full circle.

Coast Range mountainsides, like those surrounding his Los Altos home for forty-five years, provided backdrops for the 1976 novel, *All the Little Live Things*, as well as for major portions of his Pulitzer Prize–winning masterpiece, *Angle of Repose* (1971).

His sense of place and sense for the West as a region involved a good deal more than setting, a good deal more than the skill to evoke a landscape or the feel of a town, what they used to call "local color." Stegner was a regional writer in the richest sense of that word, one who managed to dig through the surface and plumb a region's deepest implications, tapping into the profound matter of how a place or a piece of territory, whatever its term may be, can shape a life, character, actions, dreams.

Something elemental about the West emerges, comes pushing through his prose. You feel it in numerous individual works, but more impressively in the body of his work taken as a whole, the novels and short stories, the histories and biographies, together with his labors as an active environmentalist—the wide-ranging output of his long and amazingly productive career.

Built into these works are levels of perception that come at you sometimes all at once, sometimes singly, like strata seen in a canyon wall. There is the physical and geological West, as an awesome stretch of the earth's landscape. There is the legendary West, as a vast repository for illusion and fantasy and improbable hope. There is the cultural West, forever locked in its love-hate embrace with the cultural East. And there is the historical West, with its violent and rapacious past that must be understood if we are to survive the present, not to mention the future.

In Stegner's world you do not find many shootouts or Apache raiders looming at the mountain rim to swoop down on a hapless wagon train. "The western past," he said in 1974, "in a lot of people's minds, is the mythic past of the horse opera, which is no past at all. It is an illusion."

Among his few cowboys is Ray Wiley, in the vintage story "Carrion Spring" (*Wolf Willow*). Ray's adversary is not a band of outlaws. It is the weather. In the brutal Saskatchewan winter of 1907 he watches thousands of cattle freeze to death. At the taut conclusion, while carcasses rot in the spring thaw, the cowboy decides to stay on, to gut it out, in spite of this disaster. Why? He can't exactly say. There is a challenge of such magnitude, he can't bear not to try again. There is also something about the land, the very look of the land. Just as winter turns to spring, the spark of hope flares one more time.

A more characteristic hero in Stegner country is John Wesley Powell, the real-life subject of his novelized biography *Beyond the Hundredth Meridian*. Powell was a naturalist, an explorer, a nineteenth-century visionary whose showdown came not in the streets of Dodge City but in the halls of Congress, where his plan for a manageable water policy for the western states was shot down by the heavy guns of expansionism and runaway development.

Published in 1954, this is essential reading for anyone who wants to understand the role of water in the evolution of western America. The sixty pages describing Powell's harrowing boat trip down the Colorado and through the Grand Canyon are in themselves worth the price of admission. And the issues Powell raised in the 1870s and '80s, raised again by Stegner in the 1950s, are still with us, supporting his contention, as both historian and novelist, that the past illuminates the present—a family's past, a river's past, a region's past— as surely as a coastline or a prairie or a mountain range can bear upon one's character, one's dreams, one's worldview.

I feel compelled to mention one more book, less known and seldom talked about these days, because it has been out of print for a number of years. But it had a good long life, after it was published, during the final year of World War Two, and it represents another defining feature of Stegner's vision. He titled it *One Nation*. As time goes by, this book becomes, in my opinion, ever more significant. It's a pioneer-ing study of the United States as a mosaic of many coexisting peoples. These sentences come from the Introduction:

> No other nation on earth has had the opportunity the United States has had to bring so many peoples and cultures together into one society, to learn from all of them, to grow by the contributions all have made. It follows that no other nation, despite the tragic failures of our principles in many instances, has come so close to promoting a real brotherhood of man. Without our minority groups and the diverse strains of our culture, American society is a pale imitation of Europe. With them it is something newer and stronger.
>
> But it follows just as surely that our failure—if we fail—to make a place for everybody in that society will be a blow disastrous to the hope for peace in the world. For if *we* cannot do it, within the boundaries of one continental nation, under one democratic government, with a tradition of political ideals as high as any nation ever aspired to, how can it be done in the world of nations whose sole tradition has been suspicion, spheres of influence, and balances of power, and whose blood burns with hatreds generations old?
>
> The problem of the populations of America, the problem of making one nation from the many races and creeds and kinds, one culture from all the European, Indian, African and Asiatic cultures that the promise of freedom has drawn to our shores, comes to a head in our time. Its solution is the absolutely essential first step of a process which is historically inevitable, but which can be materially hastened by the efforts of any American with the imagination and good will to work at it.

This sounds like something that could have been written fairly recently, perhaps within the past couple of years. Such ideas are very much in the air these days. But Stegner did not write this book last month. Or last year. *One Nation* came out in 1945, when very few people dared to talk this kind of talk. In 1945 my wife, Jeanne, was still in an internment camp called Manzanar, along with ten thousand other Americans of Japanese background. That was the climate in 1945, and his was one of the few voices speaking out with fervor that there was another way to look at individuals and to think about their histories and their humanity. It is just one more example of what he has done for us all, over the years, as a writer, as a historian and storyteller, as a man of the western United States.

Last February many of these concerns were still on Stegner's mind. In Sacramento, the Center for California Studies was holding its annual conference on the state of the state. "Reassembling California" was this year's theme, and the three-day event was dedicated to Wally, as a writer and a teacher whose work had touched just about every aspect of Far Western life. Knowing he would be on hand, a large crowd turned out for a Friday morning panel called "The Range of Vision: Wallace Stegner and the West." Four of us had been invited to speak: Patricia Limerick, a University of Colorado historian; Al Young from Palo Alto, a former Stegner Fellow; Gerald Haslam, a writer and editor from Sonoma State; and me. At the end of the session Wally took the stage and talked for about ten minutes. This was one of his last public appearances, and for most of us there it was the last time we would see him.

We had talked about his fiction, his historical work, about his time in Washington, D.C., when Stewart Udall was Secretary of the Interior, and about the writing program he established at Stanford. Several questions from the audience had touched upon the role of regions and places, and he came back to this, our attitudes toward the places we inhabit, invoking Mary Austin, and finally invoking John Wesley Powell.

He was right more than a hundred years ago when he said that in the West there is enough water for about a fifth of the land. And that means no matter what you do with it, whether you're going to manufacture with it, whether you're going to have cities, going to use it for agriculture—there is water for about a fifth of the land. And thank God that will leave us some open space, I think, for quite some time.

His voice, as he said these things, was a voice I had been hearing for over thirty years, on and off the page, a voice that requires you to listen, a voice both deliberate and spirited. There was something of the minister in Wally Stegner, though not the haranguing kind; he was a scrupulously moral writer but not a moralizer. There was something of the prophet about him too, but not the Jeremiah kind. His grasp of history gave him a window on the future, but he leavened his warnings with compassion and a careful, hard-earned wisdom.

As he spoke that morning I remember thinking that he looked remarkably fit for eighty-four. He had vigor. His eyes were bright. His newest book was in the stores—*Where the Bluebird Sings to the Lemonade Springs*—and he had readings lined up. At the time there was every reason to believe he would be with us for a good while longer. It made his untimely death in Santa Fe last month a double shock. He passed away too suddenly, and too soon. But his works live on, and they will be with us for a long time to come, a lifetime of solid prose. In six decades of writing he gave us twenty-eight books, plus countless essays, articles, and stories, along with a way of looking at America and at the American West, and a way of seeing more and knowing more about ourselves.

(1993)

Money and Trust

This piece first appeared as a foreword to the anthology *Writing Home: Award-Winning Literature from the New West*—fiction, non-fiction, and poetry by former winners of the Joseph Henry Jackson and James D. Phelan Awards. It includes work by several writers who went on to achieve wide recognition, among them Ernest Gaines, Philip Levine, Wendy Lesser, Frank Chin, Dagoberto Gilb, Leonard Gardner, Jane Hirshfield, and Al Young.

The stories and essays and poems gathered in this volume all speak for themselves. But something has to be said about these two awards, which have given so many of us an early boost and have, for decades now, nourished California's thriving literary life. The Jackson. The Phelan. We refer to them as entities with lives of their own. But how did they get here? And why?

When you're starting out as a writer, you don't think much about such matters, or about where the money may be coming from. You just hope that sooner or later some of it will come your way. The first check I ever received for a piece of writing happened to have James D. Phelan's name on it. In those long-ago days—my undergraduate days in San Jose—I knew nothing about this fellow, whether he was an alumnus or the former chair of a department, whether he was alive or dead. I only knew that every spring something called the "Phelan Awards" were given out for stories and plays and poems by campus writers. For a while I was trying my hand at sonnets. They had a special category for sonnets, and eventually I submitted one I thought might be a contender. I came in third. Since I had never applied for anything, or come close to winning anything, I was very happy to take Third Place in the Sonnet Contest at San Jose State College. At the awards ceremony I got to hang out with other aspiring writers. And thanks to James D. Phelan—whoever he might be—I walked away with a check for ten dollars, which was a serious piece of money back then. I was sitting on top of the world. "Ten dollars for fourteen lines," I was thinking. "That's over seventy-five cents a line!"

Two decades would pass before I fully understood how that check had found its way into my pocket and where it fit with Phelan's numerous efforts to encourage the work of the creative imagination. The campus awards, by the way, were somewhat different from the Award being celebrated here. The intent was similar, the source was the same, but those were local, rather than statewide. Phelan had never attended San Jose State. He simply wanted to recognize younger writers in the valley where he'd enjoyed his final years.

In the late 1970s I had the good fortune to spend two months as writer-in-residence at Villa Montalvo, his palatial spread outside Saratoga, in the western foothills, perched between the broad valley and the verdant ridge. While there I learned that his father had come to California during the

Gold Rush and made a fortune in banking and real estate. Born in San Francisco in 1861, Phelan had served as the city's mayor, elected on a reform ticket in 1897. A Democrat in a predominantly Republican state, he later spent a term in the U.S. Senate, where he made some friends and made some enemies, as politicians usually do.

I have to confess that his political career has not interested me nearly so much as the fact that he named his villa for a novelist. Has anyone else done this? Towns and cities sometimes do. Oakland has Jack London Square. Salinas has the National Steinbeck Center. But who else has named his own residence after a writer of any type? It has always seemed to me to be a key to Phelan's passions and preferences, particularly since this novelist was one that few people had heard of back in 1912, when the villa was completed.

An ardent Californian, he felt a special kinship with the fellow who had coined the name of his home state. It appears for the first time in *The Adventures of Esplandian*, a novel by Garcia Ordoñez de Montalvo. Little is known about Montalvo, except that he wrote this sixteenth-century romance, a tale of preposterous adventures carried out by a bold Spanish knight whose exploits take him to "an island called California, very close to the side of the Terrestrial Paradise...."

The word is not Spanish. It is a Spanish-*sounding* word, an invented word, a science-fiction name for a fantastical place. Montalvo's novel was published in Seville in 1510, twenty-five years before the earliest explorers, sent out by Hernán Cortés, sighted and named what is now the tip of lower or Baja California.

An estate with a legacy both literary and regional: this is in perfect keeping with Phelan's tastes. Born to wealth, shrewd in business, he was also a voracious reader, an essayist too, a sometime poet who traded manuscripts with friends, and a student of European history. An exceptionally cultivated man, he was very much at ease in the company of writers, painters, and sculptors. Before becoming mayor, he had served as president of the San Francisco Art Association. His circle included some of the most eminent creative people of his day, among them the landscape painter William Keith, architect Arthur Page Brown, who designed the Ferry Building, poets George Sterling and Edwin Markham, and his long-time friend and confidante, the novelist Gertrude Atherton. To this day one of the villa's apartments is named for her.

He passed away in 1930. A bachelor all his life, with no immediate heirs, he bequeathed his Saratoga property to the people of California, with the grounds to be maintained as a public park, and the buildings "to be used as far as possible for the development of art, literature, and architecture." In keeping with his will, the Montalvo Center for the Arts now offers a year-round program of plays, concerts, gallery shows, readings, and residencies. It's an Italianate villa, with columns and balustrades, surrounded by 175 acres of gardens and forested slopes. By the time I first checked in, it had already served as an elegant oasis for hundreds of writers, painters, sculptors and composers.

He also left money to the San Francisco Public Library, the Art Association, and the Palace of the Legion of Honor. He funded the awards contest at the San Jose campus. And he set aside an endowment "which shall be used annually for awards in literature and art, to bring about a further development of native talent in California." Launched in 1935, the James D. Phelan Award was the first of its kind on the West Coast, reflecting his longtime belief in the creative spirit of his home region. Seven decades later we are all the richer for it.

Joseph Henry Jackson was another kind of benefactor. He too was an ardent Californian, though not by birth. He did not have Phelan's kind of money, but he had a legendary energy that made him a spokesman for the West and for the West Coast. In his day he was one of the most highly regarded and influential literary voices in the country.

He was born in New Jersey in 1894. When we entered World
War One he left college to organize an ambulance unit, and
later served as an infantry lieutenant. After the war, at age
twenty-five, he headed for California, settling in Berkeley. He
went to work for *Sunset* magazine in 1920, rising to editor-in-
chief. In 1930 he took over as literary editor for the *San Francisco
Chronicle* and remained there for the rest of his career.

For twenty-five years he composed a daily column,
"Bookman's Notebook." He also edited a Sunday book page
for the "This World" section. In addition, he launched a
weekly radio show called "Bookman's Guide," which ran for
eighteen years. Broadcast first over KGO, it was later carried
by the Pacific Coast Network, and eventually aired coast-to-
coast via NBC. His columns, which were reprinted in the
Los Angeles Times, together with his radio show and occasional
pieces for the *New York Times* and the *Saturday Review*, gave
Jackson a national voice. Fair-minded and even-tempered,
he was surely the most listened-to literary commentator west
of Chicago.

His influence was felt in another way, as a frequent judge
of contests, both local and nationwide. During his quarter
century with the *Chronicle*, Jackson served at various times
as judge for the Phelan Award, the Commonwealth Club
Medals, the O. Henry Memorial Awards, the Atlantic Prize,
the Harper Prize Novel, and the Pulitzer.

For most of us, this would have added up to a full-time
job. But somehow he found time to author books of his own,
more than a dozen titles, most having to do with the history,
culture, or literary life of his adopted region. The best known
today is *Anybody's Gold: The Story of California's Mining Towns*
(1941), included by the *San Francisco Chronicle* on its list of
the twentieth century's one hundred best nonfiction books
by writers west of the Rockies. Many years before the Gold
Rush had been rediscovered as a key to California's past and
present, Jackson had given us this pioneering work.

In 1944, he edited the first significant anthology of West Coast literature—*Continent's End: A Collection of California Writing*. An early champion of writers such as John Steinbeck and William Saroyan, he believed in California as a literary region with its own unique vitality and promise. It is impressive now to note the poets and storytellers he had recognized and brought together into a single volume almost sixty years ago. Among them we find, in addition to Saroyan and Steinbeck, M. F. K. Fisher, Kenneth Rexroth, Josephine Miles, Hildegarde Flanner, John Fante, James M. Cain, Budd Shulberg, George R. Stewart, Gertrude Atherton (still based in San Francisco then, and still writing), and Robinson Jeffers, whose famous poem had given the collection its evocative title.

Soon after Jackson's death in 1955, some friends began searching for a way to remember him and his legacy. This group was led by novelist and historian George Stewart and by James D. Hart, who would later become director of the Bancroft Library and who for many years served as secretary to the Jackson Award.

In his eloquent introduction to the 1970 reissue of *Anybody's Gold*, Wallace Stegner remembered those meetings:

> From the beginning it was clear what his most fitting monument would be; he had helped so many writers that he ought to be remembered through a fellowship to a young writer of promise. Prose or poetry, it didn't matter; Joe had a history of liking and assisting both. But the geographical territory from which those fellows should be drawn *did* matter, and the committee of his friends had some discussion about it before they made up their minds.

While Jackson's audience was national, his passions were closer to home. In an effort to be true to his life and work, they settled at last on northern California and Nevada, the parts of the world he had inhabited and roamed and written about and come to love. They raised some seed money to get it launched. Two years later the first Joseph Henry Jackson Award went, fittingly, to Salinas Valley writer Dennis Murphy, for his taut and compelling short novel *The Sergeant*.

In the *Paris Review* interview series "Writers at Work," Katherine Anne Porter speaks of her apprenticeship. "I spent fifteen years," she says, "learning to trust myself: that's what it comes to."

Every writer talks about the time required to find one's way. She was the first I'd heard describe the task as learning to trust oneself on the page. It immediately struck me as an essential truth. And years of disciplined practice, as she details elsewhere in the interview, is the best way to get there. But this particular type of trust can sometimes be nudged along by other means.

Back in 1967 the manuscript I submitted was a new departure for me, not new for literature perhaps, but a kind of storytelling I hadn't tried before. I had not yet published any long fiction. I wasn't at all sure I could bring this off. A short novel called *Gig*, it concerned one night in a piano bar, told by the piano player. Customers gather at the lid of his grand, and it becomes a little theatre-in-the-round, arranged not in acts, but in "sets," as a musician would conceive his evening of music, with an emphasis on the lyrics of the songs he plays, a kind of guiding scripture.

The Jackson judges that year were all writers I admired. Their recognition increased by a huge measure my belief in what I had attempted, as well as my commitment to the writer's path. The money, of course, was very gratifying, as was the author's luncheon, and the press release that followed. But what these awards are really about, in my experience, is faith. The Phelan, the Jackson, aimed at younger writers, they offer you that next increment of faith in your own imagination, what it has given you so far, what it is yet to give.

(1999)

Steinbeck's Legends

This year *The Grapes of Wrath* turns fifty. When Viking Press releases its Golden Anniversary edition, you might say that three legends are being commemorated. First there is the era itself. The Joads of Oklahoma have come to represent the great multitude of displaced families forced to leave farms and lives behind in the Dust Bowl of the 1930s and trek west toward what they hoped would be better times. The book, helped along by the John Ford film, is a legend too, a classic of American fiction. Meanwhile, among Steinbeck buffs, how he wrote his masterpiece has become another kind of legend, a story all its own.

Two years before he started the Joads on their archetypal journey, Steinbeck took an assignment from the *San Francisco News* to do a series on the predicament of the state's migrant farmworkers. It was the summer of 1936. Refugees from the South and the Midwest were pouring into California by the thousands.

At the time, Steinbeck and his wife, Carol, were living outside Los Gatos. His first major book on the subject of farm labor, *In Dubious Battle*, had just been published. Certain growers were troubled by his pro-worker leanings, and certain labor radicals did not appreciate his account of their Machiavellian strategies. But *News* editor George West, who had once met Steinbeck in Carmel, liked what he had read. He arranged to send the thirty-four-year-old novelist on a statewide tour of the fields and Hoovervilles and the camps being developed by the federal Resettlement Administration.

The result was called "The Harvest Gypsies," seven pieces that appeared in the *News* in October 1936. They were reprinted in 1938 by San Francisco's labor-oriented Simon J. Lubin Society in a pamphlet titled *Their Blood Is Strong*. His potent blend of empathy and moral outrage was perfectly matched by the photographs of Dorothea Lange, who had caught the whole saga with her camera—the tents, the jalopies, the bindle stiffs, the pathos, and courage of uprooted mothers and children. (Long regarded as a treasured but hard-to-find prologue to *The Grapes of Wrath*, these early articles have been recently reprinted under their original title, *The Harvest Gypsies*, by Heyday Books in Berkeley.)

While researching that series Steinbeck met Tom Collins, the manager of a government camp south of Bakersfield, in Kern County. Drawn to each other the two men were soon traveling companions, as Collins became his migrant-labor mentor, providing raw material—field reports and oral recollections—that would find its way into the *News* as well as into the novel.

In early 1938 the two men were traveling again through the San Joaquin, this time into fields near Visalia and Nipomo, where winter floods had created chaos in the already precarious lives of displaced migrants. Suddenly thousands were without shelter and starving. Steinbeck, who had seen a lot of hardship, had never witnessed anything like it. With Collins he spent two weeks doing round-the-clock rescue work in mud and rain. At one point Collins heard him say, "Something hit me and hit me hard for it hurts inside clear to the back of my head. I got pains all over my head, hard pains. Have never had pains like this before."

It was a crucial turning point. The need to report, as he had done for the *News*, gave way to something larger and much more urgent. Two months later Steinbeck was sitting down to write an as-yet-untitled novel. At the same time, he began the daily journal that Viking Press is bringing out as a companion to the Fiftieth Anniversary edition. Called *Working Days: The Journals of "The Grapes of Wrath,"* it was edited by Robert DeMott, formerly a director of San Jose State's Steinbeck Research Center. It covers the period of actual composition, from May to October, 1938. Judging by the details in *Working Days*, this was a novel born in pain and sustained by pain.

Part of the legend of the making of *The Grapes of Wrath* is the feverish obsession of the writing, at the end of which Steinbeck collapsed from nervous exhaustion. His journal bears this out in sometimes excruciatingly intimate detail. It is as if a closed-circuit video camera had been mounted above his desk in the eight-by-eight workroom on Greenwood Lane in the foothills near Los Gatos. These are daily, confessional glimpses of a man who, while giving voice to an American legend, is sweating and brooding, counting words and pages, fighting nausea, blacking out.

During these same five hectic months he is also nursing his wife through a tonsillectomy, buying a ranch, entertaining Charlie Chaplin and Broderick Crawford, worrying over reviews of *The Long Valley*, which came out that summer, and trying to ignore reports that his New York publisher, Pat Covici, is going bankrupt.

What emerges from these rushed entries is the picture of a man whose life is filled to overflowing, whose body is falling apart while his mind and heart are possessed with a story that will not go untold.

The published novel is over six hundred pages long. He wrote it in one hundred working days. Pacing himself relentlessly he averaged two thousand words a day, commencing on May 31, when his journal begins:

> Here is the diary of a book, and it will be interesting to see how it works out...

On October 26, the day he completed the final scene, his entry conveys both misery and relief:

> ...I am so dizzy I can hardly see the page....I wonder if this flu could be simple and complete exhaustion. I don't know.... Finished this day—and I hope to God it's good.

Steinbeck didn't get his wish. You never hear the word "good" used to describe *The Grapes of Wrath*. From day one this has been a novel with devoted fans and powerful enemies. Readers have loved it, and they have hated it. There are still people in Bakersfield who cannot discuss it in a calm voice. They have not yet forgiven him for the way he described working conditions there and for the damage they believe this did to Kern County's reputation.

In its first year the novel sold half a million copies. It has been selling ever since. Why has it endured? There are many reasons. And they are not all literary. Steinbeck's fever, for one thing. It is still in there. His book continues to tell a story that touches the conscience and stirs the blood and cuts close to the bone, with an eerie resonance for the 1980s. The great wheel turns, and once again, while the rich get rich and the poor get poorer, we are confronted with a newly visible and growing underclass of citizens who used to have at least enough to get by but now have fallen through the bottom of the economy.

Though fifty years have passed, this is still not the kind of novel that gives you much distance, historic or aesthetic. It continues to have the holding power of a documentary film. It brings to mind the kind of witnessing that has since been turned over to New Journalism. If Steinbeck had been telling this story thirty or forty years later he might have tried a non-fiction novel, along the lines of Capote's *In Cold Blood* or Mailer's *Armies of the Night*. But new journalism and the non-fiction novel had not yet been formulated, so he had to invent a form—part storytelling, part reportage, part sermon, part myth—a form to elevate and make universal the experience that had so appalled and electrified him.

(1989)

The Path of Empire

This piece originally appeared as a foreword to the reprint edition of Bayard Taylor's *Eldorado*.

Bayard Taylor was twenty-four when he left New York in June 1849, bound for California by way of Panama. Unlike the great multitude he soon would join, he was not heading west to prospect for gold or to seek his fortune in the far-off land of promise. He came as a writer in search of the story, which in that year was a very big story indeed. As a young reporter for Horace Greeley's *New York Tribune*, Taylor was being sent out to cover it. President Polk's announcement the previous December had stirred imaginations from Paris to Honolulu to Canton. "The accounts of the abundance of gold in that territory," Polk said in his State of the Union address, "are of such extraordinary character as would scarcely command belief." The world was converging on California, a legendary place that had now become synonymous with adventure, discovery, high hopes, and new possibilities.

Taylor was an astute reporter. His sure eye for the telling detail was coupled with an impassioned awareness that here was history in the making. Writing as he moved, he captured the feel and panorama of a volatile time, and wrote a book that can still hold us a century and a half later.

He was, however, much more than a reporter. That word does not go nearly far enough in describing his literary range and ambition. "Man of letters" would be more like it. Before going to work for Greeley he had already published two small collections of poetry and a travel book (*Views Afoot*, 1846), an account of his hiking tour through Europe, which went through six printings in the first year. Later in life, while continuing to write for the *Tribune* and other periodicals, Taylor would publish nine more travel books and four novels, as well as books of essays, collected correspondence, and several volumes of verse. In his day, some called him "the poet laureate of the Gilded Age," and for about a hundred years he was best known as a poet. In 1870 he brought out a translation of Goethe's *Faust*—thought at the time to be the pinnacle of his career—a work so well regarded it led to his appointment as U.S. Minister to Germany. Though his poems continued to be anthologized well into the twentieth century, *Eldorado* stands today as his most enduring work, a classic study of this formative moment in the life of California and the nation.

At the outset Taylor was not entirely sure his trip would lead to a book. He was the 1840s version of a television crew on assignment to provide the eyewitness account of a fast-breaking national and international event. Greeley had asked him to send back a series of "Letters" to the *Tribune*, which Taylor began to compose as soon as he departed. In his opening chapters we can see the form: "From New York to Chagres," "Crossing the Isthmus," "The Pacific Coast of Mexico." But once he reached San Francisco, the idea of a book-length narrative clicked into focus.

In a letter to his publisher, George Putnam, on September 30, 1849, Taylor wrote, "There is the richest material in the world to work upon, and I feel quite certain of doing something with it which may be of lasting credit....I left the question unsettled in my mind until I should see something of the country, but before the close of my second day in San Francisco, my determination was taken."

The quest for gold intrigued him. But he knew that was only part of the story he would have to tell. With Mexico defeated, an old government had dissolved. The next one had yet to take clear shape. Out of near anarchy, new towns were sprouting. On its own singular terms, a new society was being formed. In our own time, as we strive to comprehend the kind of place California has become, it helps to look again at those embryonic days. Taylor's first description of San Francisco reminds us, among other things, that by 1849 cultural diversity was already a feature of West Coast life:

> The streets were full of people hurrying to and fro, and of as diverse and bizarre a character as the houses: Yankees of every possible variety, native Californians in sarapes and sombreros, Chileans, Sonorians, Kanakas from Hawaii, Chinese with long tails, Malays armed with their everlasting crisses, and others in whose embrowned and bearded visages it was impossible to recognize any especial nationality. We came at last into the plaza, now dignified by the name of Portsmouth Square. It lies on the slant side of the hill, and from a high pole in front of a long one-story adobe building used as the Customs House, the American flag was flying.

Between late August and late December, Taylor would travel by mule across the Central Valley and into the Sierra foothills to mingle with miners and observe their techniques. He would take a schooner through the delta and upriver to the bursting town of Sacramento. He would visit missions

and ranchos and walk from San Francisco to Monterey, where
forty-eight delegates had gathered to frame a constitution
for what they hoped would be the Union's thirty-first state.
His report of this convention is the best that has survived and
provides us with a unique window into the two-month debate
that would chart the course of an as-yet-undefined region.

Crucial issues were on the table. "The clause prohibit-
ing Slavery," Taylor notes, "was met by no word of dissent."
(Had it failed, as some delegates hoped, California could have
been aligned with the Confederacy.) Another clause "prohib-
iting the entrance of free people of color into the state" was
passed, but then, in a second round of voting, "was rejected
by a large majority." These same delegates made California
the first state to adopt a constitutional provision allowing
married women the right to own separate property.

The convention's most heated debate centered on the location of an eastern boundary. The final decision literally shaped
a good part of the future of the western United States. And
Taylor watched it all.

In the fall of 1849 California was so new, no one had yet
agreed on where it began and where it ended. Some wanted a
boundary to follow the ridgeline of the Sierra Nevada range.
Others believed it should extend clear across to the Rockies,
to embrace the enormous region recently acquired as a result
of the Mexican War. Maps of the day tell us "Alta California"
contained not only the coastal strip, with its string of missions,
pueblos, and presidios, but all of what is now Nevada and most
of Utah, along with parts of Arizona, Colorado, and Wyoming.
Leading voices on the Boundary Committee argued that these
were the original and authentic dimensions of California as
claimed by Spain and Mexico and thus should be honored.

When their proposal came before the convention, a majority actually voted for it. If that vote had stood, California
would not only be a thousand miles long but nearly a thousand
miles wide. In addition to Orange County, Silicon Valley, and

Yosemite, it would include the Great Basin, the north rim of the Grand Canyon, and Salt Lake City. But as Taylor reports,

> At the announcement of the vote, a dozen members jumped up, speaking and shouting in the most confused and disorderly manner. Some rushed out of the room; others moved to adjournment; others again protested they would sign no constitution embodying such a provision. In the midst of this tumult the house adjourned.

In the week that followed, eight or ten more proposals were put forth, prominent among them a line to be drawn midway between the Sierras and the Great Salt Lake. According to delegates John Sutter and General Mariano Vallejo, this had marked the outer edge of Mexico's civil jurisdiction.

In the end they adopted a proposal based on calculations by "Mr. Hastings, a member from Sacramento." He was the notorious wagonmaster and trail-guide author who had persuaded the Donner Party to take an untested route south around Salt Lake, a "cut-off" that cost them weeks of travel time. By 1849 Lansford Hastings was a thirty-year-old lawyer and speculator selling subdivided lots on the river south of Sutter's Fort. It was his idea to run a line eastward of the Sierras, with the long angle south and east toward the Colorado.

Nowadays this dogleg line seems inevitable, an eternal feature of the state's profile, depicted on book covers, maps, and license plates. Reading Taylor's account, one sees that the line could have been drawn just about anywhere from the Central Valley eastward. The very size and future look of the new state was in the hands and in the minds of four dozen delegates wrestling for advantage as they searched for boundaries in a boundless terrain.

While Taylor watched the politics and described the boomtown ferment, he was ever attentive to the lands he passed through, the natural spectacle that was like no other he had seen. Though his poetry has not lasted, there is often a music in his prose, as he conveys his own wonder. Between convention sessions he hiked across the Monterey Peninsula to Cypress Point, then a remote coastal outcropping:

> The extremity of the point is a mass of gray rock worn by the surf into fantastic walls and turrets....In the narrow channels between the rocks, the pent waters roll inland with great force, flooding point after point and flinging high into the air the purple flags and streamers of seaweed, til they reach the glassy, sheltered pools that are quietly filled and emptied...

Taylor sees through a kind of zoom lens, which is a main source of this book's continuing readability and holding power. Close-up and poetic perceptions can live side by side, page by page, with his assessment of a Constitutional Convention and what it says about the place of the West Coast in nineteenth-century America.

Today we hear more and more about California's complex role on the Pacific Rim. His narrative reminds us how long this transoceanic role has been in the making and how it was first imagined. With patriotic zeal he voices his pride that "the new highway to the Indies, forming the last link in that belt of civilized enterprise which now clasps the world, has been established under my country's flag...." The delegates' long debate, like the Gold Rush, had its own inherent drama; but for Taylor it was one more step in a westward expansion that extended beyond this shoreline (hence his subtitle, "Adventures in the Path of Empire"). It was a view he shared with those who had engineered the Mexican War in order to gain control of California's harbors. They foresaw an American empire that would reach much farther than the continent's outer edge: San Francisco Bay would be our gateway to the Pacific, ensuring access to the wealth of Asian trade. (Three years later, when Commodore Matthew Perry steamed into Tokyo Bay, with orders to

open Japan to the West, Bayard Taylor was with the fleet, on
another assignment from the *Tribune*.)

The last quarter of his book, none of which had previously
appeared in the paper's series, recounts Taylor's event-filled
trip home from San Francisco, via Mazatlán and Guadalajara,
across central Mexico to Vera Cruz, north from there by ship
to Mobile, Alabama, and eventually on to New York. This
should not be regarded as an afterthought or an epilogue.
It is an essential feature of his journey. Bringing us back to
where he started not only gives Taylor's story a pleasing
symmetry; it provides, in a single volume, a rare microcosm
of the complete Gold Rush pattern.

As J. S. Holliday documents in his monumental narrative
The World Rushed In (1981), for most of those who flocked
here from 1848 to 1850, California was not a final destination.
The majority of argonauts did not linger more than a year or
two, taking what they could find before they turned around
and went back home. He calls it "the gold rush cycle." By
identifying and charting this cycle, Holliday redefined the
Gold Rush for contemporary readers; and Taylor's round-trip
journey is, in a way, its embodiment.

He stayed here a total of four months, finding his personal
Eldorado only after he had returned to Manhattan. An instant
hit, his book was published in New York and London in the fall
of 1850, went back to print in both countries before the year's
end, and went through multiple editions in the decades that
followed.

Something should be said about the scale and rather aston-
ishing speed of this achievement. Between the day he left New
York and the day his book reached the stores, some eleven
months had elapsed. That includes writing time, travel time,
production and distribution time. His trip had occupied eight
of those months, with two for transit each way. The two
volumes of the original edition came out to four hundred

and fifty pages, some of it composed en route, some after he returned. And this was long before the days of typewriters, tape recorders, Xerox machines, or laptops. Notes, drafts, final manuscripts—everything had to be written out by hand. There was no mouse to click if he happened to change his mind.

Eldorado was Taylor's fourth book. In the next twenty-eight years he would write forty more—like a man obsessed, said those who knew him. But this was the one that has lasted, the story of a young man's journey to what was then the farthest corner of the known world, and still shining light on the world we all inhabit now.

(2000)

Another Kind of Western
(with Jeanne Wakatsuki Houston)

At the County Museum in Klamath Falls there is a relief map of the region where Oregon and California meet, showing two large bodies of water, Lower Klamath and Tule Lake. It shows how this country looked in the 1870s when Captain Jack, the famous Modoc chief, held off the U.S. Cavalry for five months by holing up in the lava beds with what remained of his beleaguered tribe. A hundred years later those lakes are almost gone. Near what was the center of one sits the town of Tule Lake, a cluster of pale buildings surrounded by vast potato and onion fields. Old lake bottoms make good crops, though you'd never guess it from the look of the town, which is bleak, sunbaked, seemingly abandoned most of the day. *The Last Picture Show* could have been filmed at Tule Lake, or *The Misfits*, or *A Fistful of Dollars*.

We were there to film another kind of Western, based on the book my wife and I wrote, *Farewell to Manzanar*. She was seven when she was evacuated with her mother, grandmother, and nine brothers and sisters, and shipped two hundred and fifty miles inland to a square-mile compound of tarpapered barracks. She spent three and a half childhood years there in a high desert valley east of the Sierras. Thirty years later, in the summer of 1975, we traveled up to Tule Lake to watch some of her memories be turned into a two-hour dramatic film, the first to deal specifically with the World War Two internment. We were confident that the film would be true to our script. We'd co-authored it with director John Korty, whose previous picture had been *The Autobiography of Miss Jane Pitman*, winner of nine Emmy Awards. What we didn't foresee, what soon began to impress everyone, was how the making of this film became a rare event in itself, another kind of reenactment.

When I saw those rows of black barracks the first time, back in 1942, they didn't mean anything to me. I was still excited and feeling the sense of adventure after our long bus ride—the first trip I'd ever made outside Los Angeles County. Approaching them thirty-three years later I was filled with apprehension, uncertain what I would feel, yet intensely aware that I would be affected in ways I couldn't anticipate. I had already been back to the ruins of Manzanar, three times, while we were writing the book. The impact of the original trip, the flood of memories it triggered, was what gave rise to the book in the first place. So the initial shock was past. At Manzanar, where almost nothing remains, I had conjured my own images of what it had been like when ten thousand of us were eating and sleeping and walking the streets and living our lives. When nothing remains, you fill the empty spaces from inside yourself.

At Tule, Bob Kinoshita had so convincingly recreated the look of the camp, it was like driving into a photograph I'd seen many times. It didn't really hit me until the photograph came to life, until I saw people wandering among those barracks, dozens that first day, standing outside the mess hall waiting for their call to the first scene. After that I was close to tears most of the time. They were dressed in clothes from the forties, fedora hats, double-breasted suits,

calf-length flowered dresses, clumsy-looking oxfords. There was a
lot of kidding, like people do at a costume party. But underneath
it ran a poignancy much deeper than nostalgia. Many of them had
been interned at places like Manzanar, Tule Lake, Heart Mountain,
Minidoka, Topaz. For this film, they had driven sometimes two or
three or four hundred miles (one man planned his summer vacation
so that he could drive out from New York City with his family) to put
on the clothes they used to wear, to be extras, to play themselves or to
act out scenes their parents had lived through.

Soon after Pearl Harbor was bombed and war was declared,
the federal government authorized the removal from the West
Coast of anyone thought to be a security risk. This mandate
was carried out along racial lines. By the spring of 1942, 110,000
people of Japanese ancestry had been evacuated from their
homes and farms and ranches to ten inland camps. Two-thirds
of them, like Jeanne and most of her family, were native-born
American citizens. Each camp was built to a common master
plan, somewhat like an army base, with tarpapered barracks
arranged in blocks, guard towers spaced around the perimeter,
the whole enclosed in barbed wire. Administered at first
by the army, the program was soon turned over to a new
agency, the War Relocation Authority, who managed it until
shortly after the war ended in 1945.

There were two camps in Arizona, two in Arkansas, one
each in Colorado, Utah, Wyoming, and Idaho, and two in
remote parts of eastern California—at Manzanar and at Tule
Lake, just below the Oregon border. John Korty chose
Tule Lake as the film's principal location partly because it
was easier to reach from his Mill Valley headquarters, partly
because it was the only one of the ten with original barracks
still standing. Fifteen years earlier a local investor had bought
them from the government and was now leasing and selling
units to low-income families. This had been the largest of the
camps, holding 18,000 people at its peak. By 1943 hundreds

of barracks had been erected here—a few miles south of the town. About forty remained, among spotty lawns, dusty pick-ups, and a few struggling trees planted over thirty years ago by internees.

To restore the wartime look, art director Robert Kinoshita, a veteran Hollywood designer, who'd been interned at Poston Camp in Arizona, covered one row of these remaining barracks with lath and black tarpaper. He rebuilt one interior using knothole-riddled pine planking. He reconstructed a sentry post with a pagoda-style roof, like the one still visible at Manzanar, and a high wooden guard tower nearby. With some skillful intercutting of Sierra landscapes it would be hard to tell that we were four hundred miles north and west of where the actual events took place. Both camps were located in dry, flat valleys between mountain ranges. Both were at an altitude of four thousand feet, where summer heat runs into the nineties most of the time, and the wind very dependably stirs up sand and blows it through your clothing and stirs up thunderheads with little warning. It made no difference which camp former internees spent time in, they all remembered the dust, the relentless heat, dry landscapes, and a sense of exile.

The crew brought along wind machines for some of the outdoor scenes. They didn't need them. During the first shot—of some Nisei carpenters raising a scaffold—a cloud of dust and sand came rolling between the barracks. It darkened the sun and sent hats flying more persuasively than any special-effects man could hope for. That was the first of many very eerie, time-warping moments, when life on the set began to repeat the life in camp. The climate had not changed. The buildings had not changed. Spontaneously, people found themselves reacting in similar ways. We began to talk about this, to remember.

The shooting days were long and tedious, with a lot of waiting between scenes. Inside the barracks—formerly living quarters but now used for make-up and wardrobe and an actors' lounge—it was just too stifling to remain for long. Outside there was no shade, no relief, not even any grass to stretch out on. So we gathered in the mess hall, chatting, sweating, sipping lemonade or ice water, trying to catch a few wafts from the fan. The mess hall had been there in 1942—one for each block of fourteen barracks—when the first arrivals had to gather and talk about how they were going to cope with this disruption in their lives. After lunch one day I watched an elderly couple in old-fashioned clothes smiling and muttering in Japanese—which I have never been able to understand—and for a moment all time was erased.

The children fared the best. They didn't seem to mind the heat. Almost immediately a gang of set-urchins formed. Children whose parents were involved with the picture teamed up with children who already lived there and had come hanging around the set. Two of our kids were among them, our boy-and-girl twins, age eight—near the age I was when my family arrived at Manzanar. By the end of the first day the mix of sweat and dust had streaked their arms and faces black. Their clothes were heavy with dust and mud. They didn't want to leave. They loved it. They were all playing hopscotch in the near-dark, their lines drawn in the dust with sticks, their laggers loose rocks picked up outside the mess hall. Their pockets were filled with tiny shells grubbed out of the sand—residue from the centuries when this whole valley was under water. This had been one of the first things kids did at Tule in the forties. In the early weeks of the internment, with no playgrounds, no movies, no radios or swing sets, they collected shells from the old lake bed and strung them into necklaces and bracelets. They looked for obsidian arrowheads, and played hopscotch in the sand.

One day it rained very heavily. Afterwards I was walking from the mess hall under a heavy sky when I heard someone playing the piano, rehearsing a scene for a camp talent show that would be filmed that night. For days we'd heard nothing outdoors but wind and the rumble of car engines. The sound of music in this desolate setting made my spirits soar, the same way it had when I was nine *and ten. I became a kid again, walking through mud puddles, humming the tune, but aware this time of how much music had added to our lives back then. The most amazing thing was that the man playing the piano now was the same man who'd shared so much of his music with us in camp—Lou Frizell. The tune was "I'll Remember April," an early forties hit. Even his style was recognizable. It was a total flashback. I remembered singing in the school glee club he used to direct. And that started me thinking about all the things we did in camp to amplify, to beautify life, in spite of the adversity—the musical shows, the tea gardens, the flower arranging, traditional dancing, watercolor paintings of the mountains.*

Lou Frizell brought his own memories to this location. In 1942 he was just out of college. Manzanar High School was his first and only teaching job. He spent three years there and is still remembered by Jeanne and many others as a man whose talents and enthusiasm enriched camp life. Old yearbooks show him directing plays, musicals, choruses, and orchestras. Right after the war he left for New York and went on to become an established performer, with dozens of stage, TV, and film credits behind him (*Summer of '42, Front Page, Streets of San Francisco,* etc.). A jovial and seasoned character actor, he returned to play one of the handful of Caucasian speaking roles—a music teacher named Lou Frizell.

All the other leading and supporting roles were played by Asian Americans—Yuki Shimoda, Nobu McCarthy, Clyde Kusatsu, Pat Morita, Mako, Seth Sakai, Momo Yashima, James Saito, Dori Takeshita, Franklin Abe, Akemi Kikumura. This fact alone made the production unique. And the performers were proud, aware of their opportunity, involved in much more than a professional way. What you felt from them on the set was a kind of reverence.

Akemi Kikumura was an actress with the East-West Players in Los Angeles and a graduate student in anthropology at UCLA. She played an important supporting role, as Jeanne's sister-in-law, a woman in her early twenties who enters the camp with a babe in arms, and remains there to bear a second child while her husband volunteers for the U.S. Army and gets shipped overseas. Akemi's experience was similar to what many felt who were too young to remember the internment itself but whose families went through it. Before she was born her parents and older brothers and sisters had been removed from their West Coast home to the most easterly of the camps, Rohrer, in southern Arkansas, where they spent two years.

"No one in my family has ever talked about it much," she said. "Being in this film opened me up to what went on there and why we are the way we are now. My family is a lot like the family in the film. I'm the youngest of eleven kids. Seeing the barracks at Tule, where some of my other relatives were interned, playing the role of a young mother in the prime of her life, bearing children in this situation—I just understand my mother and older sisters a lot better. It's like reliving a part of my family's history and understanding it for the first time."

Jimmy Nakamura was not a performer. He was another Manzanar veteran, who drove up from San Mateo to work as an extra, and then stayed with the company when it moved down to the prison farm at Santa Rita, behind Oakland, where the riot scenes were staged. This sequence was based on an actual riot that broke out in December of 1942. A protest over conditions inside the camp, it was triggered by the arrest of a young cook, and it ended a few hours later when the military police opened fire outside the camp jail, wounding several demonstrators and killing two. Jimmy Nakamura, at age eighteen, took part in that uprising. Thirty-three years later he played a demonstrator in the dramatized version.

"I wasn't sure if I wanted to be in the riot scene," he said, "especially when I saw the machine gun props. But somehow I found myself moving with the mob. During the actual riot, we chanted, 'Free Harry!' because it was Harry Ueno, the cook, who'd been wrongfully imprisoned. In the movie they changed some of the names and some of the characters, and we were supposed to say, 'Free Joe!' But with all the torches, and the running of the mob, I found myself shouting, 'Harry! Harry!' It was unbelievable how I seemed to be going through the same thing all over again. When the guns started firing I felt the same terror. It really hit me the next morning when I woke up. I cried for hours...the tears wouldn't stop."

Yuki Shimoda had also been eighteen, and living in Sacramento when his family heard the news that the Japanese had bombed Pearl Harbor. A few months later they were all shipped north—to Tule Lake. After the war and a degree from Northwestern, he pursued a career in the theatre, eventually enjoying long runs on Broadway in *South Pacific, The King and I, Teahouse of the August Moon, Auntie Mame.* After the film version of *Auntie Mame* brought him to Los Angeles in 1967 he performed in numerous TV shows and feature films. Now, at age fifty-two, he had come back to the camp he'd spent one year in, to play the lead role of Jeanne's father, Ko Wakatsuki.

"Many times I have asked myself, Why do I train, why do I work to improve my craft? When I read this script, I felt that the role of Ko was the role I have been preparing for all these years. In one way or another, I think we all feel that way. As Asian American performers we spend too much time playing cooks and servants and officers in the Japanese navy— because these are the roles offered to us. I can remember when even these roles were much harder to get than they are now. It was not very encouraging, in *Teahouse of the August Moon*, when I coached David Wayne, Eddie Bracken, Larry Parks, and Eli Wallach to play the role of Sakine, and it never seemed to enter anyone's mind to offer the role to me.

"Here in this picture, we finally have a chance to play roles we can identify with at the gut level. It allows us to portray Japanese Americans experiencing the full range of human emotions. The feeling on the set is like no other picture I have

worked in. Everyone knows how important it is to get each
scene right, and everyone is pulling together."

*Yuki's first day at Tule Lake they filmed my father's return from
North Dakota. He'd been picked up by the FBI a few weeks after
the war started and shipped to an all-male camp for Japanese
aliens, an army prison at Fort Lincoln outside Bismarck. Nine
months later he rejoined us at Manzanar, a man transformed by
the bitter cold of that region, and by the shame of being accused
of disloyalty to a country he'd lived in for thirty-five years. As the
cameras started to roll, down by the main gate of the reconstructed
camp, as Yuki climbed out of the bus, I realized he had become
my father. Somehow, because of his age, his lifetime as an Asian
American man, his memories of what his own family had been
through here at Tule, and his years of professional experience—
he made the scene so real I was watching myself relive the moment.
The same wind was blowing. The sky was overcast. All Yuki did
was stand there in his overcoat, trying not to lean on his cane, while
his wife and his youngest child clung to him weeping; but in his
face there was all the pride, the humiliation, the stubbornness, the
shattered dignity.*

*I began to cry. When the scene was over I looked around. Tears
shone in the eyes of everyone—John Korty, the cameraman, all the
extras and spectators, the other actors, the crew, and even Yuki,
who'd been stoically playing the man who would not let himself
break down. The actress playing my mother, Nobu McCarthy, had
called up such a show of grief at what had happened to her man,
when the scene was over Yuki took her in his arms. Nobu grew up
in Japan, spent the war years there as a child. She has her own deep
reservoir of stored-up feeling and memory. They leaned into each
other's arms, weeping and laughing, not only for the scene but for
the reasons so many were moved that afternoon, releasing emotions
welling in each of us, for the re-creation of these images, in this
setting where many similar scenes had taken place, releasing our
pasts in this deep, communal way.*

The last days on location were something like the last days of the camps. All the extras had left. The principal players and most of the crew moved on down to Santa Rita where some hospital scenes were staged, and the riot. Only a few workers remained, to dismantle the guard tower, tear down the signs, peel tarpaper off the barracks and let the dust re-coat them. In Jeanne's memory it already resides in the same place as her childhood memories—a windswept dream. Driving past it now, on Highway 139, south of town, if you didn't know what to look for, you'd never know who had been there.

(1976)

Where Does History Live?

When we first moved into this house I did not know it had a history. I did not know of its links to what many regard as a defining episode in the exploration and settling of the American West: the saga of the Donner Party. I did not yet understand how a house can contain a story and how that story can catch hold of you, send you back in time trying to reimagine a family's legend, trying to reenter the mythic years when California was about to be invented.

In 1962 I was just out of graduate school, hoping to get started as a writer, and this was simply the cheapest place we could find—a neglected Victorian in a seacoast town seventy miles south of San Francisco, a block back from the edge of Monterey Bay. In those days—before the University of California opened its campus here in Santa Cruz—buildings like this one were being torn down, more trouble than they were worth, it was said. Two stories high, with an alpine roof and a pointed cupola, it hadn't been painted in thirty years, and for the last two it had stood empty. The front window was broken out. Where a wide staircase rose to the second-floor verandah, the latticed siding had fallen away, softened by decades of well-salted morning fog. The old stairs were layered with blackberry vines.

No one in the neighborhood seemed to recall who owned it, but eventually we found them, on the far side of town. In the end we got the whole place for seventy-five dollars a month. So we moved in, with our first daughter, then going on two. And only later did we begin to hear the story this house had to tell. Little by little, as we came to know our neighbors and met local old-timers, we picked up bits and pieces of lore.

Built by a sea captain, in a style called Carpenter Gothic, it had once been a manor house surrounded with gardens and presiding over a sizable tract of land, though all of that had now been sold off, parcel by parcel. For a number of years it had been owned by descendants of a pioneer family named Reed, or perhaps Lewis. Toward the end of her long life a woman named Patty Reed, or Patty Lewis, had lived here, one of the younger Donner Party survivors, or a relative of one of those who'd come staggering out of the Sierra Nevada range after the devastating winter of 1846/47. Before and after World War One she had lived here with three unmarried daughters and her bachelor son. Maybe she had died in one of these upstairs rooms sometime in the 1920s. Maybe some of the vintage furniture inside the house—the maple rocker, the carved sideboard, the ancient pedal sewing machine—had once belonged to her...

Such details added to the mystique and aura of the place, but not in a way that fed my literary imagination. As the years went by, as I began to have some luck with publishers, my focus was more and more on contemporary fiction and wrestling with current events. From my reading I knew a bit about the history of California and its role in the opening of the West, but as a writer I'd never felt compelled to reach back that far for my material—not until an old friend called with an unexpected proposal.

We'd gone to high school together in San Jose, about thirty-five miles from here, where he still lived. Recently elected president of a venerable men's club—one of the oldest in the state—he was looking for someone to compile a volume that would celebrate the club's one hundredth anniversary. I took it on in part because the money was good, in part because I soon saw it as a rare opportunity. Here was a unique window into the formative years of my home region. I would be privy to the minutes of a very influential social club and to the full roster of its early members. This had included men like Paul Masson, the vintner who brought champagne to America, Senator James D. Phelan, and San Jose mayor Barney Murphy of the adventurous Irish Catholic dynasty that once controlled some three and a half million acres in California, Nevada, Arizona, and Mexico.

I began by arranging an interview with the club's oldest living member, a fellow named Frazier Reed II. He was eighty-five then, a retired insurance salesman, still spry and active. His condo overlooked a golf course on the outskirts of San Jose. His clubs and cart were parked in the portico. As he ushered me in, I was startled to see on the wall of his entryway a large black-and-white photograph of our cupola-topped Victorian thirty-five miles away in Santa Cruz. (By this time, I should note, two more children had come along; what we'd envisioned as a short-term stay had become permanent. No longer renters, we owned the place.)

"My God, Frazier!" I exclaimed. "That's my house!"

"Well, young fella," he said, with an ironic smile, "it may be your house now. But it should have been my house."

"What do you mean, your house?"

"That's a long story. And don't think I hold a grudge against you for living in it now. But my name was right there in her will, ya see. And then the night before she died she rewrote it."

"Who was that? Patty Reed?"

"No. Not her. It was my cousin, Patty's last daughter. I was the next in line, ya see, and she just went and gave the place away…"

Under the spell of a wily attorney, that daughter, at the final moment, had willed it to the local chapter of a fraternal lodge, the Native Sons of the Golden West. Decades later a framed seventeen-by-twenty-four-inch black-and-white blowup of the manor house in its heyday still hung on Frazier's wall, bespeaking a lifelong affection for what could have been his. Though no longer bitter or resentful about his disinheritance, he was more than eager to talk about those days. When he saw that I was eager to listen, the story came tumbling forth—the story of this house, and of his great-aunt Patty Reed, and of Patty's father, James Frazier Reed, who, with the two Donner brothers, had organized the infamous wagon party out of Springfield, Illinois, in 1846. A prosperous businessman with land and connections (Springfield attorney Abraham Lincoln had been a personal friend), he'd decided, in the middle of his life, to sell off all his holdings and head for California, two thousand miles west, already being advertised as a realm of boundless opportunity.

We never did talk about the men's club. That would wait for another day. As my keen interest piqued his memory, he spent the afternoon recounting the long odyssey of the great-grandfather for whom he'd been named. A proud and headstrong ancestor, part Scotch-Irish, part Polish, James Frazier Reed had stayed with the struggling wagon party as far as central Nevada, where he was banished after killing a teamster with a Bowie knife.

"Killed him in self defense, of course," said Frazier, "since it was the teamster John Snyder who started it." (I would later learn that the motives of both men are being debated by scholars and descendants to this very day.)

Forced to leave his wife and four children behind, Reed crossed the Sierra Nevada and reached Mexican California just ahead of the same snows that trapped his family at what is now called Donner Lake. He tried to return with a rescue party but found the mountain trails already blocked with impassable drifts. During the next four months, as he waited out the winter weather, he set forth to mount a larger rescue effort, traveling on horseback through the turmoil of an ungoverned and lawless region, from Sutter's Fort to the Pueblo of San Jose, to the U.S. naval detachment anchored in San Francisco Bay, then across the raging, mile-wide Sacramento River at flood time. These months would find him entangled in the final stages of the Mexican War and the prophetic cross-cultural struggle for control of California and its precious ports.

Meanwhile, in the mountain camps—made of hastily thrown-together lean-tos and log sheds—the snow piled higher and higher. In all there'd been eighty-seven travelers in the loose-knit band, half of them under the age of eighteen. During these same four months, three dozen died from exposure and starvation. Some resorted to consuming the dead for their own survival. By spring of 1847 their grim and desperate fate would be broadcast around the world as a cautionary tale from the Far West: the Land of Promise is really a Land of Two Promises, where the fabled landscape can turn against you without warning and become a deadly adversary.

Though Reed's wife and children were reduced to skeletons, they weren't among those who consumed the flesh of others. He was finally able to bring them out of the high country and into the fertile lowlands of Santa Clara Valley, where he prospered once again. He joined the Gold Rush, acquired a lot of land, built a ranch house, and became a major player in the early development of San Jose.

His younger daughter, Patty, married a man from New York named Frank Lewis, who died young, leaving her widowed at age thirty-eight with four of their eight children still living at home. By that time, thirty years had passed. Both her parents were gone, as well as most of the family's assets, lost through poor management after her father died. To support herself and her children Patty accepted an offer to run a new beach-front hotel in Santa Cruz. That was 1879. She lived here for the rest of her life. After one of her sons made a small fortune in the candy business (perfecting the world's first nickel candy bar), he bought the manor house that would be Patty's home for her last ten years.

As a favored nephew, Frazier Reed II had often made the trip from San Jose to visit her while he was growing up. On the day I met with him he still remembered the original lay-out of the gardens. He remembered how all the rooms had been furnished. He remembered sitting at a dining room table that had come from his great-grandfather's house, said to be the table on which the Great Seal of California was designed, in 1850, when San Jose was for a time the new state's first capitol. He remembered who slept where and confirmed that his Aunt Patty—eight years old when the wagons left Springfield—the woman who'd nearly starved to death in the Sierra snows, had indeed passed away in July 1923 in what is now our bedroom.

When I left that day my head was buzzing. I came home ignited by the notion that this house itself, as her final perch and resting place, somehow had a role in her family's noto-rious and emblematic journey west, from Illinois, across the plains and through the Rockies, to this final edge of the farthest shore.

As soon as I'd finished up a couple of other projects, I went on the road. Setting out to retrace key portions of that jour-ney, I followed the wagon party's route from Fort Bridger in Wyoming through the mountains of central Utah and out to the Great Salt Lake. I held closely to an infamous cut-off recommended by the trusted trail guide, Lansford Hastings, which James Reed and several others believed would save the

party weeks of travel time, but proved to be their undoing.
I found the bleak and treeless site in central Nevada where
Reed had stabbed John Snyder, and from there followed his
route of exile past the desert sink where the Humboldt River
disappears into the sand, into the vaulting Sierra Nevada
range, the climb through Donner Pass, and down the other
side to Sutter's Fort, now surrounded by the city of Sacramento. I traced his looping pilgrimage over the Coast Range
and through the onetime villages and mission towns that
clung to San Francisco Bay.

Meanwhile I began to read whatever I could find on the
family, on the Donner Party, its origins and its personnel, on
the status of the American Dream as of 1846, which has been
called "The Year of the Great Migration," when a thousand
families for their thousand different reasons set out to cross the
continent. I read the published works, the memoirs and full-
length chronicles, such as George R. Stewart's classic *Ordeal by
Hunger*, then began to haunt the various libraries and archival
holdings where the letters, diaries, manuscripts, and old periodicals are housed: the Bancroft at U.C. Berkeley, the California State Library in Sacramento, the San Jose Public Library's
California Room.

From my interview with Frazier Reed II I knew this house
had become a final repository for all the Reed family holdings. He'd told me that in 1946, after Patty Reed's younger
daughter passed away, everything had been donated to the
Sutter's Fort Museum—items of furniture, old photos and
daguerreotypes, the famous four-inch ceramic doll Patty had
carried with her from the mountain camp, land petitions
and deeds handwritten in Spanish and in English, bills of sale,
notes to Reed from George and Jacob Donner, hundreds of
letters and, in its original leather pouch, the penciled pages
of a trail diary James Reed kept during the rescue effort he
led in early 1847. It was a major cache of Donner Party mem-
orabilia, and in Sacramento I finally came upon the bulk of it,

still stored at the reconstructed fort, in a seldom-visited upper room, behind an unmarked door—644 items called the Reed Family Documents Collection. Again my head was buzzing, this time with a vivid awareness that this collection, so valuable for historians and guarded by the family for a hundred years, had all been stored for decades right up here in the very attic where I now work.

Maybe that had something to do with how I finally found a way to tell the story, or begin to tell it.

One morning at my desk I was thinking I had read enough and traveled enough and it was time to make a start. I knew I wouldn't recount the entire pageant. The cast was too large and varied and unwieldy for a novel to encompass. Moreover, that had been attempted several times, both in fiction and non-fiction. And rather than dwell on the cannibalism, as most other writers had done, I would look for ways to keep that offstage, while focusing on a single family, the husband, the wife, the four children. Guided by my interview with his great-grandson, I would follow James Frazier Reed, whose dreams and contradictions, whose banishment and odyssey seemed to capsulize something essential about the whole episode. Outspoken and willful, he made some decisions he later regretted. But so did they all, a mismatched bunch who found themselves stuck with one another in unforgiving terrain. There's no question that Reed had contributed to the communal misfortune. This was in fact what drew me to him, as a character. While his own pride made him a culprit, he was also capable of a redeeming compassion and true courage.

Given all that, given what I thought I'd come to understand, I was still gripped by the anxiety that's always part of beginning a novel, the sense of stepping out into uncharted terrain. In the case of the Donner Party, though every mile of their journey has been exhaustively tracked and studied and sifted, numerous mysteries still remain. The truth of what happened a hundred and sixty years ago still floats somewhere between the often-conflicting testimony of those who survived, the stories and memories passed down through their descendants, and the best guesses of the many writers and researchers who've grappled with some piece of the tale or with the whole of it. The survivors' words are almost always colored by the all-too-human desire to cast their own family members in the best light. What's more, between family and family there were old resentments, bred by frustrations and setbacks on the trail, which in some cases lasted for decades. You can see evidence of this in the very layout of the mountain cabins.

One would think that a band of travelers marooned at six thousand feet and hunkering down for the winter would find a way to stick together. In fact, the reverse was true. It's worth a trip to Donner Memorial State Park, outside the mountain town of Truckee, just to see how far apart the cabins stood and what those spaces say. At Donner Lake there were three main cabins. One occupied by the Murphy family stood about a hundred and fifty yards from one occupied by the Breen family. From there to a third cabin, occupied by Margaret Reed and her children, was about a quarter of a mile in the opposite direction. From there it was another eight miles to the site where George Donner's wagon broke down, where he and his brother and their families dug in. Once the relentless snows began to fall, sometimes piling ten and twelve feet above the flimsy roofing, it might be days before you learned what had transpired in another cabin. It might be weeks. It might be years.

I was mulling all these matters, shuffling my notes, suspended, you might say, in the humbling void between the known and the unknown, when from somewhere I heard a voice, one I instantly recognized. I would not call it an actual sound in my head, nor was it the quaver of ghostly sentences rising out of shadowy cobwebs at the far side of the attic. Rather, it was the distinct sense of a certain way

of remembering, a way of speaking as the elderly woman
Patty Reed might have spoken in the years when she lived
here, before she died in the bedroom downstairs, a woman
of the late nineteenth century thinking back upon her child-
hood, a charged memory from that time, as she recalled the
day her father was banished. I wrote a line:
"Rivers are often compared to snakes."
I looked at that and wrote another:
"And it is not by chance."
And more lines began to follow:

Every river I have ever seen goes curving and looping from
where it starts to wherever it ends up. The Snake River, which
I have not seen, is one example. The Humboldt is another. For
a while it was called the Mary's. But that is one they could just
as well have called the Snake, in my opinion, instead of naming it for a fellow who never even saw Nevada. It makes an evil
mark through a devilish place, and I am glad I have not had to
go anywhere near it since the time we made the crossing. We
had to stand by that river and watch papa ride out on a starving horse with his head wrapped in a bloody kerchief and his
hat split to fit around the bandage. He was wearing buckskins
then like some of the other men, trousers and fringed tunic, so
elegant when we left Fort Laramie, all smeared and dark now
with firesmoke and sweat, and nothing in front of him but
sand and chalk and bare mountains. I can tell you it was the
hardest day of my life up to that time and the hardest day for
mama too, though we would all have worse days before that
trip was done. She had put one husband in the grave. Now she
had followed her second husband to the very end of the world
and was surely imagining that she could be widowed again at
thirty-two. She looked as if it had been her who took the knife
blow to the chest, not Snyder, as if it was her life that flowed
into the sand beside the river. I know now that she wanted to
fall down and quit right there, but she braced herself against
the wagon so she would not falter. She had decided to be

strong for the rest of us, and I have to say that from that day forward she was strong in ways none of us had seen before.

This passage is not where the published book begins. As things turned out, it's located about fifty pages in. But the writing began that day, as more pages flowed outward from those opening lines; and Patty Reed's voice would become a central feature of the novel. It would give her a role equal to her father's, in a narrative running on a double track. An omniscient voice follows Reed's progress from the time he leaves his family to the time he rejoins them. In a parallel sequence called "The Trail Notes of Patty Reed," she speaks from her verandah here in Santa Cruz, looking out at the ocean and looking back seventy years and more, finally coming to terms with her family's legacy and the riddle of her father's life. Throughout, her memories are triggered by the shoreline and the changing light across the water:

> The ocean I see is not what we came searching for. The farthest border of the land was not our goal, but the land itself. I should say *his* goal, the farthest land my father could envision, where he would be his own man at last.

Patty's voice, wherever it came from, gave me a way into this novel. Playing one narrative voice against the other gave me a way to reenter a history that had already been recounted many times. I saw that a strong and contemplative female presence could balance the restless male urge to pull up stakes and make the headlong continental crossing. As I say this I am reminded of a remark by the gifted short story writer Grace Paley: "To get the story told you have to tell two stories. The second comes rising up next to the first, or sometimes comes rising up inside it, and it's the telling of the two together that makes the story."

The showdown between James Reed and young John Snyder is a crisis for the beleaguered caravan, symptomatic of the bad luck and bad chemistry that put their wagons at the tail end of the Great Migration of 1846. It is a family crisis too. The fight itself, the argument, the trading of blows, the stabbing, is narrated in the omniscient voice, with an emphasis on the drama and on Reed's rising anger, his self-doubt, his remorse. That scene is soon followed by Patty's recollection of the day (as in the excerpt just noted), the daughter's voice a kind of counterpoint, opening up a wider range of feeling. And if this is successful, two or three layers of emotional engagement are added to the known and verifiable detail. While a sensitive eight-year-old watches the departure of a father she fears she may never see again, an eighty-year-old woman, with the hindsight of age and long experience, is looking back upon that childhood day. At the same time she's in touch with what her mother was enduring; having been a mother herself, a wife and a widow, Patty now knows much more than she could have known as a girl.

The desert terrain is accurately described, the time of year, the angle of light. Various wagon party members who bore witness are all in place, named by name. Reed on horseback, his head wound bandaged, the man who wounded him now freshly buried in the sand—all such information has its source in a letter, a diary, an interview. To this, Patty Reed, in her "Trail Notes," brings a kind of memory that is historically probable yet is not part of anything she left behind. In real life she didn't keep a diary or journal. It's one of the liberties a novelist will take. I have to find a way to see through her eyes, or perhaps listen more closely to the voice I hear when I'm at my desk in what used to be her attic.

You don't choose your material, Ernest Hemingway said; it chooses you. That was certainly my experience with *Snow Mountain Passage*. In all I gave three years to the writing. Now that it's done and published and making its way in the world of books, I can still sit in the rocking chair Patty Reed sat in eighty-five years ago. I can look into a beveled mirror she once looked into, above the oak-paneled fireplace. From the verandah I can regard her view of Monterey Bay, which still glitters and beckons, and consider that on the day we moved in, back in 1962, her story, her family's story, was already waiting here, inside the house.

It is a mysterious process, discovering a history this way. On the coast of California, which has been characterized by so much movement and restlessness and drift, very few of us have lived anywhere long enough to have that sense of grounding that comes from centuries of residence, with all the generations of ancestors and ancestral spirits close at hand. At any given moment, I've heard it said, half the people in this state have lived here ten years or less. It is my luck to be a native, born in San Francisco of parents who emigrated from west Texas during the Great Depression. Back in the mountains of Tennessee I have relatives whose families have lived in the same county since the end of the Revolutionary War. But I have never lived there. I live here on the western shore, where for most of us history is passed on not by blood but by osmosis. And sooner or later it will work on you, whether you want it to or not. Old voices are always in the air, in the towns and in the soil, waiting to be heard.

(2006)

PART FOUR

SOME FICTION

A Family Resemblance

It wasn't a bad-looking car, a 1984 Citation with AM/FM, air conditioning, automatic transmission. Baby blue. Not my first choice for getting around, but my mother had enjoyed it. I started out thinking I could get thirty-three or thirty-four hundred, which seemed to be a fair price at the time, according to the classifieds. I was prepared to take less. I had to get rid of it. I wasn't planning to drive it, and storing it was not an option.

After the ad came out half a dozen people called. Three stopped by the house to look at the car, among them Harold Wang, a medical student from Shanghai. He drove it around the block and haggled in a preliminary way, then said he wanted his cousin's opinion. For reasons too trivial to go into—let's say it was mutually convenient—we agreed to meet a second time in a parking lot at the edge of San Jose, a Safeway lot on a long boulevard of malls and discount stores.

I had decided I would let Harold have the car for thirty-two, or even a bit less, if he could come up with the money right away and not keep me waiting. I liked the way he had presented himself. He was twenty-six or twenty-seven, a clean-cut fellow—dark slacks, sport shirt—in his second year at Stanford and obviously under a lot of pressure, as graduate students always are. He had brought along his young wife and their new baby and a couple of people who stayed in another car while we talked. One of them was his father. They were all from mainland China. Though the father did not open his mouth the whole time, I could tell he had coached the son on how to shop for a car in the United States. The son was in a way performing for the father, trying to be shrewd and manly in these negotiations.

I liked the family unity, since this was the way I had grown up, among relatives who had come west during the 1930s, new to this coast and sticking together while they made their way.

I also figured Harold had access to the necessary cash. I had only seen the father from a distance, but he had a prosperous look about him. At our second meeting, as a matter of fact, I was certain Harold carried an envelope full of bills in his coat pocket. He was as ready to buy as I was to sell. Or almost as ready.

The cousin he brought along was younger by four or five years, a small and careful fellow, also from mainland China. He wore running shoes and sunglasses and an acid-washed jacket, blue denim streaked with white. He could not speak much English but he knew something about cars. He tapped around on the doors and fenders searching for bondo patches underneath the paint. He examined the spare tire and the muffler and the door latches and the seals around the windows. He opened the hood and listened to the engine and held his hand at the end of the exhaust pipe to feel the engine's pulse. He tried the brakes and the horn and the lights and the radio. Finally the hood was shut, the engine was silent. It was just a matter of reaching an understanding.

Harold offered me twenty-nine hundred. I told him my absolute bottom price was thirty-one. Anything lower and I would be losing money, I said. We both knew he wanted the car and we knew what the final price would be. Yet Harold was procrastinating. It wasn't the money, really. I didn't feel that. It was a matter of trust. We had not yet crossed some final threshold of trust.

I had the feeling that he needed to be reassured about my opinion of the car, or about my loyalty to this transaction. Or perhaps he needed to be reassured about me. I was after all an unknown quantity, not simply a fellow with a car for sale, but a foreigner, the mysterious other. If I were in Shanghai trying to bargain in Chinese with someone I did not know, for something in this price range, I would surely feel the same. I wondered if they had classified ads in China, and I wondered if it would be the first time Harold had thought of handing over this much cold cash to an American.

Standing in the Safeway lot at 3 p.m. on a sunny, blue-sky afternoon, we had reached this curious impasse when a woman came toward us, pushing a shopping cart between the diagonal rows of cars. She looked to be in her late fifties, and she wore a neck brace that made her back too erect. She had short red hair and the kind of white skin that turns to flame when anything unexpected occurs.

Between the rows she stopped, with a tight and cautious smile.

"That's my car," she said.

A Dodge two-door was parked in the next slot, eight or ten years old. We had all inadvertently gathered next to it.

"We just happen to be standing here," I said. "They're looking at my mother's Chevrolet."

"Your mother's?"

"By chance," I said.

"What are you talking about?"

Her hand held the cart as if its push bar were the guardrail at a drop-off cliff.

"I mean, it's by chance I'm parked next to you."

"I just don't know what to expect anymore."

She was speaking to me but looking hard at Harold, whose sallow and scholarly face had turned severe as he pondered his cash flow.

"Sorry," I said, for the three of us.

"It's been broken into so many times I've lost count. They chip the glass, they ruin the doors. My life has been threatened. I'm a teacher. But do you think that makes any difference? Right outside the classroom I have had things happen."

"I know the feeling," I said.

We moved well away from the Dodge, giving her plenty of room. Harold was now consulting in Chinese with the cousin, who kept looking at his watch. Harold explained to me that a brother had dropped them off and would soon return. Time was becoming a factor. His jaw muscles were pumping. He had to make a decision. He stared at me, then he stared at his cousin's wrist, as if the watch held the answer to the riddle of this moment.

Our tense reverie was broken by a long, grinding scrape, then the clunk of thick metal. About thirty feet from where we stood, the woman had jumped a circular divider. Her Dodge now straddled it. Inside the car she twisted and turned, as if pursued. She lurched into reverse, scraping the underside again. When the front tires met the divider, she shifted into low. The car lurched forward, and the rear tires hit the island, which was the height of sidewalk curbing. She was stuck.

She opened the door and called out to anyone within earshot. "What did I do? What did I do?"

This was a huge parking lot that merged with other huge lots, all filled with diagonal rows of empty vehicles. There was no one else around.

"You went over that divider," I said.

"Oh my God! Did I ruin the car?"

"Just a scrape," I said. "When your wheels fell, the body hit."

"I didn't see it! I didn't see it! With the three of you so close I thought I ought to get out of here."

She was outside the car, next to the open door, her face red with accusation and alarm.

When Harold asked if the Dodge had front- or rear-wheel drive, her brimming eyes went wide.

He held his hands low in front of him to make a lifting motion. "Then we will know where to lift," he said.

She did not seem to hear this. Or perhaps she did not believe he would understand her reply. She spoke to me. Her eyes were aimed at me, as if I were Harold's interpreter.

"It's too heavy to lift," she said. "It's a very heavy car. Can't you see that?"

The cousin had his hands on an invisible steering wheel, telling her with sign language and broken English to cramp it tightly, then inch the car back and forth. He was moving toward her grille, while Harold approached the trunk, ready to organize a lift. They were both talking, signaling. The woman's eyes leaped wildly from one to the other, then looked at me across the roof, asking me to translate their cryptic messages. These eyes said she was prepared for the worst.

I guess I wanted to put her mind at ease. I dropped down on all fours to peer at black tire scuffs on the concrete curbing and at her car's crusted underbelly, searching for dents and hanging parts. I thought about my Levi's, which were recently washed. I thought about my life and the ludicrous indignity of this scene: all I wanted to do was get rid of a car for a reasonable price and there I was on the asphalt squinting at this unknown woman's oilpan and tie rods and grimy axle.

"Is it ruined?" she cried. "What if it won't drive? I can't take this car back to the shop. I couldn't face taking it back."

"It's okay," I said. "I really don't see anything here. Just get in and do what that fellow says."

She looked at the cousin, who pantomimed another tight turn of the wheel. Above the brace her neck and cheeks seemed to fill with blood that could not escape.

Still on my hands and knees I said, "Cramp it hard to the right, then back up as far as you can."

"This car has been trashed so many ways. It's been to the shop for everything. I never find out who does it. The police aren't any help."

I ducked again to examine the muffler, the rusty tubing. "I don't think anything has happened. Really. Just get in and give the wheel a try."

By the time she slid onto the front seat I was around on her side of the car, standing at an angle that happened to block the sun. I must have looked ominous to her. She froze, staring straight ahead. By a freak of timing, Harold's brother appeared just then. He pulled his Toyota pickup into the slot she had vacated, hopped out and looked around, but said nothing, evidently grasping the situation.

Unfortunately he too wore sunglasses and an acid-washed denim jacket. As he moved toward the front of her car, joining the cousin, the glasses and the jackets had the look of a uniform they both shared.

In all three of these fellows you could see the family resemblance now, narrow faces with black hair angled across high foreheads, and all equally somber as they waited to see what the woman would do—while she waited to see what we were going to do. I could imagine what was running through her mind: we were some kind of trans-Pacific shopping mall gang working our way down the California coast, and now we had surrounded her, the cousin and the brother in front, Harold behind, me looming on the driver's side. She was trapped, and outnumbered. She was babbling.

"I hear something in the steering wheel. Do you hear it? When I turn the wheel like this? My God! It *is* something. What did I do?"

"You didn't do anything," I said. "It's going to be okay. Try cranking it hard to the right."

With the car in reverse she gripped the wheel and tried a tight turn. The effort squeezed her face with pain. She could not make the move. Her eyes, when she turned to me, were full of terror and defeat.

I hunkered next to the window. "Is it your arm? Your neck?"

Her shoulders slumped. Her tears began to fall.

"What happened?" I said.

"It was whiplash," she said. "Somebody braked in front of me. I never saw who. I didn't hit them but I got thrown around. It's the second time it happened. Do you know what it's like to be completely out of control? And to realize that nothing you have ever planned for yourself is going to work out? I think I am having a nervous breakdown. I don't even know what I'm doing here. I never come to this part of town."

The way color rose into her face had been reminding me of someone. Now I saw that her sense for the pointless anarchy of this moment reminded me of me, while in coloring she resembled my mother. I felt my own tears welling. I almost reached through the open window to touch her arm. Perhaps I should have. I had seen my mother in a similar state of mind, after she'd been sideswiped in heavy traffic. For weeks she had the highway jitters and the late-life jitters, and being a widow had not helped matters much. From where I hunkered I could see this woman was on her own. Her manner told me that, and the single sack of groceries and something about the interior of the Dodge, the way the seats were strewn with paperwork, bits of clothing and Kleenex and receipts, the backseat as well as the passenger side. This was how my mother's car had looked before I cleaned it up to sell, a car no one rode in but her.

"Would you like me to try it?" I said.

She couldn't answer.

"Scoot over," I said.

"Oh no. No. Please. I'll get out."

As if she had to choose between the car and her life, she surrendered the wheel. I slid in. With my eyes on Harold hand-signaling in the rearview, I cramped it and inched backward until the tires touched concrete. In low I cramped it the other way and watched the cousin and the brother in their matching jackets waving and winding their hands in the air, with their eyes on the front tires, calling out one-word instructions.

"More! More! Stop! Stop! Okay! Okay!"

It took five moves in each direction, and for those couple of minutes we were allies, liberating the Dodge. When the front wheels finally cleared the divider, their three faces opened in sudden grins.

The woman was grinning too, a wild grin. She was giddy, on the edge of crazy laughter. She had been prepared, I think, to see me disappear with her car. In the driver's seat again she only wanted to flee. She shifted fast and the car lurched again.

"What am I doing here?" she called out the window. "None of this makes any sense. I never shop at Safeway!"

We watched her swing a wide U-turn into the next aisle, speeding for the exit lane. Harold said nothing about this episode. Neither did I. It was hard to know what to say. Yet there was no doubt that she had brought us closer together. Her panic had cleared the way. I knew he was ready now to make another offer.

I was thinking Harold would be getting the car for a decent price, one to make his father proud. And I was thinking again about my mother, who had started life in rural Oklahoma and in some ways never left. She would have panicked at the sight of any three or four men standing around in a parking lot for no apparent reason. If she had come upon an Anglo in Levi's and three young men from China outside Safeway, well, it would have made her dizzy; the foreign faces would have been enough to push her sense of peril to the limit.

"I can pay three thousand," Harold said at last. "But no more. I do not have more than that."

I waited a moment, as if weighing this proposal. "To sell the car for that amount, I would have to have it all in cash."

He nodded and reached inside his coat for the bulging envelope.

While the cousin and the brother observed from the backseat, we sat in front, where I filled out a notice of sale and passed it to him along with the pink slip and a tire warranty from Sears, and a battery warranty. He counted out thirty one-hundred-dollar bills and asked me to count them. Then we shook hands.

The brother and the cousin left first in the pickup, followed by Harold in the Citation, hunched forward, nervous with responsibility. I had expected the money to bring more satisfaction than it did. Watching him leave I felt abandoned. I stood there on the asphalt while the car turned right at the intersection and the flow of traffic carried it away.

The boulevard sounds receded with that car, as if an invisible screen had closed behind it. In this strange stillness, as the taillight winked its final wink and the baby blue trunk disappeared, I wondered why I had kept to myself the collision that once mangled her rear fender. I wondered why the cousin had not noticed the repair, and if he had, why he hadn't mentioned it, thinking then of the many things we never mention. My mother's passing, for example. I had not mentioned that to Harold either. She had lived a long life, so it came as no surprise, but it wasn't something I was ready to talk to anyone about.

The afternoon breeze fell away. Alone among the rows I found myself inside a tent of silence. An awful yearning gripped me, and then the fear that can stop you in your tracks, the fear of what is not yet known, which will sometimes take in everything imaginable. I couldn't tell you how long it held me there, how long I stood watching the long parade of silent cars.

(1989)

Gasoline

Gas, *coined by the Belgian chemist*
J. B. Van Helmont (1577–1644), was
derived from the Greek word "chaos."
—*Webster's New World Dictionary*

Like a driver whose lungs cry out for air, Charlie roams the town in search of gasoline. His tank is almost empty. Far to the left his needle flutters over the lonesome letter E.

He knows this needle well, knows its every habit. The fluttering means he still has a gallon, maybe a gallon and a half. In times past he might have toyed with this, pushed on down the road testing how many miles he could make after the fluttering stopped and the needle flopped over playing dead. It was a little flirt with destiny he used to love. Today he can't afford it. Such pastimes depend on stations at every corner, unflagging supplies of fuel at all hours of the day and night. Some say those days and nights are gone forever. At eleven on a Thursday morning, each station he passes is closed or not pumping. It makes Charlie's eyes itch. It is like waking up in the wrong country, or on the wrong planet.

For as long as he can remember, the stations have been there, like the streets, like the sky. From the earliest days of his childhood the pumps have beckoned. Charlie can recall a time when managers gave you things, rewards for buying gasoline. Here, take this plate, they would say, take this set of dishes, this quart of Pepsi, this teddy bear. My pumps runneth over, they would say. Now the pumps are drying up. And no one can explain it. Some say the world supply of fuel is running out. They wag their heads and say your next tankful could be your last. Charlie doesn't accept this. Others say that oil profiteers, perhaps the Arabs, are to blame. He isn't sure about the Arabs. He has never met one. But as he speeds along past the laundromats and taco bars, the drive-in car washes, the drive-in banks, the muffler shops and stereo warehouses and tire outlets, as his anxious stomach begins to flutter like the needle on his gauge, it helps to have someone specific to point a finger at. It occurs to him that Arabs might be lurking behind all our addictions. Coffee. Hashish. Horse racing. Sexual excess. Gasoline.

A gauzy layer of fumes and car heat hugs the boulevard. In the near distance a yellow pole emerges from this layer, and atop the pole a large square sign says MARTY'S GAS AND GO. His heart leaps. Something tells him Marty's is open and pumping. Some vibration rises through the street fumes to charge the morning air around the sign. As he nears the corner, he sees cars lined up beneath a metal canopy that shades the four pump islands. Hoses connect each car to a pump, and drivers stand holding hose nozzles shoved into their cars while they watch numbers change inside the little windows on the pumps. Charlie is astonished at how good this makes him feel, like arriving home after some exhausting journey.

A single line of cars snakes outward from the pumps and down a cross street that meets the busy boulevard. It looks to be at most a line of thirty-five or forty. This doesn't bother him. Half an hour's wait is a small price to pay compared to lines he's heard of, or compared to no fuel at all. At this station it could be less than half an hour. They only pump gas. There are no mechanics, no racks, no batteries for sale, no fan belts or road maps. Just the four islands of four pumps each, tied by computer to the tiny white office set back from the canopy, where the cashier sits watching lighted numbers come up on her console. Most days the cashier is the only one on duty. This morning a young lad has been hired to direct traffic on and off the quarter-acre asphalt lot. With his long blond hair, wearing jeans and a T-shirt that says TODAY IS THE FIRST DAY OF THE REST OF YOUR LIFE, he flags cars between his apple-crate barriers whenever spaces open at the pumps.

As Charlie eases past the waiting cars he removes his dark glasses. In the eyes of his fellow motorists, he sees a look of well-being that seems to match his own. In the way these drivers willingly take their places and obey the blond attendant, he sees long-starved communal instincts rising to the occasion. It comes very close to patriotism, this sharing of small inconveniences to keep the larger show on the road. Charlie is reassured, gripped by an unexpected rush of comradeship.

He has reached the next corner and swung wide, preparing to U-turn and pull up behind the final car, before he realizes the line turns the corner, to avoid blocking the intersection, and continues up a side street.

He sees another forty-five or fifty vehicles, maybe more. He sees campers, delivery vans. His throat goes dry. His eyes are dry. Blinking, squinting to see how far the line extends, his eyes burn in the dry heat. The block behind was a mix of homes and small businesses, a chiropractor's bungalow, a pet hospital. This street is all residential, part of a subdivision, with small lawns, new trees spaced between interchangeable ranch-style houses. The street curves out of sight, and the line of vehicles follows the curve.

As he moves along the line Charlie sees a different look on the faces waiting. These folks don't have Marty's pumps to

spur them. Trees and houses block their view of the big sign
catching sunlight. He sees boredom here, edging up on anger.
By the time he has passed a dozen cars there is fury in the
eyes of certain people who try to stare him down. He slides
the glasses back on, just as a woman sitting in a dune buggy
with an exposed engine gives him the finger. Three cars later
a man in a rusting white Mustang with spoke wheels backs
up a foot and rams the next car in line, a perfectly restored
Cadillac hearse with paisley drapes across the rear windows.
The Cadillac driver leaps out. In his rearview, Charlie
observes these men toe-to-toe and ready to punch.

Then he loses sight of them, as he follows a long, suburban
horseshoe loop. Two-thirds of the way around, after he has
passed seventy-seven more vehicles, including numerous pick-
ups, an Airstream trailer, and a two-ton rent-a-truck, another
street branches off, cutting deeper into the district. Again the
line takes the corner, rather than clog the little intersection. This
too is a curving street, and again the line curves out of sight.

These houses are a few years older and more expensive. The
trees are higher, shading the sidewalks and the larger, greener
lawns. This used to be a walnut grove. Full-grown walnut trees
stand near each house, mingling with acacia, liquid amber, date
palms, and spreading ivy. Someone has parked a roadster at
the curb. It causes the line of waiting cars to bulge like a boa
constrictor with undigested prey. There is a craziness about this
maneuver. These drivers enjoy the opportunity to create some
true congestion. As he inches past, Charlie enjoys being forced
to the opposite curb. He laughs to himself. It keys him to the
mood. These people are feeling reckless. The pumps are so far
away, their plans for the morning have all been scrapped.

He passes a van with bubble portholes and flames curling
outward from the wheels, filled with high school kids dressed
for the beach. They have given up ever getting there. Giggling
helplessly one girl has sprawled on a sloping lawn under one
of the walnuts. Two others sip German beer as they swirl to
urgent drums and a thundering bass line.

A few cars ahead he sees a motorbike rigged like a vendor's wagon. It is parked in the street near a Plymouth Horizon, and the woman straddling the seat holds a white styrofoam cup under the spigot of a five-gallon thermos. Charlie slows down, opens his window to the welcome aroma of fresh coffee. For hours he has smelled rubbery false air coming through his vents and the false leather mustiness his naugahyde upholstery gives off when the sun hits it. This coffee happens to be French roast, pungent with chicory. The aroma fills him with affection for whoever brewed it and thought to bring it clear out here. Nearing the motorbike all he can see are sandals, jeans, flaming copper hair. As he stops he pulls the glasses off again. Though he has been told dark glasses look dramatic in some sinister and compelling way, he has a hunch that this time eye contact might be more effective. She turns, and her eyes gaze directly into his, blue and confident, so confident he almost looks away. He wants to say something memorable.

He says, "How much is the coffee?"

"A dollar a cup. No refills." Her voice is soft, her eyes brim with merriment.

"For French roast," he says, gaining control of himself, "that's a pretty fair price."

"I make my money on the baklava."

He glances at the wide shelf above her handlebars where gleaming pastry squares are stacked in a white carton, their layers of translucent crust thickened with honey and grated nuts. He inhales. The holiday sweetness blending with chicory stirs all his appetites.

It makes him bold. "What else do you do?"

"I sometimes read cars."

"You mean professionally?"

"Your radiator, for instance, it is on the verge."

"Of what?"

"And you yourself."

"On the verge?"

Her words start warm light rising through his body. Charlie is thirty-seven. He has been married, divorced. The job he works at pays the bills but means less and less to him. For months now, years perhaps, something inside, elusive yet urgent, has been pushing outward. He has felt himself ever nearer to some momentous threshold.

A horn beeps. In the rearview he sees cars and trucks stacked up behind him. "Sonofabitch," he mutters.

"Catch you later." She seems ready to burst out laughing, not at Charlie, but at the very way life unfolds.

As he stomps the accelerator, roaring ahead, his first thought is to park quickly, walk back and find out what she meant. A glance at his gas gauge reminds him there isn't time. It feels immoral to drive away from such a woman, such burnished hair. Yet any delay now would be too costly. A gallon left, and Marty's is the only station open. He squints hard to quell the fierce itching in his eyes. Something solid is slipping out from under him, something as firm and as fixed as the asphalt. In the old days if you were interested in a female, a car was an advantage, your strongest ally.

He guides around more bulges where local cars are parked. With every curve in this stalled and serpentine caravan he expects to see the final car. He follows the street through a blighted tract where uprooted stumps and scaffolded foundations mix with gutted cottages half torn down. Beyond this the line slopes over a rise and down into a neighborhood set apart by a broad thicket of Monterey pine. Here the landscape changes dramatically. The colors change. One side of the pine thicket is gray with construction dust, the other side intensely green. The houses are quite elegant, two stories high, colonial in style, with white porch pillars and manicured lawns. Tall redwoods rise in groves behind the houses, which are like manor houses fronting large estates, all tastefully gathered around a cul-de-sac where the line finally ends.

Charlie has passed hundreds of vehicles, perhaps a thousand. He figures he has traveled at least two miles, more

likely three, when he pulls up behind a boat trailer attached
to the rear of an immense and glistening El Conquistador
motorhome. This is not part of the neighborhood, it is the
last vehicle in line. Through its blue tinted glass he can see
vinyl furniture, overhead area lamps, a twenty-inch Sony. Up
one side an aluminum ladder climbs to the roof where the
heating and cooling vents emerge and some deck chairs are
strapped. The trailer pulls a gleaming fiberglass launch with
red padded seats and a hundred-fifty-horsepower Mercury
engine hanging from its stern. Together the launch and the
Conquistador occupy one-fifth of the available curb space.
Above the simulated knotty pine door of the motorhome
phosphorescent paste-on letters say NESBIT'S REVENGE.

Another car pulls in behind Charlie, then another, and
another, until he can look straight across at a young fellow in
a cowboy hat driving a high-wheeled Ranchero pickup with
twin spots and a roll bar. He smirks, as if disdainful of Charlie's
Dodge. Charlie knows it isn't disdain. He has seen this smirk on
the faces of overweight women walking out of ice cream par-
lors with triple-deckers. It is the look Charlie wears on his own
face now, the guilty smirk of the gasoline junkie who must
drop everything to drive this far for a fix. Soon the cul-de-sac
has filled with cars, as the line begins to loop back upon itself
and down the opposite side of the curving street. The smirk-
ing, shamefaced drivers are shutting their engines off, breaking
out magazines, switching on some music while they wait for
the next move forward toward the distant pumps.

Into this arena of small, tentative sounds comes one large,
insistent sound, a plaintive grunt, a steady grinding. He listens.
He leans out the window. It comes from the El Conquistador.
He hears the engine catch and start to purr, then sputter and
cough, purr a moment longer, cough again, and snort. Two
smoky farts pop up between the boat trailer and the simulated
knotty pine door. Then the long motorhome falls silent.

The driver's door slowly opens. A large, heavy man climbs
out, wearing a denim yachting cap, an orange jumpsuit, hiking

boots. He slams the door and stands with hands on hips, frowning at the other drivers, who all watch him. There is nothing else to do. He turns and kicks his front tire ferociously.

The fellow in the cowboy hat lets out a rebel yell. "She's down! But you ain't whupped her yet!"

Nesbit kicks the tire again. He turns to his aluminum side ladder and kicks it so hard the bottom rung tears loose. Twice more he kicks it, shouting, "Goddam fucking Arabs!"

Exuberantly the cowboy yells, "You've hurt her that time!"

With a surprising burst Nesbit hurls himself against the door of his motorhome, like a lineman going at a tackling dummy. He bounces off, leaving a deep dent. Several drivers call out or honk in appreciation. Then Nesbit hunkers next to his injured ladder and looks back at Charlie, suddenly calm, as if this has been an audition and Charlie is now supposed to make some kind of decision.

While the two men regard each other, something inside Charlie relaxes, something he has been wrestling with since he drove away from the coffee vendor. His junkie shame dissolves. His eyes stop itching. Leaving her was not immoral, because there are two moralities, two codes in the air today, and he feels wondrously poised between them, on the verge, as she put it. Surely this must be the meaning of her prophecy. Under the Old Code you always knew what to do because in a world dripping with gasoline there was always plenty to go around. The New Code shifts from moment to moment, in a world of uncertain fuel supply. The New Code, for example, says you do not get involved with anyone whose nine-mile-per-gallon motorhome has run dry at the end of a three-mile gas line. The Old Code says any time you find yourself right behind another vehicle in trouble, no matter how many other drivers may be close by, you are the one most obliged to help. If he followed the New Code, Charlie would pull around in front of this motorhome and move ahead with the line. The problem is, the line isn't moving. It hasn't moved in some time. The cars up front stand bumper to bumper with no space for squeezing in. Until someone else moves, there's nowhere to go. So for the moment the Old Code prevails, and it pleases him that he can choose to respond in the tried and tested way.

He sticks his head out the window. "What happened, pal? You run out of gas?"

Nesbit snorts a hopeless laugh. "Do dogs bark? Could Einstein count to ten?"

"You don't have a spare can?"

"Of course I have a spare can. I always carry a spare can." He speaks loudly and distinctly, as if from a stage. "It just doesn't happen to have anything in it. Is that a crime?"

Charlie gets out of his Dodge and looks around. He feels like stretching. He might walk over and talk to Nesbit. In a second-story window of the nearest house he sees a drape pull back and a shadowy figure evidently watching this invasion, perhaps watching Nesbit in particular, since his equipment now blocks the driveway—a vast slab of concrete leading forty yards through shrubbery to a three-car garage with wisteria crawling across its shake roof.

Stepping toward the motorhome Charlie says, "As soon as this line starts to move, I guess we ought to at least push you ahead a few feet."

Gloomily Nesbit says, "This is not a sportscar you're looking at."

"Five or six of us could get it rolling."

Nesbit shoves fingers into the corners of his eyes. "Five or six of us. Jesus Christ! What a grotesque situation. I swear the goddam Arabs are going to bring us to our knees."

"You think the Arabs are behind this?"

Nesbit yanks down the chest zipper on his jumpsuit, as if the question makes him break into a sweat. He begins to fan his hairy chest with the loose orange lapels. "Do mice have legs?" he cries. "Did Benjamin Franklin wear glasses when he signed the Constitution?"

The fellow in the cowboy hat has left his pickup door open and strolled across to take a look at the dent. He squats and reaches out with reverence, touching the edges where hairline cracks break through the beige paint job. Charlie hunkers next to him, so that they make a trio hunkering out of the summer sun's fierce rays, in the shade cast by the big motorhome, picking at the asphalt and discussing the mysterious forces around them, as men have done for thousands of years when thrown together by the camaraderie of mutual affliction.

"I got a cousin drives truck," the cowboy says. "Tells me oil companies are holding fuel back just to run up the price."

Charlie says, "I have heard people say the whole thing is a false problem."

"You call this a false problem?" Nesbit says. "Down at the ass-end of a dead-end street? Five hours from the gas station, and no way to get there?"

"What I mean is," Charlie says, "some guy has supposedly invented a car that gets a hundred and thirty-four miles to the gallon."

Nesbit takes this personally. "I don't see you sitting in one."

The cowboy says, "Oil companies bought up all the patents."

Charlie says, "I heard the CIA bought up all the patents."

"Same difference," the cowboy says. "Those clowns in Washington all sleep with the oil execs—according to my cousin."

Charlie has a fresh idea to test out. "You ever get the feeling that we are the last generation of suckers?"

Nesbit slaps his forehead with violent ecstasy. "Oh my God! Did you say suckers? That is the understatement of the century! What's your name anyhow?"

"Bates. Charlie Bates."

"Listen, Bates. Guys like you and me and the cowpuncher here, we are the greatest suckers in the history of the world. Look at this. Seventy-seven thousand dollars is what I got tied up in all this gear, and I am absolutely at the mercy of some

sheik over there in Mecca or wherever the hell they live, holding on to the oil until the price runs up, then bringing the
profits over here to buy our own country out from under us.
You want my opinion, the real truth is it's the Arabs and the
Chinese who are sleeping together. They would all like nothing better than to bring us to our knees!"

Standing up he backsteps across the asphalt for a better
look at what world market conditions have done to his invest-
ment. "Look at my goddam motorhome!" he shouts. "Is there
any excuse for this? Look at that ladder! Look at that paint job!
What's it going to cost me to get this fixed?"

The cowboy leans in closer to the wrinkled body and
grins. "That is truly a dent and a half, old buddy."

Charlie says, "You think it's the Arabs and the Chinese
together?"

Nesbit throws his hands wide and yells at the sky, "Do bears
make big poopie in the woods?"

Beyond him a glint of movement catches Charlie's eye, a
glint of hope. At last the line could be moving. He stands up
to see past Nesbit. Grille to license plate the marooned cars
still wait. This glint comes from a black Chrysler limousine
squeezing through the straits where the two rows of vehicles
have bottlenecked the entry to the cul-de-sac. The limousine
is long and sleek, recently waxed, driven by a mustachioed
chauffeur. Tinted windows make it hard to see who's in back.
The windshield catches glare. The hood ornament is one foot
from the Conquistador when the Chrysler stops, without a
sound, and a triple-width garage door lifts open forty yards
up the driveway.

Nesbit mutters, "Oh shit."

Charlie says, "We're going to have to scoot her forward."

Nesbit's hands are in the air again. "One gallon will get this
baby started! That's all I need!"

"Hey, calm down. We have lots of time. I'll talk to the guys
up ahead about making a little room."

"I'll pay five bucks for one gallon of gasoline!" Nesbit shouts. "Regular, unleaded, super, supreme. Ten bucks. I don't give a cat's patootie!"

Before anyone can answer he rushes to the rear window of the limousine. "If the rest of these bench jockeys would pitch in…!"

The door's swing interrupts him, and a cultivated voice. "May I make a suggestion?"

A small dapper man steps out, his face swarthy, smooth, well cared for. He wears a navy blue business suit with striped silk tie, black shoes highly polished, short black hair, black moustache, and trimmed black chin beard. His black eyes hold Nesbit with a brooding intensity that causes the big florid face to twitch.

Carefully he says, "You might unhook your boat trailer, then push the motorhome backward into the vacated space. This should at least give me room to pass."

As he speaks, Charlie notes another glint, from the same second-story window, which now stands half open, a glint from a small mirror or, it crosses Charlie's mind, a small weapon. He turns and catches what could be a glinting reply from the house directly opposite.

To Nesbit he says, "Did you see that?"

Nesbit doesn't hear. He is transfixed by the dapper man. "Who are you?"

"I happen to live here," the man says with the proper control of his indignation.

"Are you an American?"

"I am merely suggesting a way to have my driveway cleared. Does nationality matter?"

"Does it matter?" Nesbit roars. "Is sunshine good for pimples? Could Babe Ruth hit?"

Other drivers are drifting toward the Chrysler. It's a diversion. The dapper man, suddenly surrounded, pulls out a white handkerchief and pats his shining brow. Glancing at the window Charlie sees what could be the tip of a gun barrel resting on the sill.

"Nesbit," he murmurs, nodding at the house, "how hard is it to unhook the trailer?"

Nesbit sees the window. He grabs the small man by the coat. "What the hell is going on? What's your name?"

"For Christ sake!" Charlie says. "Let him go! Look at this!"

In a flash it has come clear to him, the way this cul-de-sac is set up, the way the road curves and the pine barrier covers sight lines. This is a little realm unto itself, a low-profile retreat where random visitors are unlikely. Seven houses face the street, and dim faces have appeared in other windows. The way the vehicles follow the concrete rim, they are beginning to resemble a wagon train pulled into a circle. Nesbit seems to see it in exactly such terms. He takes the dapper man by the neck and pulls him against the shady side of the motorhome, one arm on the throat, the other up behind the lean back in a hammerlock.

"Nesbit!" Charlie cries. "Have you lost your mind?"

The chauffer has scrambled out of the limo and crouches now looking for an opening, an enormous fellow wearing a turtleneck sweater and windbreaker. His eyes glitter. His head is shaved. He comes much closer to the kind of culprit Nesbit has imagined bringing world progress to a standstill. Instantly hate flows between them like a vapor.

Nesbit says, "One more step, I'll break his arm."

The dapper man, who cannot speak, raises his free hand commanding the chauffeur to stand back.

Charlie moves in next to them. "This is insane. All we have to do is unhook your boat trailer and let these guys drive on into their garage."

"You think it's insane? I don't think it's insane at all! This guy is from Arabia!" He relaxes his throat hold. "Am I right?"

The man coughs a raspy, "Yes."

"What the hell are you doing here?"

"I like it here, the same way you do."

"That's not how Arabs talk."

"I did my undergraduate work at Berkeley."

"Now you own all these houses, isn't that true? You own the whole damn neighborhood, including the redwood trees."

"It happens that I do represent a corporation with a large and varied portfolio."

"And all these people peeking out the doors and windows, they are all your brothers and sisters. Correct?"

"One sister, a brother-in-law, and several cousins, all of whom will be deeply affected if any harm comes to me."

Deeply affected does not begin to describe the chauffeur, who is staring and jerking like a caged animal searching for a way through the bars, much as Nesbit looked just before he grabbed the Arab. Charlie wishes he could leave them alone to fight it out. Why can't he? What nameless loyalty holds him here? At any moment he expects rifle fire. People are standing in the doorways. In the street a dozen motorists have gathered, some siding with Nesbit, some with his victim. The cowboy calls, "Hey, let the little fella loose! Don't he have a right to drive up his own cotton-pickin driveway?"

Hearing this, Charlie sees what must be done. The cowboy is still living by the Old Code. If these were the days when a homeowner could expect free access to his driveway at any hour of the day or night, Charlie himself would by now be pitching in to unhook the trailer. But faced with a motorist unhinged by the lack of gasoline, Charlie has to search the New Code for guidance.

"Nesbit, listen to me. Suppose we could get this wiseass Arab to siphon five gallons out of his tank into yours."

Nesbit considers this. "I want the chauffeur to do it."

Charlie looks at the chauffeur, whose jaw muscles are ready to explode. "If we can get the chauffeur to do it, will you turn this guy loose?"

Nesbit doesn't answer.

"Look. What the hell do you want?"

"For once I want some justice! Look at my ladder! Look at my paint job!"

"You want gasoline. Right?"

Nesbit starts to laugh. "Do tires stink?"

Charlie regards the brooding eyes of the man from Arabia. He sees a survivor. Later this man may consider retribution. Right now he wants out of Nesbit's clutches and into the safety of his compound. The man's eyes signal his chauffeur, with a nod toward the Chrysler. "Use the reserve can."

Nesbit says, "You told me he was going to siphon it."

"That'll take twice as long."

The chauffeur glows with rage. If eyes could kill, Nesbit would now be sprawled on the asphalt covered with flies and maggots. For a long moment he tries to murder Nesbit with his gaze, then he walks to the trunk, opens it and unstraps a five-gallon can. He has to unscrew Nesbit's gas cap. He shoves the spout in and stands next to it smoldering.

As motorists and relatives watch and listen to fuel gurgling into the thirsty Conquistador, the charged silence is punctuated by snaps and pops from the metal can. Maybe two gallons have made this passage when Nesbit, losing patience, says accusingly, as if Charlie betrayed some lifelong trust, "I want him to siphon it."

"For God's sake, Nesbit! Gasoline is gasoline."

"I want to see this sonofabitch down on his knees in the street sucking high octane ethyl out of the back-end of that Chrysler through a hose."

With a thunk and a slosh the reserve can hits the asphalt. The chauffeur is reaching inside his windbreaker.

The man from Arabia shouts, "Raoul! Don't be an idiot!"

Raoul doesn't hear him. He draws a snub-nosed .38 from his shoulder holster and points it at Nesbit's head. "This swine does not deserve to live."

The big ruddy face loses its color. "Hey! Hey, hold it there! Hold it a second!"

His head makes an excellent target since it is several inches higher than the Arab's, so much higher that he tries in vain to shield himself. As Charlie watches Nesbit squirm for cover, his distaste turns to compassion, then to lofty detachment from the entire spectacle. Time stands still. He asks himself what he is doing in this besieged cul-de-sac at eleven thirty on a Thursday morning. And he remembers what he set out to do so many hours ago. He was planning to sell his car. Big repair bills are right around the corner. He touches his shirt pocket where the title resides, with the registration. This is really the only thing that holds him here. His car. According to the Old Code you do not walk off and abandon your car in a strange neighborhood. It's too late for the Old Code, of course, and there's no time to ponder what the New Code prescribes. Raoul is ready to pull the trigger. Part of Charlie wants him to. Nesbit deserves punishment. But not death. The instant before Raoul fires, Charlie rushes him and diverts his aim, though he can't stop the bullet, which narrowly misses the two struggling men and blasts into Charlie's radiator.

He hears the hiss of escaping steam, as outcries fill the arena, as motorists retreat, or push forward. People from the houses hurry down their drives. Nesbit's arms go limp. He sinks back against the motorhome.

The dapper man takes command, holding both hands high to restrain his relatives. "Back! It's all right! Get back inside!"

He steps up to Raoul and slaps his face. "You fool! This is precisely what we do not want!"

The chauffeur's eyes melt with shame. "He was humiliating me."

"Give me that pistol. Get into the car."

To Nesbit the man says coldly, "You have enough fuel to get started now. Please move so I can pass."

Nesbit seems paralyzed. With glazed eyes he stares at the little Arab.

Charlie says, "Do it, man, before something worse happens."

"My life," Nesbit says weakly, "you saved it."

"Never mind your life. Fire up your engine. Move it out."

He stumbles toward the cab, yanks his bent door open with a scrape, climbs in, pumping the pedal, turning the key like a robot.

Charlie squats in front of his Dodge to observe the flow of splashing water. He lifts the hood and sees that Raoul's bullet continued on through his engine. The cowboy is there next to him.

"Whooee, that little sucker tore right through her."

The man from Arabia appears at Charlie's shoulder. "My sincere apologies. Raoul is...impulsive."

"I guess the police should be notified."

"The police? What could be accomplished by notifying the police?"

Charlie turns and studies the profile of this man who now studies the ruined engine. Beads of perspiration hang from his forehead like tiny grapes. "I was hoping," the man says, "that you and I might reach some sort of...an agreement."

Again warm light starts to rise through Charlie's legs and belly. According to the New Code, when fuel is five hours away and even then unreliable, a car with a bullet through the engine is a hindrance and a yoke around the neck. Yet according to the Old Code, profit is always profit. If he could liquidate with honor, might he not then have it both ways? Might he not then take the profits and position himself for some new beginning? As if in answer, the next sound he hears is the sputtering putt-putt of the blue-eyed coffee vendor.

The sight of her copper hair elates him, fills him with high purpose. For the benefit of the waiting Arab, Charlie shakes his head, grieving one last time above an open grave. Mournfully he says, "Looks like that radiator's finished, the water pump, the short block."

The cowboy chimes in. "No telling what all else."

"That's right," Charlie says. "Who knows what else?"

"Would a thousand cover it?" the Arab asks.

"Fact is, when I left this morning what I was planning to do was sell this car. I was hoping to get eighteen hundred, maybe two thousand for it."

The Arab pulls out his handkerchief and pats his forehead. "How about twenty-five hundred?"

"There is also the inconvenience. Wear and tear on the nerves. Mental anguish."

The cowboy says, "I'd sooner see a horse get shot than my pickup."

"Three thousand is as high as I can go."

An outburst around the motorbike distracts them.

"My God!"

"What next?"

The woman has parked in the center of the cul-de-sac and seems to enjoy the commotion.

Charlie calls out, "What's happening?"

"Some fighting," a man calls back, "down at the pumps!"

Her pastry shelf is empty. She has left her thermos and her wares behind, to carry this news along the line. Charlie joins the circle.

"The story is two mean-looking dudes in a van hopped the curb at Marty's and pulled up in front of the lead car. When people started honking, one guy climbed out and stood there dangling a big machete while his buddy came around to open the tank. Some fellow filling up on the next island got so mad he just turned the hose on them, sprayed them with gasoline, then whipped out his Zippo lighter and told them to get rolling. Well, they didn't wait to see if he meant it."

She straddles her motorbike, blue eyes darting, amused and saddened, and teasing, or testing something in the eyes of her listeners, especially Charlie's, once she notes how he watches her. He isn't sure she remembers him.

"On their way out, the guy with the machete whacked off four of the hoses. This didn't sit too well with the folks who had been waiting since breakfast. With nobody in charge

232

but that kid directing traffic they had to take the law into their own hands. Three cars tried to cut off the van before it got back on the boulevard, so right where people drive out, there was a four-car pileup. That's why the line isn't moving and won't be for a while yet. They have to clear the area, get those thugs out of their van without setting them on fire, and of course the hose slashing means less pumps when things resume..."

Before she has finished, drivers are striding toward the cars, to start up and move on, or check this against radio reports. Others can't decide. "I already drove thirty-five miles this morning," one fellow complains.

"Well what the hell you gonna do?" the cowboy says, hopping into his pickup. "Camp out overnight?"

"I don't have enough gas left to go anywhere," says another, slumped against his front fender.

"We're screwed."

"We're up shit creek."

"Not me," says Nesbit, whose Conquistador is rumbling again. "They suckered me once! They don't sucker me twice!"

With noisy bravado he guns his engine and pulls out from the curb, clearing the driveway so the limousine can pass.

Raoul, wearing black shades, scowls at the steering wheel in disgrace. The Arab sits behind him again, in the velvety and air-conditioned shadows, peeling hundreds from a fist-sized wad. He hands thirty bills out to Charlie and says coolly, "Title."

"I beg your pardon?"

"The certificate of title. You wouldn't happen to have it with you."

Reaching into his shirt pocket, Charlie marvels at how often things come around. As he signs away the car, his training under the Old Code compels him to seal this deal with the proper words.

"She's got a good spare tire," he says bending, with a congenial grin. "Plenty of tread. And the jack should be right there under the seat. It's the original jack."

The Arab's reply is an invisible finger to the button that controls his tinted window. It rises between them. The car purrs forward, up the long driveway and under the wide garage door, which silently drops shut.

Charlie looks around. The doors in all the houses are closed again. The lawns are green and empty. The drapes are closed. Above the roofs redwoods rise toward the hot sun, the placid sky. Unfettered, released, he is ready to float beyond the tops of those redwoods. The news from the pumps has sent him halfway there. He swells with affection for the messenger. When he hears her voice again, it is part of this floating, part of a globe that is separate from the grinding starters, the roar of engines, the chattering newscasters and beeping horns.

"Need a lift?"

He turns and finds her regarding him with the same directness he almost couldn't handle an hour back. The difference now is three thousand dollars in his pocket and no more gas gauge to bully him. He wonders if she saw the money changing hands. Or is she seeing something else—the self-assurance rushing through him, the bursting confidence of a man on the verge? He doesn't much care. Whatever works. She has sized up the situation, the shattered radiator. Her merry smile is breaking loose a thread of sugary crumbs at one corner of her mouth. She has been sneaking bits of pastry. He wants to laugh.

"I could use a lift."

"It's snug with two. But...well, it's a way to get acquainted."

He climbs on behind her, pelvis to pelvis, belly to spine. He hooks heels on the metal stirrups. "How far you going?"

"Back down to the boulevard, for more supplies," she says, revving it with a twist of the handgrip. "It's lunchtime. People are going to need sandwiches, things to drink. I also read gas stations. These folks are in a terrible fix. The trouble at Marty's is just beginning."

"You're not worried about fuel?"

"I can make this run twenty times. We get a hundred miles to the gallon, uphill. Size is the problem. That seat all right? You on there? You can hold onto my waist, you know."

His hands explore the slenderness. A coating of gristle on the lower ribs suggests regular exercise. He figures she is thirty-four and taking good care of herself. Up close to the abundant hair he sees a few white strands you'd never notice ten feet away. As she revs it again, swinging around, he says, "How do you read these things? I mean, how did you know it was going to be my radiator?"

"How do diviners know where to dig wells?"

He lets his hands inch around toward the firm belly flesh. She doesn't mind. A breeze blows some copper hair back. With the breeze come erotic hints of chicory, grated nuts, and with this scent comes a vision of what could happen next. In a world of uncertain fuel supply, where conditions shift from moment to moment, her enterprise is just the sort of thing you might put a little cash into. Today of course would be the day to invest. All these drivers, sooner or later they'll figure something out. Tomorrow the line could be twice this size, or it could be gone. With admiration he realizes she has known this all along.

Over her shoulder she says, "What are you doing this afternoon?"

"You have any ideas?"

"On my way out here I was thinking about how that line has doubled back. If I had a partner, we could work both sides at once."

"I wouldn't mind giving that a try. I wouldn't mind at all."

She is puttering forward, past the stranded drivers. Most have held their places, figuring there's nowhere else to go. Half a dozen chose to leave, just as a string of new arrivals reached the bottleneck looking for a way to turn around. The cowboy's Ranchero was the only vehicle to get through, before Nesbit, in his rush to escape, approached the narrow exit at too sharp an angle. His bent door changed the setting on his outside mirror, so he couldn't see the boat trailer. It jackknifed, and he is boxed in on three sides, bellowing, leaning on his horn, stuck like a rhino in a revolving door.

Charlie shouts, "Nesbit!"

The big head quivers as if slapped.

"Nesbit, why don't you relax for a minute. Stand back…"

"Why don't I what?" Beneath the yachting cap his trapped eyes bulge. "Why didn't Custer wear a blindfold at the Little Big Horn? All I need is four or five feet! Get one of these other jokers to stand back! You think I can afford to burn fuel fighting my way out of this? Jesus, what a madhouse!"

His voice is behind them now. She has eased between two bumpers, up onto the sidewalk. They are taking a rise toward the next neighborhood. Soon the logjam is out of sight beyond a curve, behind the thick border of Monterey pine. It's quieter here, with the engines off, the drivers dazed or standing by their cars. A brief flexing in her belly tells him to slide his hands a bit farther, until the fingers link above her navel. In reply she presses a shoulder back, encouraging a hug. Her hair is blowing into his mouth and ears as they clear the rise and coast a while.

(1980)

Daily Evangelism

I have been trying to remember the name of this fellow I knew in college. I think it was Ferad. I have looked through the yearbook. His picture isn't there. He didn't belong to any clubs. He was an exchange student, a few years older than me. I will call him Ferad. He came from Iran but preferred his country's older name. If you asked him where he lived he'd say, with pride, "I am a Jew from Persia."

I once came upon him sitting alone in the sunlight, reading, on the steps outside our dormitory. In the moment before he noticed me behind him, I stood gazing at his cap, a small bowl of cloth held in place by coils of thick black hair that reached up around its edges. From above, you could see the pattern of intricate circles, some made of tiny squares, some made of triangles, rings of interwoven reds and blues and golds, all layered around a central wheel with eight spokes. Nowadays I would recognize its mandala pattern. Back then it held me for reasons I couldn't fathom. The yarmulke had once belonged

to his father, a devout man who lived in the city of Shiraz.
His cap had the same beguiling design you see in Persian rugs.

The college was a small, private Christian school on the
outskirts of Los Angeles, and I have often wondered what
Ferad was doing there, having to contend with people like
me, or the way I was in those days. They had a generous budget for foreign students. For a bright fellow like Ferad I suppose it meant a tuition stipend along with a chance to taste
a bit of the wider world. I see now that he may well have felt
safer in our midst than in the Moslem land he'd left behind.
I'm just guessing. Though we talked about many things, we
never talked about that.

For pocket money he worked two afternoons a week on
the campus grounds crew. That's how we got acquainted.
Ordinarily I would not have chosen such a fellow for compan-
ionship. Not back then. But you learn things, working side by
side. You can end up despising a person, or liking him more,
for what his habits show you. Ferad was easy to be with. He
knew how to move furniture and how to handle a hoe.
He was comfortable with tools and knew something about
plants. Whatever the job, he pitched right in, ready to do his
share, though never compulsive about the tasks Shorty the
supervisor would set before us. If Shorty had recently walked
away, Ferad might drop his rake and fall back onto the grass
with his hands behind his head. On the job, by the way, he
didn't wear his yarmulke. He wore an aging fedora. Underneath its brim, his eyes would glow with merriment.

"Isn't this the life?" he would say. "Isn't this the America we
all have dreamed about?"

He'd make it funny and we'd laugh together, though I
scarcely knew what he meant. I had no idea how America
looked to him, or what it meant to be from Persia or from
Iran or to be from anywhere. I had not traveled beyond
the borders of the United States, nor had I strayed very far
beyond the borders of my family's way of seeing. Most of my

relatives were guided by the words of the New Testament. Or said they were. Most everyone on that campus believed in Jesus. Or claimed to. I was among the believers. Or thought I was. Or thought I was supposed to be. There seemed no way around it. In the world of my youth you accepted the New Testament as the literal word of God and believed in Jesus as the one and only path to salvation.

That semester I had enrolled in four courses—Journalism 2, Psychology 2, Music Appreciation, and Daily Evangelism, taught by Brother Carvel Simkins, a working minister who had preached the gospel all across Oklahoma, Texas, and New Mexico. Brother Simkins was firm in his conviction that those who had repented of their sins, accepted Jesus as the Son of God, and been baptized into our particular branch of Christianity were "saved," while all others were regrettably "lost."

I'd been hearing this message since childhood and was starting to wonder how a truly loving God could be satisfied with such a lopsided arrangement. So far I had kept this and other questions to myself. As I shopped around for some path through college, hopefully through life, a part of me could still imagine a career as a preacher of the gospel. My father used to say it ran in the family. We had a cousin back in Texas who preached for what my father called "a fair-size congregation." He had come west to visit us once, when I was ten, a tall, bald-headed man, more like an uncle than a cousin. One afternoon he took me aside, put his thick hand on my shoulder, and told me he believed I was cut out to do the Lord's work. He had a baritone voice that made everything he said sound important. Years later his prediction was still with me, though I had not been anywhere near a pulpit.

Brother Simkins reminded me of that cousin. He had the same booming voice. I'd heard him preach with a passion that could lift people out of their seats. "The Bible is God's word," he would declare, "because this is how he chose to reveal his plan to mankind! If we read the Bible we can't fail to see that

there is only ONE GOD! ONE PLAN! ONE WAY to get to heaven!
That's God's way! And that is what I am up here this mornin
to tell you about. Right here in the pages of His holy book he
is offering you the keys to His kingdom. It's a wonderful gift,
brothers and sisters. Won't you take it now? Won't you open
your hearts to the one true way!"

I had seen men and women stumble down the aisle to
the front of the church, where they would fall to their knees
weeping with sorrow and pleading for redemption. I had seen
spittle rim the edges of Brother Simkins' mouth. At the sight
of these penitents, his eyes would brim and his voice would
break with gratitude.

"Hallelujah!" he would shout. "Hallelujah!"

I wanted to know that kind of fervor. I was desperate to
believe wholeheartedly in *something.* I'd recently turned eighteen and felt that time was running out.

At the first meeting of Daily Evangelism, as he rested his
elbows on the lectern, leaning toward us, Brother Simkins
made the classroom another form of church. His leathery
face seemed to want to smile. His voice was muted now,
gravelly and soothing. He held high his well-worn copy of
the Scriptures. The successful evangelist depends on the
Bible, he said, but he wanted to make it clear right from the
start that other factors could not be ignored.

Timing, for instance.

And tilling the field before you sow the seed.

"You can't just walk up to the first person you see and stick
a Bible under his nose and say, Brother, you better pay attention to me or you're gonna end up in the deepest pit of hell
and roast there throughout eternity like a hog at a barbecue.
No sir. That fella's gonna laugh in your face and go on about
his business. Before you ever say the word 'Bible,' you have
to build up some trust with that person. You have to become
his ally. You have to find the feeling the Frenchman calls 'rapport.' Any of you people know the word 'rapport'? It means

that between you and that other person there is a harmonious feeling..."

He paused there, a skillful and practiced pause, while his eyes roamed our faces, letting his message sink in.

Other students nodded with approval, and I was nodding with them.

Rapport.

Rapport.

It was a new, exotic word. I wrote it down. I let it linger in my mind, eager to see where this would lead. As I waited, Brother Simkins began to pass out the course syllabus, and my eagerness withered.

He had a system for saving the souls of the as-yet-unsaved. Its main ingredients were rapport and a set of Bible verses that had to be presented in a tested sequence. These were listed in blue ink, along with his grading scale. To get an A in Daily Evangelism you had to show proof, by semester's end, that you had used his system to convert and baptize a "Prospect" of your own choosing. If the semester ended before an actual baptism was achieved, you could get a B by proving your Prospect had expressed belief in Jesus and was poised at the lip of the baptismal pool. To get a C you had to show, in writing, that a Prospect was at least exposed to Brother Simkins' method. The written assignments would consist of "Progress Reports," describing all that passed between you and your Prospect.

He read this aloud with slow urgency and grave pauses, as if somewhere a war had been declared and we were recruits soon to be sent into combat. Now my hands were slick with moisture. I had figured that studying evangelism would be like music appreciation, where you learned by listening and no one would ever ask you to bring in a saxophone and try to play a song. Preaching to a "Prospect"—actually talking a person *into* something—this was not at all what I'd had in mind.

Afterward, in the palm-shaded patio outside, I joined some classmates to consider the task before us. A fellow named

C. W. Goodspeed did most of the talking, since he claimed to have a conversion already in progress. I knew C. W. from another class. He had a glossy voice and unwavering blue eyes.

"This young woman grew up a Methodist," he said, "but she never took to it. She'd just been adrift, waiting to hear the Lord's true word. I read her what King Agrippa said to the Apostle Paul—'Almost thou persuadest me'—and tears filled her eyes, as if she'd been waiting her whole life for somebody to read that verse to her."

C. W. spoke with the radiant face of a prophet, as if a divine hand had been guiding him through the very scriptures laid out in our syllabus. He was certain he'd have a baptism to report within a couple of weeks.

From the way he talked I could tell I knew the New Testament better than he did. I also knew he would have a Prospect in the water and baptized and dried off before I had the first verse out of my mouth. Like so many of the young preachers-to-be, C. W. was a born talker. He could talk his way through anything. I didn't see myself as a talker. That was not my calling. Part of me could still imagine that one day I might get the hang of it, but not then, not yet.

Walking back to the dorm I asked myself why I had signed up for Daily Evangelism. I couldn't remember. The idea of being a preacher filled me with despair.

I cut the second meeting. I decided to drop the course. I would sign up for something else. "The Bible as Literature." That sounded more to my liking. And yet I never got around to it. I never filled out the drop form. Why I procrastinated, I'm still not sure. It seems now, looking back, that waiting was a form of preparation, as if I somehow knew the lesson I needed was already coming toward me.

Every couple of weeks Ferad and I would spend an afternoon edging grass along a promenade that bordered one side of the campus, trimming it back from the concrete path and away from the wide circles of dirt surrounding the date

palms that lined the promenade. This was slow, patient work.
We'd been at it a couple of hours, trimming opposite sides
of the path, talking back and forth about whatever came to
mind—buying cars, Shorty the foreman, cafeteria food, the
weather, the perpetual spring of southern California, how
roses flourished here but dates never quite mature...

After the three o'clock classes started, we took a break.
The promenade was nearly empty. Shorty was nowhere in
sight. We sat back against one of the thick grainy trunks.
Half-grown dates hung above us in yellow clusters and fell to
litter the grass. Fingering one of these datelets, Ferad wondered if they ever got enough of the desert heat they needed.

It was a blissful interlude. As we sat there side by side, the
word "rapport" came to mind, and this time I understood its
meaning. An electric shiver passed through me. Disconnected
pieces of my life came together with a click. As if led by some
unseen hand, I had already accomplished steps one and two.
A Prospect had been selected, and we had just spent the afternoon building up rapport. Here was a field that had already
been tilled. Ferad and me, we had three *months* of rapport
going for us.

I saw the great opportunity before me. I felt a rush of kinship, along with the sudden awareness that here was a sinner
whose soul would have to be saved. I had never thought of
Ferad as a Prospect. I had never thought of him as lost. Yet
clearly I had been guided toward him, as he had been guided
toward me. Bible verses filled my head. I yearned to speak
them. Yet I could not speak. I closed my eyes.

The insides of my lids were coated with fire. I opened my
eyes and saw that something had happened to the light. It
was thicker than normal light. Rising from the lawn in front
of me, it had gathered into a shape, a translucent cloak of
light. Floating toward us it seemed to have the outer edges
of a garment, brightest at the top where a roundness glowed,
so bright I thought I should not look straight at it. I could not

help but look. As it drew near I could see the thickness, and also see through it, the grass and trees beyond, softened by a coating of silver.

Later on, extremes of light would come to me in other forms—in meditation, when the inner candle can flame up like a sunrise; in high mountain country, after a spell of solitude, when the burnished shine of granite peaks can fill the sky and fill your eyes with the divine glory of all creation. In those days I had only one phrase for such moments. Silently I said, "Thank you, Lord."

To Ferad I said, "Do you believe in Jesus?"

It was a way of asking him if he saw what I was seeing. His answer told me he was not.

"I have read his teaching. He was a very wise man."

"But do you believe in Him?"

Ferad always took his time. His serene gaze now aimed at me. "Do you mean, as a teacher?"

"I mean as the Messiah, as the Son of God?"

His mouth curved in a small smile. "This is a large question for such a sultry afternoon."

Exactly. It was a time for large questions. And I knew which ones they should be. Sitting with my legs crossed I was a holy man. As long as this mantle of light hovered near us, I could make no mistakes. I had it all in my head. Brother Simkins' tested formula. You started by proving that the Bible was the one true expression of God's Will. From there it was only logical to agree that we should all follow whatever the Scriptures tell us.

"I know you believe in God," I said.

"Yes, I do."

"And I know you have read the Bible."

"Of course. More than once."

"'In the beginning was the Word,'" I quoted, "'and the Word was with God, and the Word *was* God.'"

His eyebrows rose. "What has come over you?"

"Do you believe the Bible is the word of God?"

He thought about this. "It depends on which parts."

"Which parts?"

"The Old Testament? Or the New?"

"Well...all of it."

Ferad stood up. "I think I see Shorty."

I saw Shorty too, next to the administration building, checking the hoses. Soon he'd be checking on us. I would have to skip ahead a few verses. I said, "'For God so loved the world he gave his only begotten son, that whosoever believeth in him should not perish but have everlasting life.' That's from the book of John."

Handing me my clippers Ferad said, "I fear the wrath of Shorty. Maybe we should appear to be trimming around this palm."

"Wouldn't it be wonderful to have everlasting life?"

He looked down at me, dark eyes wide with uncertainty. "Are you sure there is such a thing?"

This stopped me. This was not in the syllabus. I needed time to think. I was grateful to hear Shorty call, "You boys act like it's quittin time! Your watches musta stopped. C'mon now. Git them edges trimmed before they cover up the whole dang sidewalk!"

His voice pierced the luminous air, like a stone dropped into the mirror of a still pond. The light above the grass thinned out, became the normal light of afternoon, and Shorty was striding through it with a coil of watering hose looped over one shoulder. The silvery gathering dissolved, the spell was broken.

That night, writing up my Progress Report, I tried to describe being in the presence of Jesus. No matter which words I chose, it sounded false. It sounded like something C. W. would say to advance himself. The fact is, I didn't yet have words for it. It wasn't about words. It was about light. Maybe what I'd seen above the grass had not entirely disappeared. Maybe some of it had entered me. I wasn't sure.

If I had been blessed that afternoon, why did I lose my tongue?

In the end I didn't mention Jesus, hoping the facts of what had passed between us would be enough to let Brother Simkins know I was doing the work of the Lord at last.

A couple of days later he called me into his office, a musty cubicle heaped with sheaves of paper. Volumes of Christian teachings spilled from the shelves. One wall displayed a wide four-color map entitled Bible Lands. Persia was on there, in the desert country east of Palestine, out past Mesopotamia and Babylon. An enormous copy of the King James Version occupied a reading stand near his desk, where open pages featured the words of Jesus printed in red. In the middle of his desk a space had been cleared, and my report lay open in front of him. He studied it a while, nodding.

"Son, this here's a real nice report. When you missed the second meeting, I felt a pang of deep concern, I truly did. But I can see that you have a grasp of what we're trying to accomplish here. The basic grasp, that is."

He removed his horn-rims and looked across at me, fatherly now. In the strange, muted light of his study the dark pouches under his eyes gave him a mournful and haunted look. Brother Simkins had a large nose. In class it looked pink. In this light it looked purple. Up close you could see the broken capillaries webbing out in all directions. I felt sorrow for someone who had to go through life with such a nose. It brought me closer to him.

I said, "Thank you, sir. I just wonder if I could ask your advice about one thing."

"Ask away, son."

"What do you do if a Prospect doesn't seem to believe in everlasting life?"

A gleam brightened his haggard eyes as he leaned toward me. "You have hit the nail square on the head! That is why I called you in. Your average Prospect never asks such a question.

Your average person *yearns* for everlasting life and wants to know how to achieve it. The problem here is, you are barking up the wrong tree. If I was you, I wouldn't mess with a foreigner. And don't get me wrong. I got nothing against foreigners. It's not about them. It's about time. As daily evangelizers we only have so much time. I know our people go overseas to all these various countries, and my heart goes with them, it surely does. I know we invite these young people from every which place to come here and study with a free and open mind and such as that—although in my view this makes about as much sense as bringing camels to a rodeo. You see what I'm driving at, son? Right here at home we got our work cut out for us. In my day I have gone round and round with foreigners. Lord knows I have tried. But they do not think like we do. Your Buddhist, your Hindu, your A-rab, his mind is made up. Meanwhile there are good Prospects by the truckload, folks who already think pretty much like you and me. They just haven't come clear around to our way of seeing things. Are you with me on this, son? This is the field we want to plough. This is the flock that is calling out to you to be their shepherd."

He handed the report back to me and shook my hand, as if we'd reached some kind of agreement.

Out in the courtyard, under drooping fronds, I looked again at the pages I'd written. I liked Brother Simkins. I wanted him to like me. Why then did I mistrust his advice? I couldn't put my finger on it.

The answer appeared in the form of Ferad himself, who now stepped out of the next building. As he waved, walking toward me, I took it as another sign. I felt the light returning. My heart filled with gladness. He had a jaunty way of walking. His arms swung free. He wore sandals, a loose cotton shirt, a scarlet vest. He had a collection of vests, this one with maroon and gold trim as carefully stitched as his yarmulke. He lifted his palms to a blue sky and exclaimed with joy, "When the heavens give you this, who needs books!"

Brother Simkins was advising me to find a more likely, a
more susceptible Prospect. But how could I abandon Ferad
before he'd even had a chance to see the truth and step out
onto the path of salvation?

I said, "You must be feeling pretty good about something."

With merry eyes he said, "This was my last class for the
week."

"I think we should go get some coffee."

"I'm off coffee. But I might have a cup of tea."

We ambled toward the student center. I see now that the
setting itself fed my sense of inspiration. The date palms.
The balmy climate. A man from Persia walking along next
to me wearing leather sandals and a vest. It was a scene right
off the map of the Bible Lands. Much later I would learn that
our campus and the town of Nazareth were both situated in
arid zones at almost the same degree of latitude. The way I
felt just then, we could have been walking along a road somewhere in Palestine two thousand years ago. A verse flowed
through my mind, the words of Jesus, as quoted in the book
of Matthew. "Where two or three are gathered together in
my name, there am I in the midst of them."

I'd been imagining that we would find ourselves an outside
table and talk as long as we needed to. Now I couldn't wait.
I felt I could do no wrong.

"Ferad, have you thought any more about our conversation the other day?"

I watched him blink, thinking back. "You mean the heat?
The dates?"

"I mean everlasting life. Have you thought about your
soul?"

"My soul?"

"Do you mind talking about this?"

"My soul," he said again. "Well, let me see. On a day such
as today I feel very good about my soul."

His voice was soft, his eyes were gentle. But his mouth had curved into a serene little smile that could have been a mocking smile. Had he missed the seriousness of what I was trying to say? A verse came to my mind, as if by messenger.

"What better time to join your soul with Jesus! He was sent to forgive us all, you know. The Apostle Peter said, 'Repent and be baptized, every one of you, in the name of Jesus Christ, for remission of your sins, and ye shall receive the gift of the Holy Ghost.'"

He stopped on the concrete path and looked at me. "Listen to yourself..."

"Isn't that a beautiful idea? It's from the book of Acts..."

"Why are we suddenly talking about my sins? What do you know about my sins?"

His little smile had become a smirk. He wasn't hearing me. I had to help him hear. I had to startle him.

"'He that believeth and is baptized shall be saved,'" I said, "'but he that believeth not shall be damned.' That's what concerns me, Ferad. He that believeth not shall be damned."

It seemed to work. His smile faded. He gazed at me, as if taking this in. At last he said, "So, I am among the damned?"

"I'm quoting from the book of Mark."

"And what does it mean to be damned?"

"You don't have to be damned, not if you have faith in Jesus."

"But suppose I have another kind of faith?"

"Well...what other kind?"

"What difference does it make, if I am on my way to hell?"

"This is why we need to talk. I fear your soul may be in danger."

"Now I am curious. Tell me what happens there."

"What happens?"

"Where is hell located? And once I am there, what will happen?"

This was not what I wanted to be talking about. "God is merciful," I said.

"Yet he that believeth not shall be damned. It must be a very crowded place, this hell of yours, to make room for everyone who does not believe what you believe…"

"It's not just because I believe it!"

I was raising my voice. Something in my voice and in my face caused him to step back. "I'm sorry. Relax. Relax."

"Those were the words of Jesus right before he ascended into heaven!"

"Take a moment to think about what you're saying. Isn't this a strange picture? Everyone who does not agree with you will spend eternity burning in the fires of hell?"

"It's not about agreeing with me!" I was shouting, waving my Bible at him. "It's in HERE! And this is the word of GOD!"

My voice rang across the wide lawn. A couple of girls in summery dresses walking along the path swung wide to avoid us.

In the loud silence his eyes followed them. He seemed embarrassed. He shifted his bag to the other shoulder, smiling again, but with his glance averted.

"I just remembered something. Two library books are due today. I ought to turn them in right now, so I'll be able to look the librarian in the eye."

Under a huge blue sky I watched him walk away across the grass. Though I said nothing more, in my mind I was calling after him. *Ferad! Forget it! Wait. Let's go have a cup of coffee anyhow. We'll talk about something else! Forget I even brought it up!*

That night in my dorm room I replayed the scene, wishing it had gone another way, wishing I'd saved my sermonizing for another day. Weren't his questions the same ones I'd secretly asked myself? I could have told him so and kept rapport alive. Why didn't I? What was wrong with me?

Again and again I heard my strident voice rising in the air of early afternoon. As they ran through my mind, the words did not change, but gradually the sound revealed an old, familiar note, and my regret began to subside. It occurred to me that what caused him to step back may well have been the ring of pulpit fervor. Could that anger welling up be an early form of what I'd been yearning for, the righteous passion of a true believer?

Well, yes. Of course. It had to be!

Around midnight I said a silent hallelujah and began to write it up that way, as if the look on Ferad's face had not been embarrassment but uncertainty. Perhaps I'd touched him after all, and this was the first sign of an awakening, a Prospect finally looking into his own heart.

Two days later I read my second Progress Report aloud in class. This time Brother Simkins asked me to stay after the meeting. While others filed out he stood by the rostrum, obviously unmoved by my missionary zeal. Though he didn't say so, I had disappointed him. I could see it in his mouth's sad arc.

"I can't fault your write-up, son. You got that part down. I do have to wonder about your judgment. Far as I can see, you are spinnin your wheels and gittin nowhere fast. I have already spoke my mind about this Persian fella. I am not going to repeat myself, except to say he is not going to budge and he is not going to bite. I asked you to wait here because neither one of us has much time today. These semesters go by mighty fast. You want to pass this course you'd best get busy and find yourself a genuine Prospect. You still got time to cut bait and reset your line."

Like a man looking at a rifle barrel he held his hands high. "Don't get me wrong now. I got no quarrel with Persians per se, nor with those of the Jewish persuasion. Heaven knows Jesus himself was Jewish. And John the Baptist. And the twelve apostles too. It's just tactics, son, tactics. We are

here to help people hear the call of the Lord. If that call falls
on deaf ears, you got to look elsewhere. You could pass this
course with flying colors. You still got time to make a good
solid B. I'd like to see you make a B, son. You got the poten-
tial. Where you take it is up to you."

My head was full of questions. I wanted to ask him how
you walk away from someone who might be in danger.
There was no time to ask. He had his papers packed and
his briefcase buckle snapped. With a final glance his weary
eyes pleaded with me to take heed. He reminded me then
of my high school football coach, who used to give us lec-
tures at halftime. He did not want our opinions. He only
wanted results. I held my tongue, telling myself that by
my works I would persuade Brother Simkins to see things
differently. "By his works is a man justified." So said the
Apostle Paul.

That night, back in my room, I read again what I had
written. I saw that the next step was not Ferad's, but mine.
I would have to be more saintly. I didn't care about the grade.
What did that have to do with salvation? Here was a man on
the threshold. That's how I had described him. That's what I
needed to believe. What kind of friend would I be if I did not
try once more to show him the way? I would have to recover
that luminous time when the grass turned to silver and the
verses seemed to say themselves.

Around me the dorm was quiet. I opened my Bible and
marked a few passages with strips of paper, though I knew
them by heart. I murmured the words, as a kind of incantation, the way I would one day speak passages from other
sacred texts and speak chants in other tongues and let old
mantras steady the mind.

The words of the verses lifted me—their very rhythm and
ring—and something swelled around them, a sense of right-
ness. A moment had come and must be seized. I started down
the hall.

Ferad usually studied alone, preferring his room to the campus library. His door was not entirely shut, which I took to be a kind of welcome. At the far end of the corridor, light leaked around its edges, and with the light came distant radio sounds, a jazz combo. He liked to have some background music while he pored over his assignments. I stood outside listening, Bible in hand, finally knocked, and heard him say, "Yes?"

He was at his desk, hunched over an open book. "Well hello," he said, looking up, blinking. "Come in."

"Am I interrupting a great thought?"

"Not at all."

He pushed back and waved me toward the only other chair. "Sit down, sit down. Haven't seen you in a couple of days."

He had a corner room with windows on two sides, both now covered by closed venetian blinds. His desk was in that corner, where papers were spread out, lit by a gooseneck lamp. Light rising off the paper made his face a pattern of hollows. I'd never been sure exactly how old Ferad was. Just then he looked ancient. During these long nights of study he wore his multicolored skullcap. In scarlet vest and full-sleeved shirt, sitting back against his shelf of books, he could have been a scholar from the Middle Ages.

I said, "What are you reading?"

"History. I have a test tomorrow on the Crusades."

"You're always reading for a test."

"What else is there to do?" he said with his rascal grin. "We are always being tested."

He let this hang in the air.

"My father used to say that," he said. "Do you think he was right?"

Here was an open invitation to get to the point. I composed myself, furrowing my brow as I'd seen preachers do when it was time to look sincere.

"I do think he was right. I guess that's why I knocked on your door..."

I waited, the way I'd seen Brother Simkins wait—a loaded pause.

"There's something we ought to talk about," I said.

"Yes. I feel the same." He reached over and switched off the radio. "We have been avoiding some things. It would be a relief to clear the air."

As he leaned forward into the light, I saw the sincere look coming right back at me. It was too good to be true. The evangelist *wants* the Prospect to ask questions. It means he cares. It means you're halfway there.

Ferad said, "Tell me about your family."

"My family?"

"Tell me where you live."

"It's farther north, up the coast a ways."

"Is it a warm place? A cool place?"

"I guess you could say it's a comfortable place, for most of the year at least."

"So your father's house is made of...?"

I had to think. No one had ever asked me this.

"Wood?" he said. "Brick? Metal?"

"Mostly wood, I guess. Yes, it's a wooden house."

"Where I come from there is very little wood. My father's house is made of stone. But that is in the city. Outside the city you will find others who live in tents."

I had to get back on track. This was not what I wanted to be talking about. I opened my Bible.

"In early times," I said, "many people lived in tents. The Apostle Paul himself was a tentmaker..."

He shook his head. "I'm not talking about early times. I am talking about now. There are many ways to build a shelter—wood, stone, brick, cloth, hides. Yet the purpose is the same. Do you see what I am getting at?"

I couldn't help smiling. I knew what he was getting at, and I pounced upon it.

"You're telling me that the Moslem says his house is built in the right way. And the Catholic says his house is built in the right way…"

He spread his arms wide. "Exactly!"

"I just don't believe God would do that to us, throw down a handful of keys and say, 'Take your pick, people, it's all the same. Scramble around there on the ground for a while and find one you like.' If that's the way it is, why should He go to all the trouble of sending His Own Son down to earth to guide us toward the truth. If we read the Bible we can't fail to see that there is only one way, and that is God's way! This is all I'm trying to tell you, Ferad! Accept Jesus! Put your soul in his care! You owe yourself that much…"

I stopped. My voice was rising again, strident again, and this was not what I'd meant to do. I wasn't sounding as saintly as I'd hoped to sound. I was sounding like Brother Simkins. He had spent two whole class periods on what he called "the Common Arguments." It was in my head like a tape recording. Even as I spoke, my words didn't ring true. Raising my voice was a vain, last-ditch effort to make them true. Underneath my words I was hearing a smaller voice, faint and faraway, calling from within, asking questions I wasn't prepared to listen to: If not this, what else? What else do I believe in? Where else do I look?

Ferad sat there, waiting me out, his eyes very clear and liquid, his voice liquid too, as he pressed both hands against his chest.

"Please try to understand something. I am glad to be in America, to see the life and the ways of worship. And more than ever I am content to be a Jew from Persia. I have no desire to change my faith. None whatsoever. I respect your sincerity. I only ask that you respect mine in the same way. I value your friendship. But I do not need a savior."

His words cut through me, a sword to the belly, and I bowed my head. I felt emptied and foolish.

I closed my Bible and stood up. "I'm sorry."

"Hold on…"

"You have work to do. I have work to do."

He rose from his chair, moving toward me. "I don't want bad feeling between us."

I shrugged. I just wanted out of there. "What difference does it make?"

His eyes searched mine. He was agitated, bouncing slightly, searching for something more to say. At last he reached and lifted off his yarmulke.

"Here."

A smile crossed his face, kind and generous and forgiving. "I want to give you this."

I looked down at the rich embroidery and shook my head. He said, "What's the matter?"

"You don't have to give me anything."

"Please."

"This belonged to your father."

"I have other caps. He too would want you to have this one."

"No. No."

"Here. I want you to have it."

I stood gazing at the skullcap, wagging my head. I didn't know what to do. Brother Simkins had been right all along. I had wasted his time and mine and Ferad's time. In the eyes of both of them I had played the fool.

"I should not have sounded so ungrateful," he said. "Few people have ever taken an interest in my soul. I am touched by this, deeply touched."

His eyes were glistening. I couldn't speak. As he held the cap between us on his upturned palm, a larger silence seemed to fall upon the room and the corridors and the grounds beyond the room. Lamplight rising off the desk had the brilliance of noon sunshine and made a line around the cap, giving each ring of fiber an edge, the thinnest stripe of shading. It was a small dome of red and green and gold and blue, a little galaxy of interwoven shapes, where each square and triangle had a life, and golden threads gleamed like filament.

His eyes were so insistent that I finally reached to take the cap, and I swear that something passed through the fabric, as if the threads were magnetized. In an instant my career as a Daily Evangelist came to an early end. All my sermons simply fell apart and fell away. I didn't need them. I had never needed them. My sense of failure fell away, along with a weight I hadn't known until it was gone. It had hung upon me like a shield, like a suit of armor.

"It's yours," he said. "I'll soon be going home, you know. Maybe it can be a souvenir of our times together."

"Well thanks, Ferad, thanks a lot."

I wanted to say more, but all my words had fled.

"You don't have to wear it, of course."

I wasn't sure what he meant by this, until a bit of mischief showed in his eyes.

With a sly glance he said, "Certain people might be very alarmed to see you wearing such a thing. Our friend Shorty, for example. He might drop his precious hose..."

I felt a chuckle rising. I couldn't stop it. Between the two of us, Shorty was always good for a laugh. Suddenly everything seemed funny. Ferad, filled with mirth, was trying to hold it back. My chuckle erupted to meet his, and we were helpless after that, doubled over, staggering around his room, while our hoots echoed along the empty corridor.

(2004)

Faith

Maybe it happened as the first long earth-wave rolled through our town. Maybe it was later. We had aftershocks all night. Faith, my wife, wouldn't sleep inside. No one would but me. Everyone spent the night in the driveway on cots, or on the lawns in sleeping bags, as if this were a neighborhood slumber party. I think I had to prove to myself that if all else failed I could still believe in my own house. If that first shaker had not torn it to pieces, I reasoned, why should I be pushed around and bullied by these aftershocks rated so much lower on the Richter Scale?

When the second big one hit us, just before dawn, I was alone and sleeping fitfully, pinned to my bed, dozing like a corporal in the combat zone waiting for the next burst of mortar fire. I sat up and listened to rafters groaning, calling out for mercy. I heard dishes leap and rattle in the kitchen. I listened to the seismic roar that comes rushing toward you like a mighty wind. I should have run for the doorjamb.

I couldn't. I could not move, gripped by the cold truth of my own helplessness.

I sat there with the quilt thrown back and rode the tremor until the house settled down. Outside I heard voices. They rose in a long murmur of anxiety laced with relief, as children called to their parents, as neighbor talked to neighbor from lawn to lawn, from driveway to driveway. Eventually the voices subsided, and I was aware for the first time of a hollow place within, a small place I could almost put my finger on. Describing it now, I can say it felt as if a narrow hole had been scooped out, or drilled, right behind my sternum, toward the lower end of it, where the lowermost ribs come together.

At the time I had no words for this, nor did I try to find any. From the rising of the sun we had to take things one hour at a time. We were out of water. Sewage lines had burst, contaminating the mains. Phone lines were down. Power was out all over the county, and many roads were cut off. Long sections of roadbed had split. In the central shopping district several older buildings, made of brick and never retrofitted, were in ruins. They'd been built on floodplain. As the tremor passed through it, the subsoil liquefied. Faith and I live in a part of town built on solider stuff. No one's house jumped the foundation. But indoors, everything loose had landed on the floor—dishes, pictures, mirrors, lamps. Half our chimney fell into the yard. Every other house had a square hole in the roof or a chimney-shaped outline up one wall where the bricks once stood.

The next day I was working side by side with neighbors I had not talked with for weeks, in some cases months. As we swapped stories and considered the losses, the costs, the federal help that might be coming in, I would often see in their eyes a startled and questioning fear that would send me inward to the place where whatever was now missing had once resided. I found myself wondering whether it was something new, or an old emptiness that had gone unnoticed for who knows how long. I'm still not sure.

By the third morning we had electricity again. We could boil water without building a campfire outside or cranking up the Coleman. I sat down at the kitchen table with a cup of coffee and I guess I just forgot to drink it. Faith sat down across from me and said, "What's the matter, Harry?"

"Nothing."

"Are you all right?"

"No, I'm not all right. Are you?"

"You've been sitting here for an hour."

"I don't know what to do. I can't figure out what to do next."

"Let's sell this place. Let's get out of here while we're still alive."

She looked like I felt. Along with everything else we were getting three or four aftershocks a day. It kept you on the ragged edge.

I said, "Where can we go?"

"Inland. Nevada. Arizona. I don't care."

"You said you could never live in Arizona."

"That was last year."

"The desert would drive you bananas, you said."

Halfway through that sentence my voice broke. My eyes had filled with water. It would have been the easiest thing in the world to break into heaving sobs right there at the table.

"It's too hard," she said, "trying to clean up this mess and never know when another one's going to hit. Who can live this way?"

"What does it feel like to have a nervous breakdown?" I said.

"Maybe all we need is a trip. I don't care where. Let's give ourselves a week, Harry, while we talk things over."

"That's not it."

"What's not it?"

I didn't answer. She waited and asked again, her voice on the rise, "What's not it? What's the matter, Harry? What's happening to us?"

Her eyes were blazing. Her mouth was stretched wide in a way I have learned to be wary of. It was not a smile. Faith has a kind of chiseled beauty. As the years go by, her nose, her cheeks, her black brows get sharper, especially when she's pushed. We were both ready to start shouting. Thirty more seconds we would be saying things we didn't mean. I didn't need a shouting match just then. Somehow she always prevails. Her background happens to be Irish and Mexican, a formidable combination when it's time to sling the words around.

Thankfully the phone rang. We hadn't heard it for so long, the jangle shocked us both. It was her mother, who had been trying to get through. Once they knew the houses were standing and no one had been injured, they talked on for half an hour or so, the mother mostly, repeating all the stories she'd been hearing, among them the story of a cousin with some acreage here in the county, where he grows lettuce and other row crops. Some men on the cousin's crew had recently come up from central Mexico on labor contracts, and one of them had asked for a morning off to take his wife to a local healer. During the quake the wife's soul had left her body, or so she feared, and this healer had ways to bring a soul back. Faith's mother reminded her that after the big one in Mexico City, numerous stories had drifted north, stories of people who found themselves alive and walking around among the ruins, while inside something had disappeared.

I still have to wonder why the mother called when she did. Whether it was by chance or by design, I still can't say. Probably a little of both. She claims to have rare intuitive powers. This healer, the curandera, happened to be a woman she knew by name and had been visiting for a year or so, ever since her husband had passed away. Faith had been visiting her too. Her skills, they said, remedied much more than ailments of the flesh.

As soon as her mother hung up, Faith repeated the story of the fieldworker's wife. It came with an odd sort of pressure, as if she were testing my ability to grasp its importance. I don't know. I'm still piecing that day together. Maybe Faith too was feeling some form of inexpressible loss, and maybe she too was groping for a way to voice it.

"This healer," I said, "what does she do?"

"It's hard to explain."

"Is it some kind of Catholic thing? The devil creeping in to steal your soul away?"

She shook her head. "I don't think it's like good spirits and evils spirits or anything along those lines."

"What is it then?"

"Maybe it's like the door of your life springs open for a second."

"Why do you say that?"

"Maybe your soul flies out and the door slams shut again."

"You think that can happen?"

"I'm just thinking out loud."

"It's a hell of a thing to say."

"Don't look at me that way."

"Just tell me if you believe something like that could happen."

"You hear people talk about it."

"When are you going down there again?"

"Sometime soon, I hope. It would be a good time for a treatment."

"Is that what they call it?"

"You can call it whatever you want."

"A treatment? That sounds like…"

"Like what?"

"Some kind of medical deal."

"Please, Harry. If you're going to get defensive, I don't want to talk about it."

"I'm not defensive."

"Your guard goes up."

"Gimme a goddam break, Faith!"

"I can feel it, Harry! You know I can!"

My guard goes up. What guard, I was thinking. I had no guards left. That was the problem. Everything I had ever used to defend myself or support myself was gone. I was skidding. That's how I felt. Supportless. I had to get out of there. I had to think. Or perhaps I had to get out of there and not-think.

I took off for the hardware store to pick up some new brackets for the bookshelves. I switched on one of the talk shows out of San Francisco. The guest was a trauma counselor. The theme was "Living with the Fault Line." Someone had just called in a question about betrayal.

"Can you give me an example?" the counselor said.

"Maybe that isn't the right word," the caller said.

"You feel like something has been taken away from you." It wasn't a question.

"It's almost like my body opened up and something escaped."

A long chill prickled my arms, my neck. I had just reached the hardware store. I pulled into the parking lot, switched off the engine and turned up the sound.

"That's big," the talk show host said. "That's major."

"Hey," said the counselor, "let's think about it together for a minute."

"Think about what?" the host said. "Betrayal?"

"The earth. Think about the umbilical tie. From your mother to your grandmother, and on down the line. On back through the generations to whatever life-forms preceded ours. Sooner or later we all have to trace our ancestry to this nurturing earth, and meanwhile we have laid out these roads and rails and highways and conduit pipes and bridges and so forth in full faith that she is stable and can be relied upon. You follow me? Then when she all of a sudden gives way, splits open, lets off this destructive power without even the little advance notice you get for a hurricane or a killer blizzard, why, it's like your ground-wire disconnects. It's so random…

you realize how we're all just hanging out here in empty space. Believe me, folks, you're not alone. I've been feeling this way myself for days…"

He had a low, compelling voice that sent buzzes through me. I was tingling almost to the point of nausea. The tears I had not been able to release in the kitchen now began to flow. I sat in the hardware store parking lot weeping the way a young child lost on a city street might weep for the missing parents.

When my tears subsided I tried to call the house. The line was busy. I started driving south, sticking to roads I knew were open, more or less following a route I'd followed once before, on a day when Faith's car was in the shop and she needed a ride. It only takes twenty minutes, but you enter another world. Down at that end of the county it's still mostly fertile delta land. From the highway you look for a Burger King and a Stop-N-Go. Past a tract of duplexes you enter an older neighborhood of bungalows and wind-blown frame houses from the 1920s and earlier. The street leading to her cottage was semi-paved. Beyond the yard row crops went for a mile across broad, flat bottomland—lettuce, chard, broccoli, onions. The grass in the yard was pale and dry. Low cactus had been planted next to the porch.

The fellow who answered my knock said he was her son, Arnoldo, lean and swarthy and watchful. He wore jeans and dusty boots, as if he might have just walked in by another door. When I mentioned my wife's name he did not seem impressed. Anglos never came to see this woman. In his eyes I could have been an infiltrator from County Health, or from Immigration, or someone shaking them down for a license. When I mentioned my mother-in-law's family name, he softened a little. Dredging up some high school Spanish I tried to describe my symptoms. Arnoldo spoke a little English, but not much. I touched my chest.

"My alma," I said. "Después del temblor, tengo mucho miedo. Es possible que mi alma…"

"Ha volado?" he said. Has flown away?

"Sí. Comprende?"

He looked at me for quite a while, making up his mind. He looked beyond me toward the curb, checking out the car. At last he stepped aside and admitted me into a small living room where a young mother and her son were sitting on a well-worn sofa. There was a TV set, a low table with some Spanish language magazines, a sideboard with three or four generations of family photos framed. In one corner votive candles flickered in front of an image of the blue-robed, brown-faced Virgin of Guadalupe. Between this room and a kitchen there was a short hallway where a door now opened. A moment later a pregnant woman appeared, followed by an older woman, short and round and very dark. She stopped and looked at me while Arnoldo explained the connection. The names seemed to light her face with a tiny smile of recognition. I heard him mutter, "Susto." A scare. She nodded and said to me, "Bienvenidos." Welcome. Please make yourself at home.

She beckoned to the woman on the sofa and the son, who limped as he started down the hallway. The rear door closed and Arnoldo offered me a chair. I couldn't sit. I was shivering. I made him nervous. I was sure he regretted letting me inside. He pointed to a long jagged lightning streak of a crack across the sheetrock wall behind the TV set. "El temblor," he said. The earthquake.

Again I pointed at my chest. "El temblor."

We both laughed quiet, courteous laughs and looked away. I sat down then, though I could not bear the thought of waiting. This was crazy. I was out of control. What was I doing? What did I think would happen? I remembered the day I'd driven over there with Faith and parked at the curb. I remembered the glow on her face and how I had extinguished the glow. She had wanted me to come inside with her. "What for?" I said, "There's nothing wrong with me." The idea filled me with resentment. "It's not a lot of money, Harry," she had said; "she doesn't charge. You just leave something on the table, whatever you feel like leaving."

It wasn't the money. It was the strangeness of being there with her. Faith has these dramatic, mixed-blood looks that have kept people guessing, and have kept me guessing too, I suppose. Greek, they ask? Portuguese? Italian? Black Irish? Mexico has always been somewhere on that list, but when we first started dating she would never have emphasized it. Her Spanish was no better than mine. Faith McCarthy was her maiden name. Suddenly I did not know this woman. Mexican on her mother's side, that was one thing. Going into the barrio to visit healers, that was something else. I wasn't ready for that. When did it start? Where would it lead? I remembered the rush of dread that day in the car as I realized I was looking at a complete stranger who was inviting me to some place I had never been.

Sitting there with Arnoldo I felt it again, the dread of strangeness. Who was he, after all, with his boots and his lidded eyes? Her son? He could be anyone. What if this was the wrong house?

I heard voices from the hallway. Then the young mother and the limping boy passed through the living room out the front door, and the healer was beckoning to me. I too was limping, crippled with doubt. I had no will. I followed her to another room, with a backyard view across the fields, once a bedroom, now furnished with a chest of drawers, a couple of chairs, a long couch with a raised headrest. She didn't speak for quite some time. She just looked at me. She was no more than five feet tall, her hair silver, pulled back in a short braid. I guessed she was in her 60s, her body thick and sturdy, covered by a plain dress with short sleeves that left her arms free. Her face was neutral, neither smiling nor frowning. Her eyes seemed to enter me, black eyes, the kind that go back in time, channels of memory. She knew my fear. She knew everything about me.

She asked me to take off my shoes and my shirt, nodding toward a chair before she turned away, as if occupied with some small preparation on top of the chest. My panic welled up. It was mad to be doing this, stripping down at the edge of a broccoli field, inside the house of people I'd never seen before. I imagined the old woman asking me to swallow something terrible. Above the chest a shelf was lined with jars and small pouches. Who knew what they contained? My panic turned to fury. I could have taken the old woman by the throat. I wanted to. She knew too much. Maybe I began to understand hysteria just then, how a person can start to spin around and fly to pieces. Why didn't I spin? Why didn't I run? I stood there swearing that if she tried to give me something, I would not swallow it. That was the little contract I made with myself as I lay down on the long couch.

She covered me to my neck with a sheet. From a pouch tied around her waist she withdrew a clump of leafy fragrant stems and waved it up and down the length of my body. Her lips moved but made no sound. She leaned in close, pushing her thumbs across my forehead, digging into the furrows there, digging in close to my eyes. She began to speak, a soft murmur of words that were not Spanish. Later on, Faith's mother would tell me these may have been Yaqui words, a Yaqui incantation. There is something to be said for not knowing the literal meaning of the words. If you trust the speaker to be using them in the proper way, it makes it easier to surrender. You can surrender to the sound. Is that what was happening? Did I trust the sound of the curandera's voice? Let's say I wanted to. Let's say my need to trust her outweighed my fear. Who else could I have turned to? In her hands I began to drift. I would not say she put me to sleep. I was not asleep. I did not feel asleep. I just wasn't entirely awake. My eyes weren't open. But I was still aware of being in the room. I was outside the room, yet in it too, listening to her gentle voice.

While her hands worked on my forehead, my temples, my eyes, my nose and cheeks, her voice became the voice of wings, large and black and wide as the couch, as wide as the room, as wide as the house, sheets of darkness moving toward me, undulating, until I saw that these were the wings of an enormous bird, a dark eagle or a condor hovering. It finally settled on my chest, its feet on my skin so I could feel the talons. They held me as if in the grip of two great hands. They dug in. They were on my chest and inside my chest. From the talon grip I understood some things about this bird. I knew its solitary drifting on the high thermal currents, soaring, waiting. I knew its hunger. I knew the power of the beak. When the flapping of the wings increased, I wasn't surprised. They made a flapping thunder that sent a quiver through me, then a long shudder, then a shaking as sudden and as terrifying as the shaking of the earth, with a sound somewhere inside it, the slap of a ship's sails exploding in a gale. I was held by the chest and shaken by this huge bird until my body went slack, exhausted by the effort to resist. In that same moment the wings relaxed. The hold upon my chest relaxed. I watched the bird lift without any motion of the wings, as if riding an updraft. It hovered a while, and I had never felt so calm. A way had been cleared at last, that's how it felt. Everything had been rattled loose again and somehow shaken into place. A rim of light edged the silhouette of dusky feathers. I saw the fierce beak open as if about to speak. Its piercing cry almost stopped my heart.

My eyes sprang wide. The woman's dark brown face was very close. The heel of her hand had just landed on my forehead with a whack. Her black eyes were fixed on mine. What did I see there? Who did I see?

When I got back home Faith met me at the door. She too had been crying. I'd been gone maybe three hours. She stood close and put her arms around me. We didn't speak. We looked at each other. In her face I recognized something I would not, until that afternoon, have been able to identify. Her eyes were like the old woman's eyes, that same fierce and penetrating tenderness. It swept me away. We kissed as if we had not seen each other in weeks, as if we had had the fight that nearly happened and we were finally making up. It was a great kiss, the best in years. It sent us lunging for the bedroom where we made love for the first time in many days.

In our haste we forgot to pull the curtains. Afternoon light was pouring through the windows. At first she was bathed in light, though as we thrashed and rolled she seemed to be moving in and out of shadow. Then she was above me and so close she blocked the light. As she rose and fell and rose and fell I could only see her outline. When she abruptly reared back, her arms were wings spread wide against the brightness, while she called out words I could scarcely hear. A roaring filled my ears. A thousand creatures were swarming toward the house, or a storm-driven wind. Maybe it was another aftershock. Maybe it was the pounding of my own blood.

"Oh! Oh! Harry!" Her voice came through the roar. "Harry! Harry!" as if I were heading out the door again. Had I been able to speak I would have called to her. Maybe I did call. I know I heard my voice. "I'm here!" I cried. "I'm here! I'm here!"

Acknowledgments

Many thanks to the following, where these pieces first appeared, some under different titles and in slightly different form: "The View from Santa Cruz" in *Holiday;* "The Regional Feeling" in *The Bennington Review;* "Loma Prieta, Part One" in the *San Jose Mercury News,* Sunday Perspective; "Coast Range Sutra" and "Loma Prieta, Part Two" in *San Francisco Focus;* "Clay" in *Per/Se;* "Ancestors" in *The Men in My Life* (Creative Arts Book Co.); "The Dangerous Uncle Returns" in *GQ;* "Words and Music" in the Gale Group's *Contemporary Authors,* Volume 204; "A Portrait of the Artist" in *Olaf Palm: A Life in Art;* "How Words Sink In" in *Weber Studies;* "Beginner's Mind" in *Manoa: A Pacific Journal of International Writing;* "How Selling a Car Can Almost Get You to Nigeria" in the *Santa Cruz Sentinel;* "The Days with Ray" in *Remembering Ray* (Capra Press); "Remembering Wallace Stegner" and "Steinbeck's Legends" in the *San Francisco Review of Books;* "Money and Trust" as a foreword

to *Writing Home* (Heyday Books); "The Path of Empire" as
a foreword to *Eldorado* (Heyday Books); "Another Kind of
Western" in *Mother Jones;* "Where Does History Live?" in
Rethinking History; "A Family Resemblance" on NPR's *Sound
of Writing,* Fall 1989; "Gasoline" in *Gasoline: The Automotive
Adventures of Charlie Bates* (Capra Press), 1980; "Daily Evangelism" in the online magazine *Narrative,* Fall 2004; "Faith"
in *Ploughshares,* Spring 1993.

The excerpt in "Remembering Wallace Stegner" comes from
One Nation by Wallace Stegner and the editors of *Look,* a Life-
in-America Prize Book, Houghton Mifflin, Boston, 1945.

In "The Path of Empire" the excerpt from the letter to
George Putnam comes from *Unpublished Letters of Bayard
Taylor in the Huntington Library,* edited by John Richie Schultz,
San Marino, California, 1937.

About the Author

Born in San Francisco, James D. Houston has lived for many years in Santa Cruz. From this vantage point he has explored, in both fiction and non-fiction, the western U.S. and the Asia/Pacific region. His eight novels include, most recently, *Bird of Another Heaven* (Knopf, 2007) and *Snow Mountain Passage* (Knopf, 2001), named one of the Year's Best Books by the *Los Angeles Times* and the *Washington Post*. With Jeanne Wakatsuki Houston he coauthored *Farewell to Manzanar*, the story of her family's experience during the World War Two internment, now a standard work in schools and colleges across the country. Among his numerous honors are a Wallace Stegner Fellowship at Stanford, a Rockefeller Foundation residency at Bellagio, two American Book Awards, and the Humanitas Prize. For more information, go to www.jamesdhouston.com.

HEYDAY INSTITUTE

Since its founding in 1974, Heyday Books has occupied a unique niche in the publishing world, specializing in books that foster an understanding of the history, literature, art, environment, social issues, and culture of California and the West. We are a 501(c)(3) nonprofit organization based in Berkeley, California, serving a wide range of people and audiences.

We are grateful for the generous funding we've received for our publications and programs during the past year from foundations and more than three hundred individual donors. Major supporters include:

Anonymous; Anthony Andreas, Jr.; Barnes & Noble bookstores; BayTree Fund; B.C.W. Trust III; S. D. Bechtel, Jr. Foundation; Fred & Jean Berensmeier; Book Club of California; Butler Koshland Fund; California Council for the Humanities; California State Coastal Conservancy; California State Library; Candelaria Fund; Columbia Foundation; Compton Foundation, Inc.; Malcolm Cravens Foundation; Federated Indians of Graton Rancheria; Fleishhacker Foundation; Wallace Alexander Gerbode Foundation; Marion E. Greene; Walter & Elise Haas Fund; Leanne Hinton; Hopland Band of Pomo Indians; James Irvine Foundation; George Frederick Jewett Foundation; Marty Krasney; Guy Lampard & Suzanne Badenhoop; LEF Foundation; Robert Levitt; Michael McCone; Middletown Rancheria Tribal Council; National Audubon Society; National Endowment for the Arts; National Park Service; Philanthropic Ventures Foundation; Poets & Writers; Rim of the World Interpretive Association; River Rock Casino; Riverside-Corona Resource Conservation; Alan Rosenus; San Francisco Foundation; Santa Ana Watershed Association; William Saroyan Foundation; Seaver Institute; Sandy Cold Shapero; Service Plus Credit Union; L. J. Skaggs and Mary C. Skaggs Foundation; Skirball Foundation; Orin Starn; Swinerton Family Fund; Thendara Foundation; Victorian Alliance; Tom White; Harold & Alma White Memorial Fund; and Stan Yogi.

For more information about Heyday Institute, our publications and programs, please visit our website at www.heydaybooks.com.

BAYTREE

Other BayTree Books

BayTree Books, a project of Heyday Institute, gives voice
to a full range of California experience and personal stories.

Archy Lee: A California Fugitive Slave Case (2008)
Rudolph M. Lapp

Tree Barking: A Memoir (2008)
Nesta Rovina

Walking Tractor: And Other Country Tales (2008)
Bruce Patterson

Ticket to Exile: A Memoir (2007)
Adam David Miller

Fast Cars and Frybread: Reports from the Rez (2007)
Gordon Johnson

The Oracles: My Filipino Grandparents in America (2006)
Pati Navalta Poblete